Hi,
and let
me start by
welcoming
you to the
book.

iLife Genius Guide   **Welcome...**

There are many bonuses to owning a Mac, and top of the list
must be the suite of creative applications that comes free with every
new model. Regardless of whether you are a photography fiend, a
digital video veteran or a complete newcomer to creative pursuits,
there is something for everyone in a package that caters for all walks
of digital creativity. This book is designed to help you make the most
of your Mac and the apps that come with it and provide you with the
information you need to accomplish a wide range of tasks in each
program. From greeting cards and calendars in iPhoto, through
designing your very own website in iWeb, there are hundreds of
projects to choose from all conveyed in a simple yet informative
manner. Another bonus of the **iLife Genius Guide** is that you don't
have to be using the latest version of iLife to make use of it. We've
catered for both iLife '08 and '09 with most tutorials working in both
suites. Should you still be using an older version of the iLife apps you'll
surely be tempted to upgrade when you see the great new features included.
We've got in-depth features in both sets of apps, too, so you'll be spoilt for
choice when it comes to picking your next creative task. Don't miss the
free disc at the back of the book either; there are plenty of free
goodies on there, plus tutorial files to help you follow the step by
steps. So what are you waiting for? It's time to get creative.
The possibilities are truly endless!

Enjoy the book,   **Ben Harvell**

Become an iLife Genius

Imagine Publishing Ltd
Richmond House
33 Richmond Hill
Bournemouth
Dorset BH2 6EZ
☎ +44 (0) 1202 586200
Website: www.imagine-publishing.co.uk
Thank you for supporting Imagine Publishing – an independent specialist magazine
publisher where quality, innovation and excellence are paramount.

Compiled by
Ben Harvell

Layout by
Katy Ledger, Kate Logsdon

Proofed by
Jon White, Amy Squibb, Katy Tanner

Printed by
William Gibbons, 26 Planetary Road, Willenhall, West Midlands, WV13 3XT

iLife Genius Guide © 2009 Imagine Publishing Ltd

ISBN 978-1-906078-30-0

IMAGINE
PUBLISHING

Contents...
Features...

Check out the amazing resources & tutorial files on your free CD page 258

Essential iLife Tutorials...

iPhoto 024
Shoot, perfect and share your digital photos with ease. Create amazing gifts from your pictures, publish them to the web and much more

iMovie 086
Import and edit your video footage, add themes and titles plus Hollywood-style effects. Discover how to fix imperfect clips and share your projects with the world on disc or online

iWeb 142
Now there's no excuse not to have your own website whether you want to share pictures and video with friends and family, promote your small business or get into blogging and podcasting. You'll find everything you need for online mastery here

GarageBand 190
If you're musically inclined or not, GarageBand has something for everyone from podcasting to composing. Learn how to make use of a variety of features including Magic GarageBand, ringtone creation, voice and guitar effects and more

iDVD 234
Commit your photos and movies to disc in style with the beautiful built-in themes in iDVD. Learn how to perfect your DVD interfaces, store data as well as media on your discs and backup your iLife projects for safe keeping

"Its suite of tools are perfect and exquisitely crafted, with the right balance of form and function"

iLife recipe guide **Page 14**

5

Prepare to experience the best ever creative suite from Apple, the all-conquering powerhouse that is iLife '09. Take your movies, music, photos and websites to a whole new level with our in-depth guide

Getting hold of a new copy of iLife is, for a Mac user, like becoming ten years younger. Ambitions re-root themselves, projects you long gave up on suddenly become important again, and every time you touch your camera, camcorder or a musical instrument there's a noticeable tingle of excitement as you anticipate all the wonderful things you can do with your material now that there's a new version of iLife available. And 2009 is no exception to the rule. While, on the surface at least, iLife '09 may not appear to usher in sweeping reform to all of its apps as in previous versions, the suite has certainly moved with the times and, in some cases, will re-write the way we think about using the software within it. Take iPhoto and its new ways to organise photos, sync them with social networks and create even better books. Look at the third-coming of iMovie; a grand return to form after the slight slip that was iMovie

"There's a noticeable tingle of excitement as you anticipate all the wonderful things you can do with your material now that there's a new version of iLife available"

6

'08. We're back thinking of ways to perfect our home movies and weave incredible themes between our recently shot footage. It's not about the new features; it's about the new possibilities that are now available with the unveiling of the iLife '09 suite.

Over the next few pages we're going to dig into the iLife '09 suite and root out all the very best bits and the most exciting new tricks – and we'll also show you just what's on offer as you prepare to make the leap into 2009's must-have Apple software. Some quick starter

guides will show you how the simpler techniques work and have you ready for the more complex areas of this software too. Whether you're excited about geotagging photos, fancy some creative movie editing, yearn to be taught music by your favourite artists or simply want to keep abreast of the new developments in Apple's flagship package, we'll provide you with all the answers, some rather cunning tips and a shower of inspiration so that you're totally ready to hit the ground running with iLife once the '09 versions hit your Applications folder. ▶

Contents

iPhoto

iPhoto has long been the darling of the iLife suite, existing before there was even such a thing as an iLife suite. Now a fully integrated member of the package and flagship Apple application, it has been regularly updated since its release. 2009 brings in the most significant organisation tools since the Smart Album.

With both Spaces and Places, iPhoto has become not only the ultimate tool for browsing and sorting your images, but a database of records charting all of your friends, family, holidays and other travels. And with Facebook integration now built in to the deal, iPhoto is spreading onto the web in more ways than simply sharing a photo gallery. Here are all of the new iPhoto features explained, as well as a couple of quick guides to get you started in this fantastic new version of Apple's photo app.

"iPhoto is spreading onto the web in more ways than sharing a photo gallery"

New features

Faces
iPhoto can now find faces in your photos and even identify them, allowing you to name each one and sort albums by person.

Places
Turning GPS data into simple names, Places makes the most of your GPS-enabled camera or iPhone showing the location of your shots.

Themed slideshows
Show off your photos with these great new slideshows that use face-recognition to frame people perfectly in a wide range of styles.

Online sharing
One click is all you need to upload your pictures to Flickr or Facebook with names added (and Faces included) as tags for each.

Editing
iPhoto '09 offers an enhanced set of tools, including a way to improve the colours in your shots without affecting skin tones.

Maps
A new feature in iPhoto books allows you to use Places data to create amazing maps to show where your photos were taken.

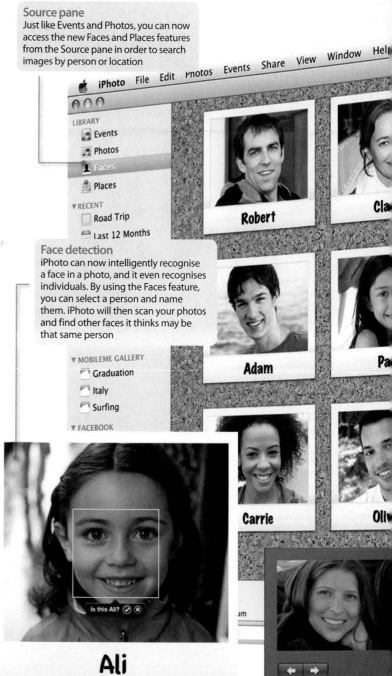

Source pane
Just like Events and Photos, you can now access the new Faces and Places features from the Source pane in order to search images by person or location

Face detection
iPhoto can now intelligently recognise a face in a photo, and it even recognises individuals. By using the Faces feature, you can select a person and name them. iPhoto will then scan your photos and find other faces it thinks may be that same person

Get started with Places in iPhoto '09

Pinpoint your pics on the map with this impressive new feature that not only allows you to chart your travels, but you can also search for a set of photos from any given location. Here's how…

1: Find the photos
Here we have an event that does not have GPS data applied. Click the 'i' button to flip the event and begin adding location information.

iPhoto

Ali

Theo

Kelly

David

Sarah

Mon 10:50 AM

Search the world
The Places interface shows a world map with pins positioned in all the locations where you have taken photos. You can zoom in and out of the map to locate specific snaps, or view them all at once

City of Light
Jul 31, 2008
44 photos
Paris
Our wonderful week in Paris with the Family.

MobileMe   Facebook   Flickr   Email

Online sharing
These two buttons allow for one-click uploading of a set of images to Facebook and Flickr. If you have added names in Faces then they will be added as tags in your photos on Facebook too

2: Name the place
All you need to do now is to begin typing the location in which the photos were taken, and iPhoto should auto-complete it for you.

3: Back on the map
You can now use the Places view from iPhoto's Source pane to locate all of your events on a world map, with photos denoted by red pins.

Get started with Faces in iPhoto '09

Let iPhoto take the hassle out of naming the people in your photographs by searching your library and finding the same faces in different shots. Here's how to tell iPhoto exactly who's who…

1: The name game
Head to your iPhoto library and open a photo that features people you want iPhoto to recognise in future images and click Name.

2: Name some names
Boxes will automatically appear around faces in your photo allowing you to input names, which iPhoto will use for future reference.

3: What's my name?
The next time you import pictures, iPhoto will ask you to confirm faces it recognises.

New book theme

Make the most of Places in iPhoto by using a new Travel Book theme that includes maps alongside all of your photos from around the world, or simply around town.

Summer at the Baltic Sea

iMovie

Let's face it, nobody was particularly happy with iMovie '08. It had a revolutionary new editing system, but it also dropped a number of the best features from iMovie HD. Apple clearly noticed this issue and swiftly made the original available for free to iLife '08 users. Fortunately, the revolution has continued into iMovie '09 – creating a happy compromise between iMovie HD and iMovie '08. The same editing layout remains, but with a host of new and improved features that offer the control users want alongside idiot-proof functionality. If anything, iMovie '09 offers the best of both worlds with handy menus that appear during drag-and-drop editing so you can define exactly what you want to do with an audio or video clip, or a sequence of footage. Prepare to be wowed by the best iMovie release yet.

> "If anything, iMovie '09 offers the best of both worlds… prepare to be wowed"

New features

Advanced drag and drop
Add clips with ease by dragging and dropping. Include transitions, slick cutaways and inserts too.

Precision editor
Use a magnified view of your footage for complete control. Trim and tweak your clips, adjust audio and define titles with ease.

Themes and maps
Amazing new themes will bring your movie to life and can be added at the start of a project (or to one you have already put together).

Video Stabilization
All the clips you thought were unusable due to a shaky hand can now be fixed and used in your iMovie projects with this new tool.

New titles, transitions and effects
Quickly preview and apply new titles, transitions and effects from the browser and click to add them.

Library browser
Like iPhoto for movies, this new feature lets you browse all your footage in full-screen mode to select clips or just review your shoot.

Stills or movies in themes
You can drop a photo into a theme or include a video clip to add a moving image to your chosen theme animation and give your project a professionally edited feel instantly

New themes in iMovie '09
Add a new theme to your iMovie project and the application will automatically add footage to create an amazing sequence in minutes. Choose from Scrapbook, Photo Album, Comic Book or Filmstrip for a variety of styles to suit your movie.

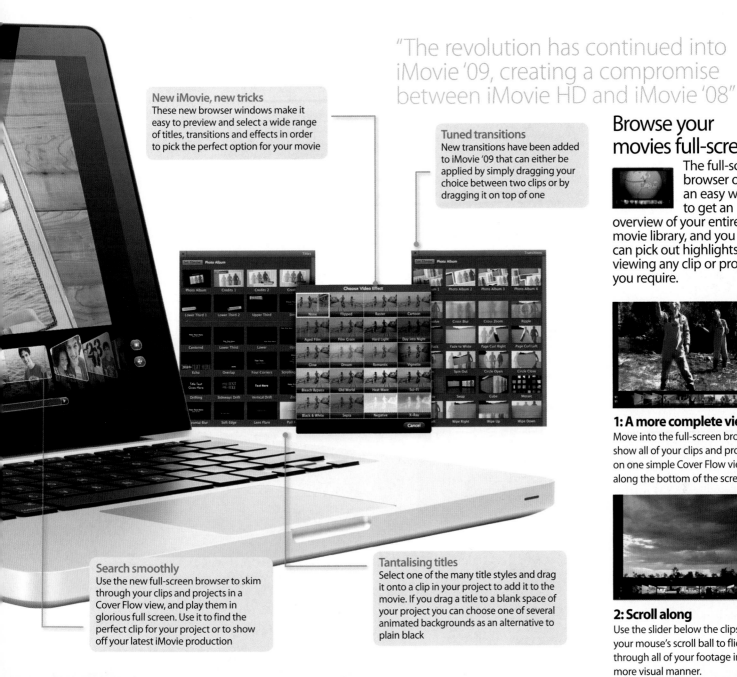

New iMovie, new tricks

These new browser windows make it easy to preview and select a wide range of titles, transitions and effects in order to pick the perfect option for your movie

Tuned transitions

New transitions have been added to iMovie '09 that can either be applied by simply dragging your choice between two clips or by dragging it on top of one

Browse your movies full-screen

The full-screen browser offers an easy way to get an overview of your entire movie library, and you can pick out highlights by viewing any clip or project you require.

1: A more complete view

Move into the full-screen browser to show all of your clips and projects on one simple Cover Flow view along the bottom of the screen.

2: Scroll along

Use the slider below the clips or your mouse's scroll ball to flick through all of your footage in a more visual manner.

Search smoothly

Use the new full-screen browser to skim through your clips and projects in a Cover Flow view, and play them in glorious full screen. Use it to find the perfect clip for your project or to show off your latest iMovie production

Tantalising titles

Select one of the many title styles and drag it onto a clip in your project to add it to the movie. If you drag a title to a blank space of your project you can choose one of several animated backgrounds as an alternative to plain black

3: Pick the clips

Buttons next to the Cover Flow display allow you to choose between clips and projects, and you can even skim the clips you select.

►

GarageBand

While the core features remain largely untouched, GarageBand '09 provides some great new options for budding musicians. Guitarists will rejoice with the addition of some amazing guitar rig setups and stomp box effects that mimic those of the greats, and these are endlessly customisable. Plug in your guitar and you're off and running with sounds like Brit Pop, Seattle Sound and Woodstock Fuzz. For those new to music or thirsty for improvement, you can now learn your instrument from right inside GarageBand itself. The Basic Lessons teach you with videos and annotations, and Artist Lessons enlist the help of popular musicians like Sting, Colbie Caillat and John Fogerty to help you master their own hit songs.

"GarageBand '09 provides some great new options for budding musicians"

An artist in your own home
Invite a music legend to teach you how to play their songs, such as *Roxanne* taught by The Police frontman Sting, at a pace that suits you

Learn from the best
At present you can pick from Sting, Sarah McLachlan, Patrick Stump, Norah Jones, Colbie Caillat, Sara Bareilles, John Fogerty, One Republic and Ben Folds to teach you hit music. The lessons can be downloaded from within GarageBand

MacBook Pro

Artist Lessons Previews

Sting · Sarah McLachlan · Fall Out Boy · Norah Jones
Colbie Caillat · Sara Bareilles · John Fogerty · OneRepublic
Ben Folds

New features

Basic Lessons
For piano or guitar, these nine lessons show you the basics at your own speed – with the ability to slow things down if you need to.

Artist Lessons
The cream of today's musical talent show you how to play their songs from right within the GarageBand interface.

New Guitar features
Make your guitar sound like the legends of fretwork with new effects and rigs that sound great and are displayed in 3D for complete control.

Magic GarageBand jam
Stop practising alone and invite a full band onto your Mac with Magic GarageBand, which now plays in full-screen mode.

Jam with the band
Set up your band and jam away on your chosen instrument in full screen with Magic GarageBand. You have complete control of which instruments and parts are used, and you can even record your song into Magic GarageBand too

Take your first guitar lesson

 Pick your instrument, select your skill level and start learning how to play in minutes with this excellent new learning feature in GarageBand '09.

1: Select a lesson
From the new look Project Chooser, select the Learn To Play option and pick an instrument and a lesson from the subsequent screen.

2: The lesson interface
The lesson will now begin playing with an introduction. You can pause and slow down with the controls found below the video window.

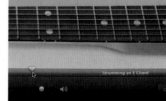

3: Navigate the lesson
If you need to move back and forth in the lesson to speed up your learning or go over a topic, drag the playhead along the timeline.

New & updated features

New themes
If your site is starting to look a little tired you can pick from a set of new themes added to iWeb in the latest version of iLife.

Add new widgets
Widgets in iWeb get even better with the addition of a countdown clock, iSight photo and RSS feed reader for your sites.

Notify Facebook
When you publish your new site or an update to an existing page, iWeb can now automatically notify your friends on Facebook.

Manage & publish
Take complete control of your pages and publishing options, whether you're uploading to MobileMe or an FTP server.

iDVD

Some said iDVD was on its way out with minimal updates in iLife '08; the birth of the Blu-ray disc and the growing popularity of the internet for sharing movies and photos was preferred to the physical format. Still, it returns in iLife '09 but, unfortunately, only with the addition of some attractive new themes.

Just because the app hasn't been hugely altered that doesn't mean it should be overlooked, however. For iPhoto and iMovie projects, iDVD is the final piece in the puzzle when it comes to sharing your iLife creations, and these new themes will stand to make things even more interesting.

iWeb

iWeb is the newest addition to the iLife suite, added as part of the package in 2008, and as such hasn't seen too many changes in this instalment. Rather than overhaul iWeb in iLife '09, Apple has simply made some of its existing features even better than before. New themes, new widgets, notification for Facebook friends when you update your site and updated management options make it even easier to create rich, exciting and interactive websites with iWeb. The new themes will also help those growing tired of the existing page designs to liven up their online creations.

Some of the updates may not provide wholesale changes, but some offer the opportunity to use your imagination to create cool new features on your site. The RSS widget in particular will provide a simpler way to include feeds on your page – whether you want to offer the latest news or information from another of your iWeb sites or blogs.

> "New themes, new widgets and updated management options make it even easier to create rich, exciting and interactive websites with iWeb"

New themes in iWeb '09

Make your site look its best with a set of professionally designed themes for iWeb, now including Leaf Print, Fine Line and Layered Paper.

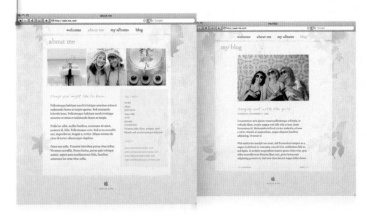

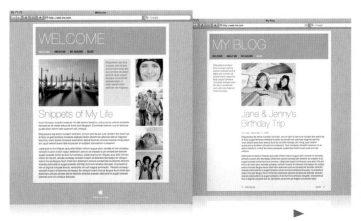

▶

Quick recipes for Apple perfection

The iLife kitchen offers a comprehensive range of implements, for the budding cook or the accomplished chef. Here's how to get the best out of all your digital ingredients

Whether you're preparing a quick photo slideshow for one, a complete movie for the family, or a three-course multimedia experience for your colleagues, iLife is the first place to turn. Its suite of tools are perfect and exquisitely crafted, with the right balance of form and function to make the experience a delight, and let you serve up sensational results.

In this day and age it's not just the finished product that matters; every moment of our time is precious, and it's always worth being able to cook

something up in time to meet the demands of your never-satisfied Flickr stream and blog.

With all that pressure it's understandable if you feel like giving in and getting a take-away from one of the ever-present photo-booths in Boots. It all looks so simple and quick, and it even says "No computer necessary" on the side of the machine – but don't be fooled. Only by preparing your own can you be sure just what goes into it, not to mention the standards of cleanliness (remember, there might be a Windows machine under that in-store packaging!). With that in mind, here are 20 recipes that

will transform your output without taking over your life. There's nothing here that you won't be familiar with, as each recipe has been tailored to work with the everyday ingredients we find in our camcorders, cameras, or even in our iTunes library.

At the risk of extending the metaphor past breaking point, each recipe also owes a lot to the means of preparation! Our digital kitchen is built around five appliances: GarageBand, iDVD, iMovie, iPhoto and iWeb.

You'll find recipes for each of these here, so whatever your tastes are there's something for everyone. Whether that's creating an invisible band to play alongside with, building an online photo gallery that others can contribute to, or making an interactive photo on a DVD.

Follow any one of the quick recipe cards included in the following pages and you'll discover that iLife isn't just your kitchen – it is also your

supermarket. Not only are all the tools you need to prepare, flavour and present your digital dishes present, but – especially in the field of film and photo – there's plenty of help in picking the best before you start. To borrow a phrase from computing rather than the kitchen, "Garbage In Garbage Out" (or the inevitable acronym, GIGO) is a lesson to us all. That's why iMovie makes it so easy to find the perfect moment.

Finally in the chef's supply chain, you, your friends and your family are gardeners too – for it is you that actually shoots the content in the first place to provide the raw materials. Just as gardens can be anything from a window box to a commercial estate, so too can your work be taken on any number of devices. But unlike the supermarket analogy, it's your material. You shot and wrote it. So pick a recipe from our selection over the next few pages for inspiration and get going!

> "Our digital kitchen is built around five appliances: GarageBand, iDVD, iMovie, iPhoto and iWeb. You'll find recipes for each of these here"

Top projects ★★★★★

 ## YouTube photo documentary

Everyone is using YouTube to express their opinion these days. Whether you've got a minority view, or you're hoping to avoid becoming a minority, here's the place to start

Ingredients

Photos of your subject
Some inspired words
iLife sound effects
YouTube account

Whether you're campaigning against a bypass, highlighting concerns about UFOs, or feel you have anything else that needs to be shared with the world, YouTube photo-videos provide the perfect mechanism. You don't even need a camcorder! Set exactly the tone you want with a stirring soundtrack and ram your message home in block capitals.

Just create a new 4:3 project, then click on the Type icon beneath the main viewer. Drag the Centred Type thumbnail from the browser into the timeline and edit the text to the title of your movie. Switch to the Photo Browser and choose a photo that helps tell your story.

To keep your viewer drawn in, click on the red End rectangle. Move it so that it's centred on a focal point in the picture, so when you play it back it'll appear to slowly close in on it. For a final flourish, locate the Super Stager sound effect from the library and add it to the main title clip. This adds a sense of menace lasting 35 seconds, though you can repeat it if you like.

 ## Album in an instant

iPhoto can help you lay out a great book, but there's no need to have Apple print it – you can do it yourself!

Ingredients

Photo collection
Captions

One of iPhoto's signature features, which is also one of the most time consuming, is the ability to prepare and print a bound book of your photos. It's easy to fall into the trap of thinking that it's the presentation that's the important part, and certainly you'll get a fine result if you're prepared to pay for the lavish bindings that Apple can create for you, but a vital part of their quality lies in the design – and you can print that at home.

Living in a world where we often see documents that have been produced entirely in a word processor by someone without any design training, the virtue of good design is easy to see. Apple's suggested layouts are clean, the captions are aligned with the pictures, and there is a grid that is followed automatically.

So Apple's quality is in no doubt, but rather than let your mouse pointer creep towards the Buy Book icon, click File Print. Once the pages have printed you may find that trimming and binding them is a bit tricky, but hopefully you'll have a family member keen to help out. Try not to trim the pages on the binding edge too much, and just use a stapler. Admittedly it's not hard-bound, but turning through the pages is still a great way to share your pictures, and it's ready in minutes!

 ## Share your thoughts

Blogging has swept from the internet sidelines to the mainstream. It's time you added your voice

Ingredients

A thought
Another thought (the next day)
Links

If the word 'blog' still brings slightly techy connotations to the mind, it's time to think again. Every major news outlet, print or broadcast, will have at least one blog, and usually many more delivering an interesting mix of timely fact and opinion.

The excitement of blogging is that you don't need to write for a big name. The financial bar for entry is no longer multi-million pound presses and distribution networks, just a few megabytes of webspace.

Blogging is a great release for a creative writer, and you'll find it helps you organise your thoughts. It's also a great way of keeping traffic up on your site.

The only question is what to write about? The answer: whatever interests you or your site's visitors. If your blog is more of a verbal release than a commercial enterprise, you could blog about current events. Add links to other commentators, and the result is a world-wide voice for your views.

Due to Copyright laws, remember the term 'fair use'. People can mention your sentences to comment on them, but it's better to put a link to your site, and vice-versa. You don't want anyone stealing your material!

One hour iMovie

Driving movie

Sprinkle over a travel movie for added flavour

Ingredients

Camcorder footage
Footage from passenger seat
Race car SFX
Left wipe

It's always nice to get away, but to take an ordinary travel film and give it the rich flavour of a road movie then you'll need to cut in some clips of the journey itself. This brings viewers further into your experience, giving them a chance to quickly absorb the feeling of distance covered.

Of course it's important to avoid over-seasoning; the effect we're after is a quick hint of montage, without the lingering aftertaste or the stereotypical music ringing in the ears. That's where Apple's sound effects step in, and by blending them in we'll get the flavour perfect in moments.

Shooting your footage needn't be a hassle. Grab the camcorder, hold it steadily and shoot through the windscreen, occasionally fixing on a target and turning to follow it as it passes. Concentrate on things that hint at the character of the region, like route signs or signs that warn of dangerous roads.

Simply take a clip of your vehicle at the start of your trip, or a shot of you and your travelling companions. Follow it by dragging in a Wipe transition, then a 2-3 second clip of forward motion, looking down the road ahead. Follow this by a second of a panning shot of a passing object. Ideally your final clip should show you arriving at your destination.

Sprinkle with the Race Car Drive By sound effect from iLife's collection, inserting it just before each panning clip so it reaches its peak as the sign passes.

The retro look

iMovie '08 can make your footage look ancient

Ingredients

Video footage
A sense of timelessness

It's been the subject of some complaint that iMovie has taken away all sorts of visual effects, but in reality a lot of them are still there, simply accessed in a different way. One of the old classics is giving a clip the feel of having been recorded either in the not-so-distant past, when we were all excited by super-8 film, or perhaps from a little further back when film itself was a technical marvel!

Given the latter simply involves applying a sepia tone and, if possible, having every member of your cast wearing vast comedy beards, we'll plump for the former option, the super-8 look.

Old film is characterised by two things: the aging of the film stock itself, which creates a yellow tone to the footage, and the occasional misstep in the feed. The first is replicated by dragging the whole clip to be aged into the project, then clicking the Adjust Video button. Click on a yellow-orange shade in the colour wheel and notch the saturation up a little.

Click OK and begin skimming along the video in the viewer. Click and drag along the video in the timeline to highlight everything from the beginning of the clip until you reach a point you'd like to add a misstep. From the menu choose Edit>Split Clip, then re-edit a few frames from the end of the first clip.

You can also split a section of the video off then click the Crop button. Move the cropped area up or down to give the impression of juddering film. Repeat this effect several times, adding variations and, if you've got one, a projector sound effect.

Narrated holiday

Do you wish that your holiday stories had the polish of a TV travel show, rather than leaving you stammering for the end of an anecdote?

Ingredients

Built-in microphone
Camcorder footage
Mobile phone videos
Photos
iMovie

The great thing about holiday videos is just how easy they are to make, especially since the entire family can now get in on the act thanks to iMovie's ability to import a variety of digital video formats – like mobile phone videos. The only problem is that all the variety can be a little bit confusing.

In a way it's like having your own outside broadcasting unit, with multiple sources that all need to be managed before a single organised signal is sent out to the viewer. One way to keep things consistent is to give the video, very literally, a voice. More specifically, your voice.

Once you've prepared your clips in order in the timeline, and added any effects you wish to use, it's time to put your words together. Some people like to write a script, while others find it better to skim to the section they would like to audibly annotate, then press the Space bar and ad-lib, or practise a few words until they've got the fit. Play around a bit and decide which method you prefer.

To record your voiceover, simply click the Microphone icon near the middle of iMovie's window, and a pop-up window will appear. To be sure the correct input is selected say a few words while keeping an eye on the levels charts, then finally click on the point in the video you'd like to begin commenting on.

You'll be given a gentle countdown, then you can talk away until your heart's content. And if you make a mistake, don't worry. Just hit Escape and your blooper won't even be recorded. Assuming, however, that you're a radio star (but not intent on killing video) then you'll only need to click at the end of your recording. The volume of the clips beneath will automatically be 'ducked' to a gentle atmospheric hum beneath your stately elucidation.

Live music video

iLife is all about sharing your talents, so if you love to perform, what better place than in front of a camera?

Ingredients

Video footage from one or more cameras
Clean sound recording
MiniDisk recorder
Clips to splice in

This is a project for the connoisseurs out there, who don't mind spending a little bit of time perfecting their art. Like a spaghetti bolognese, it's easy to produce an acceptable result, but a little harder to master it. Your first video will be ready to go in moments, but you can spend as long as you like tweaking details to achieve perfection.

There are those that will tell you that it's impossible to record music with a camcorder microphone and, for the most part, they're right. If you're lucky they'll pick up the ridiculously bassy sound that you tend to get at gigs, but more likely everything will be distorted beyond all recognition.

Instead, take a recording directly from a spare output at the mixing desk and import it using GarageBand's ability to record from your Mac's input socket (you may need to switch this from Internal Mic in GarageBand's Preferences). Trim it at either end.

Save it and return to iMovie, then open up the Music and Sound Effects Browser. Navigate to your GarageBand list and drag the recording you just made to a new video project.

Now import the recording from your main camera, which was running the whole time. Drag it as a single video clip onto the timeline, where it will instantly be enveloped by the sound recording.

Click on the long clip and select the audio icon (located third from the left, along the top of the icons that appear over the first frame). Use the menu to reduce the volume to zero, and close it. Now click and drag near the top-left of the enveloping soundtrack filed. Move it til the recording matches up with the video. This may take a little experimentation, but from then on you're free to tinker away 'til you get it right.

"This is a great way of adding your own designs or logos to your footage. But our example here is simply something fun and different to do"

Thought bubbles

iMovie's effects are fun, but sometimes you'll want to leave a more personal touch on the video. Why not add something from your graphics program?

Ingredients

Video
Photoshop Elements or equivalent
.png with transparent background

One of iMovie's better hidden tricks is the ability to overlay transparent .pngs on top of video clips. It doesn't get a lot of press from Apple because you cannot create transparent .pngs with iPhoto, but if you have a tool that will, then you're ready to create a video mashup.

PNG is a photo file format much like JPEG, but it also allows each pixel to have a degree of transparency. For this project it's vital that you can create a speech bubble on a transparent background, which is where Photoshop Elements steps in.

Create a new file of approximately video-format dimensions, making sure the Transparent option is ticked. Now draw a thought bubble (you'll find these included in Photoshop Element's Custom Shape Tools). Still in your image-editing program, add whatever text you want into the bubble. If you use layers it'll be easy to edit the text and save several different versions of the file – you'll need to create a file for each thought bubble you want, and indeed for each position on screen that you want to use it. Make sure you export the files in the PNG format, and save them somewhere convenient. You'll need them visible in a Finder window.

Finally begin editing your clips together in iMovie. When you've reached one where you'd like to add a thought bubble, simply drag it from the Finder over the video. Before you release the mouse it should appear blue, then the overlay will be indicated as a blue line above the clip. You can trim the duration by dragging the end of the line. If you were feeling a little more serious-minded, this is a great way of adding your own designs or logos to your footage. But our example here is simply something fun!

Quick iLife tip

Black and white video
Any clip you put into the iMovie timeline can be rendered black and white, simply by clicking on the Video Adjustments button in the top-left of its timeline strip. Just set the Saturation to zero, and tweak the Contrast until you're happy with the result.

One hour iPhoto

Online album

This is the quickest one in the book, a virtually instant Web Gallery and (depending on your connection speed) time to make a cup of tea

Ingredients

Digital camera
Photos
.MobileMe account

This is the classic recipe for the internet age. Take on two aging technologies, print and film, and blow them both out of the water – saving time and money along the way. The simplicity belies the beauty of the process, and it's time to get reacquainted with it. Simply connect your digital camera to your Mac with a USB cable, and switch it on. Unless you've asked it not to be in the Preferences, iPhoto will leap to life, ready to download all the pictures on the memory card to your hard drive, showing a procession of thumbnails as it goes.

Your photos will automatically be grouped into events, which by default will be all the photos taken on a single day. You can see all your pictures by clicking on an event and the Play button, but you can also share them with the world. Doing so is as simple as clicking the Web Gallery button. In the menu that pops down you can add a touch of Web 2.0 to the experience. If your friends promise to share photos, check the Allow Uploading box. They can now log on in any browser and upload photos to the same page.

When they do, you'll know about it – their pictures will appear in your iPhoto gallery ready for you to look at, print and enjoy just like the others.

Classic wedding invite

Why spend hundreds of pounds on wedding stationery when your computer can do it for you in minutes?

Ingredients

Picture of the bride
Picture of the groom
Picture of the venue
List of guests

Due to the extravagance and expense of wedding services, you may not want to go all out for invitation cards – but you'll want them to look tip-top nonetheless. Simply locate a picture of the bride and groom from your iPhoto library, create a New Card Project, and drag each picture from the main library to the New Project shortcut in the sidebar. Aim to have the couple looking in opposite directions.

Now click on the card project in the sidebar, and select the two-photo design. Drag each picture from the thumbnail bar along the top of the page into position on the card, each looking towards the centre of the card so they seem to look at each other. Once in place, a single click on each one will pop open a Zoom slider and a Hand button. Use the slider to scale the pictures so their heads dominate the frames.

For a touch of class, use the Settings dial to pick Black and White for both images (this also helps them match). Now print the card onto card-sized paper in two stages: print all the copies of the front page at once, but edit the invitation text each time and make one-off prints of each inside on the opposite side of the same pages. Now you just have to choose!

"Take on two aging technologies, print and film, and blow them both out of the water – saving time and money along the way"

Digital exposure

If you have thousands of images but want to feed their exposure correction cravings with just a few clicks, here's the solution

Ingredients

Digital camera
Manually exposed photos (or photos shot in snow)

Exposure can go wrong for all sorts of reasons, whether a user error or a failing of the automatic exposure meter built into the camera. In either case, it's good to know that iPhoto can correct them.

Snowy environments used to be a big problem for compact cameras, and indeed SLRs in Auto mode, since the unusually white appearance of most areas of the image tricked the camera in to stopping down until the snow was much darker than it should be. While the circuitry is more sophisticated these days, it's this kind of problem that will affect a whole shoot.

Another way to end up in the same situation is over-cautious manual exposure settings. It is possible to recover information from shadow areas of a digital photo, but not overexposed highlights, so it is common to stop down rather than risk losing data. If you've done this, you'll likely want to restore the exposure in all the shots equally.

The solution is the Copy and Paste buttons in the Edit Inspector window. Click on the first photo in the Event folder and it will be highlighted with iPhoto's yellow border. Click the Edit button and open the Inspector using the Adjust button. The slider at the top is called Exposure, and it simulates the effect of adding to (or decreasing) the camera's Exposure value. When you're happy click Copy, then scroll to the next picture in the thumbnails. Click Paste to apply the same effect to any of your photos.

Art piece

Digital photography has brought the colour darkroom to the home – minus the chemical smell. But what of the past?

Ingredients

Single image
Printer

For all the sophistication of modern computing, we now all have the ability to tint and print full colour prints without the chemical expertise that was needed just a few years ago. Old habits die hard. Monochrome prints have a certain indefinable timelessness that makes them seem a little more artistic than many colour prints.

In time this will likely change, as our tastes tend to, but for now it's something we can exploit to turn a good picture into a great print. That, after all, is the flexibility that digital offers us.

Choose one of your favourite photos for the black and white treatment, then click Print. A range of options will appear to the left of the picture, and from this list choose which one you want to use. The Double Matte gives you a strong border that might challenge some pictures, or really draw the eye in.

When you get to the Preview page, click on the image to highlight it within the frame. The Adjust option will become available. Click on it and choose black and white from the Inspector that appears.

You can bring out the best of darker areas of your shot with the Shadows slider, and add interest to the brighter areas with the Highlights slider. The Contrast slider should be used to taste. When you are ready, click Print. The original file will remain in colour in your iPhoto library.

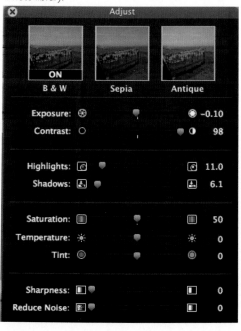

"We now all have the ability to tint and print full colour prints without the chemical expertise that was needed just a few years ago"

Always find your favourite

Sometimes there is just too much, and to get a real taste it's important to concentrate on the finest ingredients

Ingredients

iPhoto gallery
Rated photos

There are times when you want to get involved with your photos, by updating the descriptions, tweaking the contrast a notch or two, or making delicately shaded photo creations. There are other occasions where all you want to do is see your favourite shots as quickly as possible.

To be ready for those times, iPhoto invites you to take advantage of the time-honoured rating system. In other words, as you browse your pictures for the first time, press Cmd and a number key (1-5) to give an honest appraisal of the quality of your picture. A five should be the absolute best – sharp focus, smiles, great composition and lighting. The other numbers you'll develop your own feel for, but be careful not to be over-generous! Sure, every shot you take may be at least a three, but then you've effectively reduced your ratings to three possible star ratings.

With all that in place, finding your favourites across every album is simply a matter of creating a new Smart

Quick iLife tip

Favourite photo
If you don't like the shot that iPhoto has put at the front of a particular event, then simply skim over the large icon with your mouse. Hover over a picture you prefer and tap the space bar.

Album and choosing My Rating as the criteria. Set it to Greater Than 4, and click OK. A new, purple coloured album icon with a cog on it will appear in the sidebar, which you'll be able to click on the moment you load iPhoto, and you will be taken straight to your favourites in future.

If while you're browsing though, you feel that one of the photos should be relegated from a 5 star status, then you can simply press Cmd+4, or an even lower replacement star rating. The picture will be immediately reclassified and dropped from the favourites album.

If, on the other hand, you feel that some pictures should have made the cut, but you're not seeing them, you'll need to browse through them using the ordinary folders. Perhaps it would be worth making a Greater Than 3 star folder too?

One hour iWeb

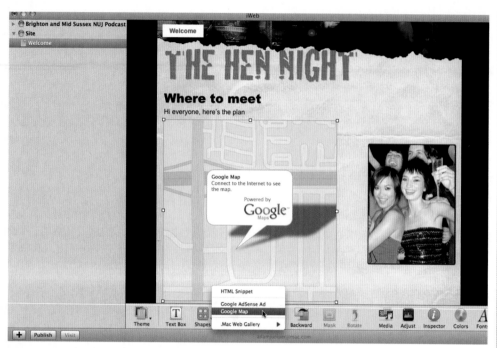

Pinpoint party planning

Bring people together with a guide from above (Google Maps, that is)

Ingredients

Internet connection
Event coming up
Planned location

If you've ever found yourself needing to bring together a group of strangers with just a few phone numbers, then you'll know what an uphill struggle it can be. Remember those scrappy photocopied plans that maids of honour or best men would send out before hen nights and stag dos, with vague crosses on maps or impenetrable lists of directions? Well, these days your problems can all be solved by building a simple page in iWeb. Not only can you write all the plans (and schedules) in strict detail, you can also keep them up to date.

Quick iLife tip

Website Widgets
You can add a wide range of extras to your iWeb site using the HTML Snippet function and code from other sites. Check out some of the excellent widgets found at **www. widgetbox. com** that can offer anything from clocks to scrolling RSS feeds and games.

"Your problems can all be solved by building a simple page in iWeb… just click Create New Site and pick the right theme for your event"

Simply click Create New Site and pick the right theme for your event – the Night Life one seems appropriate if you're trying to build some excitement. Choose the style of page you want (the simple layout of the Welcome page is ideal for a simple description of the plan).

To illustrate matters, however, there's no need to draw your own map. Just click on the Web Widgets icon at the bottom of the page and choose Google Maps. A map will appear on your page, and a small dialog box where you can type the address you're aiming for. Anywhere in the world is acceptable, and different addressing systems will work.

While you can see the dialog, you can also pick whether the map should appear in standard form as a Satellite, or as a Hybrid. You can also choose whether the address bubble and Zoom controls should be available to viewers.

If security isn't a major concern, then all you need to do now is circulate the URL to everyone you're hoping will attend. Afterwards you can add a page to the same site with some relevant funny pictures, or add a link to your iPhoto share and encourage others to upload their pictures.

Raking it in

If your site is doing well for visitors, you should be doing well for cash

Ingredients

Website
Webpage

At the risk of leaning a little too hard on the fourth wall, have you considered creating a website to share your cuisine creations with the world? It might surprise you to learn that one of the most popular uses of the internet is to swap recipes, and that means there's traffic out there.

Thanks to Google, traffic can be a valuable commodity to you, and all you need to do to take advantage of it is to install the AdSense Ad web widget onto your pages to get some of the action. iWeb will even get you going with an AdSense account if you've never used the service before.

AdSense looks at your page and adds advertisements that are relevant to the text in it, so you don't need to worry about your page suddenly being a portal for some of the internet's less salubrious service providers.

On any page you like just click the Web Widget button and choose Google AdSense Ad. In the pop-up pick a size and shape for your advert – they are measured in pixels, the standard units for web design.

iWeb will likely choose a suitable colour scheme for the ad, but if you'd like it to stand out a little more click the drop-down menu and choose an alternative.

Drag your advert to its final position on the page, then widen and shrink the iWeb window a little to ensure that you're happy with the positioning and it responds correctly to different monitor sizes.

For a recipe site, the list of ingredients will be one place Google looks for keywords. This means there might be advertisements for suppliers, and any time anyone clicks on one of them, it's pay day for you. But don't expect to become a millionaire.

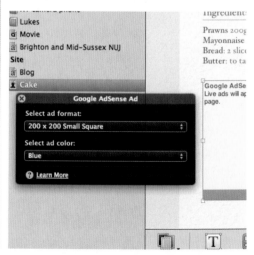

Baby central

Looking after a baby takes over your life, even before you start managing the adoring crowds!

Ingredients

Your baby photos
Friends' baby photos
Baby videos
Friends' links

We have heard it been said that if you want to simulate the experience of having a new baby, you just need to set the alarm clock to go off three times in the middle of the night, every night, and burn a £20 note each time.

There are a few differences of course, not least that your friends and family won't be interested in seeing or taking pictures of that. A real baby, on the other hand, can quickly become the focal point for the attention of many interested parties, and if you are lucky enough to have a technically equipped mother or mother-in-law it might not be a bad idea to consider a website to bring all those pictures together. Once again, iWeb has all the right tools to make it a simple matter. Create a new iWeb site and choose a suitable theme. Somehow the Baby one seems most appropriate, and starting with a Welcome page seems like a sensible idea too.

Apple's design has space for two photos – a great spot for your favourites – and you can always update it whenever you update your site.

Where this theme really comes into its own, however, is with the ability to add much more of your own iLife content and make it accessible in the same location as your friends.

To add your own photos, just click Add and choose the My Albums option. If your friends have just sent you a great Flickr link, for example, you can drag a photo straight from a page in Flickr. You can also list their page and add a hyperlink using the Inspector.

Don't forget video too. Ask your friends to put their creations up on YouTube, and link using the Web widget. Your own work can be found straight from the Media pane, using the video template.

Create a site of your favourite things

Give the world a flavour of the things you love

Ingredients

YouTube video
Pictures

If you'd like to bring a little of the modern experience to your iWeb site, then why not share some of yourself with an About Me page? There are some great templates to get you started, but the best thing is being able to include links from other sites so people can share the things you love.

From the New Page section choose the About Me page, and begin replacing the template text with something more suited to you. To replace the pictures click the Media button to open the floating Media pane. Now you can start dragging your favourite pictures and photos from your iPhoto collection onto the Apple originals.

What about something from a little further afield? If you're adding a list of your favourite bands, why not add links? Simply highlight the name of the band and, in the Link Inspector, add the URL (including the leading 'http://' bit). You can copy and paste this straight from Safari.

This is a good start, but old fashioned links are a bit 20th Century. What about bringing the content to you? Actually, that's often even easier than creating your own content, thanks to automatically generated sharing code snippets.

In your browser head for your favourite video in YouTube. If you were just to copy the link, people would have to leave your site to follow it. However, look to the right of the video and you'll see a block of text with the word Embed above it.

Click in the field and press Cmd+A to select all the text, then Cmd+C to copy it onto the clipboard. Now switch back to your iWeb page and click on the Web Widgets icon. From the pop-up menu pick HTML Snippet, click in the empty text area and press Cmd+V to paste the snippet into place.

A quick thank you

After a special event, send everyone a quick smile to say thank you

Ingredients

Single photo
Message for many
Email addresses

After a big day, like a wedding or christening, there are bound to be far too many people to thank personally. Why not let a simple smile do all the work for you? Create a new site in iWeb, and pick a simple Welcome template. Open the Media panel, select the happiest picture you can find and drag it into the waiting space on the template.

Unless your photo has exactly the same format, it might not look quite right. You can alter the shape of the picture box by double-clicking on it (you'll notice that the cropped areas of the picture appear partially transparent around the edge).

Click Edit Mask in the pop-up, and crop the picture using the corner handles. Now click on the picture again. The corner handles will reappear, but you won't be in Edit Mask mode, so when you resize the picture it will alter the size on the page. You can also drag it back into position.

Once you've finished and added your message, all you need to do is direct visitors to it. Click the Publish button. Once the site is online, an email with a link will appear. Now just add the email addresses of everyone you want to send it to from your Address Book.

One hour GarageBand & iDVD

Instant rock band

Always wanted to play with a band, but couldn't bear the looks you might get if you hit a bum note? Well, we have the answer…

Ingredients

Any instrument you like, including your voice
A dash of creativity

Why not let GarageBand rustle up some perfectly tempered playing buddies for you? They'll never complain when you hit a wrong note, or storm off if they don't get their sherbet.

Launch GarageBand and choose Magic GarageBand. In the window that follows, pick Rock (or the genre you've always seen yourself playing in), then click Audition in the lower-right. Some seemingly possessed instruments should now appear on your screen arranged as a band. Now click Play to hear what sort of backing you've got.

Not happy with one of your invisible brethren? Put the spotlight on the offending instrument and choose an alternative from the list that appears below.

Finally choose your own instrument by clicking the empty area at the front of the stage, and then simply hit Create Project.

A GarageBand project with loops is generated, just waiting for you to add your own unique sound. Place the playhead and click Record!

"Some seemingly possessed instruments appear arranged as a band. Now click Play to hear what sort of backing you've got"

Pro podcast

Although the name implies nothing but teen angst music, GarageBand is a great tool for recording podcasts and getting onto iTunes

Ingredients

Microphone (built-in or external)
Logo picture
Script (optional)

Whether you're looking to take on internet celebrities Alex Albright and Kevin Rose, or just narrowcast to a few select listeners, podcasting is a great way to reach a wider audience – and GarageBand will help you record your message and make it sound good too. How? Well, launch GarageBand and click Create New Podcast Episode. If you've done it before you might want to use a previous episode as a template.

The male and female voice tracks are self-explanatory – just click the record icon and speak into the mic. The clever stuff comes with the jingles, a vast wealth of which can be dragged in from the Media Browser's Audio tab. Another trick is the Podcast Track, into which you can drag images that can be seen on colour-screened iPods and iPhones.

Photo disc with slideshow

One of the most useful things iDVD can do doesn't include a single moment of video

Ingredients

Photos in iPhoto
Blank DVD

The great thing about using iDVD to make a slideshow disc is that you can kill two birds with one stone; you can back up high-resolution files from your computer at the same time as adding your snazzy slideshow.

This can be done in under a dozen clicks of the mouse! Launch iDVD (one click) and pick New Project. Now give it a name and choose your format. Select the Media tab, choose a selection of photos you want to use and drag your newest event to the DVD background.

Drag another copy to the DVD drop zone to avoid the template looking too blank, then double-click on your slideshow title and choose Settings. Tick the Add To DVD-ROM option, then click OK.

At the risk of going beyond the 12 clicks, you're free to add as many slideshows as you can fit on the disc. You can also alter the transitions between images, then, when you're happy with your finished project, click Burn.

Quick iLife tip

Automatic backup
If you like the idea of the high-res backups in the iDVD tutorial, you can set the program to automatically add files to the data area of the disc with a simple tickbox in the Preferences dialog box.

Interactive photo guide

iDVD menus can stretch on for many courses, so why not give each a little personality?

Ingredients

A background image

iDVD doesn't restrict you to using its own templates – you're more than welcome to replace the background with your own video or image. Since you can also position the buttons wherever you like, this makes it possible for you to create your own interactive image.

Launch iDVD and create a new project with a theme that allows for a large background image, like Stretch Extras. Locate your picture in Finder or use the Media pane, then drag it onto the background. In this case we're using a panorama we made in Photoshop, which serves as an ideal point of reference for the videos and slideshows we've got.

As you add slideshows, drag them from their automatic position to pinpoint the spot on the picture you want. Use the Inspector to set the label to the left or right of the icon and, perhaps most importantly, the Size slider to reduce it to a pin size.

This technique can be used for a wide range of projects, from documenting a vacation and using a shot of the city or town as the main menu, or for more practical uses – like showing off your new home to your friends with slideshows included for each room of the house.

Wireless keyboard

The wireless Apple keyboard is quite exceptional – not only for its weight and cable-free functionality, but it's remarkable slender form

iCandy
Wireless keyboard

Places

RECENT
Road Trip
Last 12 Months
Last Import
Flagged
Trash

ALBUMS
5-Star Photos
Our Family

MOBILEME GALLERY
Graduation
Italy
Surfing

FACEBOOK
Road Trip

Robert   Claire   Ali

Adam   Pani   David

Carrie   Olivier   Sarah

Edit   Smart Album   Slideshow   Book   Calendar   Card

Search

14 faces in 1,023 photos

Theo

Sean

Liz

Kevin

MobileMe   Facebook   Flickr   Email

iPhoto

Features

Tutorials

iPhoto is a truly stunning application. Not
only does it allow you to store your digital
photographs in an easy to use, easy to
organise interface, but it also allows you to
get creative with those photographs to get
even more out of them.

25

The complete guide to iPhoto'09

Everything you need to know about Apple's best ever version of iPhoto. Import, organise, edit and share your digital photos the Apple way…

Getting started p28

Organisation p30

Editing p32

Sharing p34

Photo is one of those apps that really does it all. Well, within reason. It won't tell you next week's Lotto numbers or make you irresistible to your preferred sex, but it does offer everything you need to get photos on to your Mac, fix problems like red-eye, tweak and crop your pictures, and get them organised so you can always find the ones you want. In conjunction with other iLife apps, iPhoto also makes it easy to share your pics with other users. And in the latest version, as part of iLife '09, it has even more great features. There's little more you could ask of it.

However, it does ask a few things of you. To get the maximum benefit from iPhoto, you really need to make it the centre of your digital photo world. It's no good storing pictures in random places all over your hard disk and expecting iPhoto to manage them for you. Instead, you should get into the habit of importing all your image files into iPhoto and keeping them stored in its library. That way you'll have every picture easily to hand in one place, and you can make full use of iPhoto's management functions to keep track of your collection.

In this article we'll take you through iPhoto's many functions and introduce you to all the little wrinkles you might not have noticed. You'll find out about the different ways to get pictures in from your digital camera, phone, iPod, or just about anything else with a USB socket, and how to set things up for the greatest convenience. We'll point out a few pitfalls to avoid (yes, even downloading a few photos can occasionally end in tears) and we'll also troubleshoot some common problems and misconceptions.

We'll then move on to examine how iPhoto can organise your images. Albums, events, keywords and folders – what are they all for and how do they work together? Geotagging and face recognition are the buzzwords du jour, but how do they actually help you sort your snaps in iPhoto '09? And what's so smart about a Smart Album? Knowing the ins and outs before you plough into a pile of photos can help you make sure iPhoto's working its hardest for you, without that nagging feeling that you might be missing something.

Finally, we'll take a tour of iPhoto's built-in image-editing tools. Photoshop they're not, but for most users they provide the perfect balance of approachability and functionality. Whether you're shooting with a £500 DSLR or your iPhone, dragging a few sliders in the right directions can make the difference between 'ho-hum' and 'wooh!' when you show off your photos to your friends. Which, of course, we'll also show you how to do.

By now you're probably so excited that you wish we'd wrap up this introduction and get on with elucidating the satisfyingly usable wondrousness that is iPhoto. So we will… ▶

The complete guide: Getting started

Preferences

Get your image management just the way you like it by utilising iPhoto's Preferences

General
Decide what a double-click does to your photo, select an app to open when you connect a camera and more.

Appearance
Speed up iPhoto, change the background colour and edit the Organize view options.

Events
Edit Event appearances, choose a time frame for auto-split and edit the double-click options.

Sharing
If you don't wish to share your entire library with other users, simply tick the albums you do want to share.

Web
Check your iDisk storage usage as well as set your options to include location data in uploaded photos.

Advanced
Set your import options, RAW format information and geographical look-up details from this tab.

"It's worth checking that your camera battery is fully charged before beginning an import"

Like the other iLife apps, iPhoto is included with Mac OS X and can be found in your Applications folder, as well as being listed in the Dock by default. When first run, it displays a Welcome box offering a quick tour of the features, which is well worth a look at. What it won't do automatically is show any of your pictures, so your first task is to import them. We look at the options for this in more detail in the Importing box-out below.

If you've got images already sitting on your hard disk but not yet in iPhoto, you can either choose Import To Library from iPhoto's File menu or just drag a folder of images from the Finder to iPhoto's main window. The same method can also be used to get images from a USB drive, from a memory card reader, or from a CD or DVD – as long as they're stored as standard image files, like JPEGs for example.

It's equally easy to access pictures from digital cameras, mobile phones and other portable devices. When you connect a device to your Mac via USB, its memory will usually appear as a drive in the Finder. Open this and work your way through the folders to find where images are stored; they'll most often be in a folder named DCIM (for 'digital camera images'), but some hardware makers prefer to use their own names, such as 'Pictures'. Again, you can either use iPhoto's Import To Library command (the shortcut being Shift+Cmd+I) or drag the folder to iPhoto.

An even easier way to get photos from your camera, mobile or other device, including iPhones and iPods, is to make iPhoto activate every time you plug your device into your Mac. To do this, go to iPhoto>Preferences. In the General tab, click the drop-down menu labelled 'Connecting camera opens' and choose iPhoto. In future, when you connect any relevant device, iPhoto will appear and show you the images stored on it. Select the ones you want – use the Shift and Ctrl keys in the usual way to add multiple images – or opt to import them all. If, like us, you tend to take quite a lot of photos, be prepared for a bit of a delay – especially if your camera uses RAW format. It's likely to delay while iPhoto previews all the available images, and then while they download. You're free to do other things in iPhoto while this is happening though, then come back to the Import screen by clicking the name of your camera (often 'NO NAME') under Devices in iPhoto's left pane.

It's worth checking that your camera battery is fully charged before beginning an import. Most cameras don't draw power from the USB lead, so if the battery runs out while the import is in progress, it'll stop. You'll then have to choose whether to delete the imported pics and start again, or to keep them and work out which ones you still need to import. The latter is normally

Importing

There are many different ways to add photos to your iPhoto library from most common storage devices

USB
A USB stick or hard drive-based device offers a simple way to import photos

Camera/card reader
iPhoto imports image files directly from your camera or phone, or from other USB devices. These will appear under the Devices heading in the Source list.

Hard drive
To import images from a folder, whether on your main hard disk, an external drive or another Mac on your home network, use File>Import To Library.

CD or DVD
Pictures on disc can be imported in the same way as from other folders. Most formats will work and photo CDs are best imported directly into iPhoto.

iPhone
By default, iPhoto will open when you connect your iPhone to your Mac and appear as a device in the Source pane so you can import images quickly.

made easier by iPhoto's option to 'Hide photos already imported', which appears during the import process. Although it's less common with modern hardware, turning off a device without warning while it's connected via USB can put its memory card into a state that won't allow data to be read until it's reformatted. This could mean losing all the remaining pictures, unless you take the card to a camera shop or data recovery specialist who can rescue the files. So it's well worth remembering not to unplug any device (or let its battery run out) before you tell iPhoto to eject it or you click the Eject icon beside its name in a Finder window.

You'll notice there's an option to 'Autosplit events after importing'. Splitting your photos into events is a quick way to organise them. If you take your camera to the fairground on Monday, a rock concert on Tuesday and the beach on Wednesday, and then download your pictures, your photos are sorted into three events. You can give each event a suitable name.

After importing images, you're returned to iPhoto's main display where the default view is Events. Each event is represented by a large button that shows a sample image from that set of pictures, with the event's title shown below (or the date if it's untitled). When you roll your mouse over a button, the sample thumbnail changes from a cropped-in view to the full image, and you can roll your mouse over this to page through all the photos in the event. Like one of them better? Right-click it and choose Make Key Photo to use this image for the button.

Double-clicking an event brings up thumbnails of the pictures it contains. Alternatively, click Photos in the list to the left (known as the Source list) to view all your pictures. You can scroll through thumbnails using the vertical scroll bar to the right, and adjust their size to make the photos bigger or see more at once by using the slider in the bottom-right corner. There are several other ways to view your photos too, as we'll see in a moment.

You should be aware of where all these photos are stored. By default, iPhoto leaves your original image files alone and creates a new copy of each photo within your library. This is contained in a single file called 'iPhoto

Icons explained

Flag
This lets you mark pics that you're thinking about doing something with. Click Flagged to see the current flagged images.

Hide
If your collection includes images you don't want at the moment, but would rather not delete, just hide them.

Slideshow
Select any number of pics and click here for an instant slideshow. You're offered various settings before you click Play.

Keepsakes
iPhoto includes interactive templates for books, calendars and greetings cards, which you can buy through Apple.

MobileMe
Click here to create an album of the selected photos in your MobileMe Gallery, which others can view via their web browser.

Create a new album
Albums are a simple way to categorise your photos. Click this button to add your own, give it a name, then drag photos in.

Enter full-screen
If you're working in iPhoto at the same time as other apps, you can make its window small, then quickly switch to a full-screen view.

Edit
Click here to access iPhoto's editing features. In Preferences/General, you can opt to make this activate an external editor.

Facebook
Click here to publish the selected photos as a Facebook album. You'll need to go through the usual Facebook rigmarole.

Flickr
iPhoto can even link automatically to your Flickr account to upload your selected photos without any faffing about.

Email
Click here to attach the selected photos to a new message in Mail. You get the option to automatically reduce their size first.

iWeb
With iWeb, it's easy to transfer from iPhoto. Select the pics, go to Share>Send To iWeb, and choose what to do with them.

Merge/split events
This button allows you to split a selection of photos into two Events or merge two Events into one. Select the images and click the button.

Show/hide info
Info about the current image or album appears in the bottom-left. Click this to hide it if you're short of space.

Name
Click this to identify people visible. It's a great way to organise pictures, and iPhoto will try to spot the same person in other photos.

Rotate
Click this button to rotate any number of selected images anti-clockwise. Hold the Alt key to swap the rotation.

Library' in the Pictures folder within your home folder (the one named with your username inside the Users' folder on your hard disk). You can see what's inside by right-clicking the file icon and choosing Show Package Contents. Your original photos are stored in Originals, while the results of any edits you've made within iPhoto are in Modified. It's important never to change or re-arrange anything within this library, as it'll hopelessly confuse iPhoto. However, in an emergency – for example, if iPhoto becomes damaged and you can't access your library – you could copy the image files out of these folders to a safe place. And don't forget to back up! ▶

⚠ Troubleshooting
If iPhoto isn't working, there's usually a simple explanation

I put some of the images in my iPhoto library into new folders. Now lots of my photos have disappeared!

Never make changes to your library – it's designed to be managed only by iPhoto. You may need to copy all your image files to a fresh location, then re-import them.

Something went wrong when I was importing pictures. I asked to keep the ones imported so far, but I don't see them in iPhoto.

Close iPhoto and launch it again. With a bit of luck, you'll see an alert saying a number of photos have been found.

Things don't seem to work as they should in the iPhoto window. For example, I can't move pictures from one Event to another. What's wrong?

You may need to rebuild your library. Hold down Cmd+Opt and launch iPhoto. Try rebuilding the permissions.

When I've taken a photo with the camera held on its side, why does iPhoto import it the wrong way up?

Some cameras don't record the info in a format iPhoto can understand. Try adding images via the Finder rather than importing them directly.

The complete guide: Organisation

iPhoto '09

Organisation methods

Events

By default, all photos taken on the same day belong to the same Event. In iPhoto>Preferences>Events, use the 'Autosplit into Events' menu to alter this. You can re-split existing events by selecting them in the main window and using Events>Autosplit Selected Events. Or if a group of photos has been wrongly split into multiple events, select them all and choose Events>Merge Events.

Places

'Geotagging' means recording the geographic location of a photo. If you use a device with built-in GPS, such as an iPhone 3G, your photos should automatically be geotagged. Click Places to see a world map showing all the destinations among your photos and click any of the pins to show the photos that were shot there. Or click the second View icon below the map to show the locations as a list.

Faces

An obvious way to sort photos of people is by the people who are in them. iPhoto '09 uses face recognition to identify faces so that you can label your photos with names. While browsing photos, click the Name icon to show a box around the face in the current image. If it detects the same face already named in another photo, it'll ask you if it's them. If iPhoto doesn't spot a face at all, click Add Missing Face.

"Once you get the hang of it, you'll begin to see how logical and flexible the system is"

iPhoto provides numerous ways to sort and group your photos, including events, albums, keywords and folders. These all work in conjunction with each other, and each photo may be assigned to several. It's still the same photo, not a copy, so when you make changes to it they'll be reflected in all the places where that photo is listed. Equally, you can delete an album without affecting the photos inside it. Once you get the hang of it, you'll begin to see how logical and flexible the system is.

The Source list in iPhoto's left-hand pane lets you narrow down which photos you see on the right. Under Library, you can click Photos to see all of your pictures sorted according to the criteria you choose under View>Sort Photos. By default, they're still organised into events, then sorted within each event. To ignore events, untick View>Event Titles. You can also click Faces to list all the people you've named in your photos, then double-click a person to see all their pictures, or click Places to see a map showing all the locations where your pictures were shot and pick a location to see its photos.

Under Recent you get more options, including Last Import, which is handy if you recently added a bunch of unsorted images and now can't find them, and Trash, where you can rescue any pictures you deleted within iPhoto and now realise you need (as long as you haven't opted to empty iPhoto's trash in the meantime). Click Flagged to see only the photos that you've flagged by clicking the Flag icon in the bottom-left. Use this to mark files temporarily while you're deciding which photos you want for a particular purpose.

Below this, the Albums list is your chance to organise your own pictures. It's up to you how you do this, but if you used albums for pictures taken during a particular session or at a particular location, you'd be duplicating the functionality of events or places. Instead, albums should reflect the content of your images. Think of them

as categories or genres, such as food, portraits or sports. To assign a photo to an album, drag the photo to the album. Remember, you can assign the same photo to as many albums as you like.

To describe content more specifically, you can use keywords. Having assigned a picture to a sports album, adding keywords such as 'football', 'championship' and 'goalkeeper' would give you more to go on when

No GPS? No problem

If you have a GPS-enabled camera then the location where you took each picture is recorded within the image file. iPhoto will read this and use it to sort your pictures by location. Click Places in the Source list to see where in the world your photos came from.

If your camera doesn't have GPS but you carry some other GPS device, you can use extra software to work out the locations of your photos and feed this information back into the image files. See **http://tinyurl.com/7cdm7j** for a list of suitable software.

Alternatively, click the 'i' icon in the bottom-right of any untagged photo or event, then click 'Enter photo location' and type a place name to find it.

Conneticut weekend

Whistler
28 Sep 2006 - 13 Dec 2008   20

Zaca Lake

Emma's Party

Camping

Ice climbing - New Zealand

Emma's Party   Camping

View options

You can adjust the size of an image with the slider at the bottom of the iPhoto interface, but Full-Screen mode is a must for editing.

iPhoto's Standard view for editing images

The larger Full-Screen view in iPhoto '09

searching later. To show the Keywords palette, press Cmd+K. Click Edit Keywords, then use the plus, minus and Rename buttons to add your own keywords.

To apply a keyword to a photo, select the photo and click the keyword (or press its shortcut key). To see the keywords that have been assigned to each photo in the main pane, tick View>Keywords, or press Shift+Cmd+K. With this option activated, you can also click below any photo and type a new keyword, which is added to your Keywords palette if it doesn't already exist. To sort your photos by keyword, go to View>Sort Photos>By Keyword.

Notice the special 'checkmark' keyword, which looks like a tick. This is handy for temporarily marking selected pictures. You might want to add your own task-based keywords to mark all the images that you're going to colour-correct or re-crop when you get round to it.

The usefulness of keywords depends on how many pictures you take and how often you'll need to refine a search according to exactly what's in the frame. Rather than spending ages on it, make time for an intensive keywording session a bit later.

You can find photos by keyword – as well as titles, descriptions and dates – using the Search box at the bottom of iPhoto's window. Another way to display only those pictures that match a particular keyword, or indeed two or more keywords, is provided by iPhoto's next image-management trick: Smart Albums. The idea here is that instead of manually adding photos to an album, you tell iPhoto to include all the pics that meet certain criteria. As you make changes to your collection, the Smart Album automatically updates. Go to File>New Smart Album and you'll see how it works. Using the drop-down menus, set the filter to whatever you want, then click the plus button if you want to add more criteria. You might keep a number of Smart Albums permanently on the go – for example, using the Camera Model filter to separate your iPhone snaps from your DSLR shots – and create extra Smart Albums as a way of searching for what you want.

Get info window Make sense of your photo's information

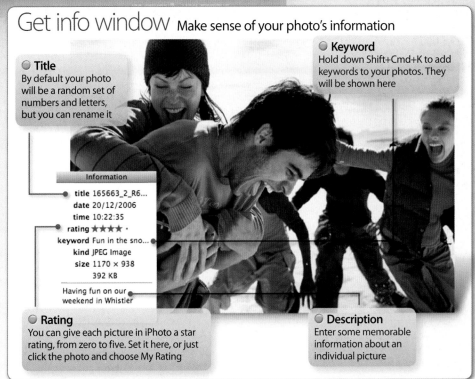

Title
By default your photo will be a random set of numbers and letters, but you can rename it

Keyword
Hold down Shift+Cmd+K to add keywords to your photos. They will be shown here

Information
title 165663_2_R6...
date 20/12/2006
time 10:22:35
rating ★★★★ ·
keyword Fun in the sno...
kind JPEG Image
size 1170 × 938
392 KB

Having fun on our weekend in Whistler

Rating
You can give each picture in iPhoto a star rating, from zero to five. Set it here, or just click the photo and choose My Rating

Description
Enter some memorable information about an individual picture

Finally, you can give each photo a rating. Like keywords, these are only shown below each photo if you activate the relevant option in the View menu. To rate a picture, select it, hold the Apple key and press a number key from 0 to 5. If a photo is so bad it isn't even worth zero, hide it by pressing Apple+L. It still exists, but won't be seen unless you tick View>Hidden Photos, in which case it'll appear with a cross beside it. As you've probably twigged, you can now sort your pics by rating or create a Smart Album for, say, all those with three stars or more. ▶

What is Metadata?
Metadata is information that's stored along with an image. Unlike options specific to iPhoto, such as what album a photo belongs to, metadata is part of the image file and can be read by other applications. If the Information icon is activated, you can see the metadata for the current photo above this.

The complete guide: Editing

It's all very well sorting your pictures by date, location and content, but you've still to exploit another great benefit of digital photography: instant editing. iPhoto is no Photoshop, but it has its own very useful editing tools built in, and with a little practice you'll soon be using them to turn just-good-enough pictures into really sparkling ones.

There's a choice of methods to activate iPhoto's editing tools. By default, you select a photo in the main window and click Edit in the toolbar at the bottom. The selected image fills the window and the toolbar changes to show the editing functions. However, in iPhoto>Preferences> General you'll find several other options. First of all, you can tell iPhoto to edit a photo when you double-click it, rather than just magnifying it. You can also use the drop-down menu labelled 'Edit photo' to choose exactly what happens when you activate editing. 'In main window' means the iPhoto window stays the same but with the editing tools displayed and 'Using full screen' means you get a full-screen view while you edit. But if you prefer to use a separate editing app, such as Photoshop, choose 'In application', then select the program file.

Regardless of your preferences though, you can choose to edit any image either within iPhoto or externally by right-clicking it and picking Edit, Edit Using Full Screen or Edit In External Editor. Note that this only works while browsing multiple photos, and not when one photo is already magnified.

Before we look at the editing tools, a quick word on how they affect your image files. As we've mentioned, iPhoto stores any edits separately from the original image. This means you can undo any adjustments at any time; just right-click the photo and choose Revert To Original. If you use the Crop or Adjust tools, you can even re-edit your changes later (the options you apply remain active and can be reset or tweaked).

If you have a high-end camera that shoots RAW images, you can use iPhoto to manage and edit these shots too. iPhoto will process RAW files from most cameras, but you can't adjust the RAW conversion. Your photo will appear as a thumbnail just like other images, but the Information panel reveals that it's in RAW, and when you open it in iPhoto's editor a 'RAW' badge appears below it. If you make changes and click Done, the image is resaved as a JPEG (though the original RAW file still exists). Inevitably, this reduces quality. So in iPhoto>Preferences>Advanced, you can tick the option 'Save edits as 16-bit TIFF files' to retain as much image data as possible.

The most basic edits are rotation, cropping and straightening, and these are the first three options in iPhoto's edit toolbar. When you click Crop, the view zooms out a little so you can see the edges of your picture, and a crop box appears, slightly smaller by default. Adjust the box by dragging its corners, then click Apply. If you need the final image to be a particular shape tick Constrain and choose the appropriate ratio from the menu.

To straighten a picture, you first need to spot what isn't straight. As a general rule, if you can see the horizon in the scene then make it horizontal, and if you can't then find something near the middle of the frame that should be vertical, and make it so. When you click the Straighten icon, iPhoto shows gridlines to help, plus a slider to rotate the image.

The next edit option, Enhance, is a one-click operation designed to make pictures clearer and bolder. It won't improve every photo, but it's worth trying on any that look slightly dull. Press Ctrl+Z to undo any changes you make if necessary. The Redeye tool, which counteracts the satanic effect of flash, is almost as easy to use: click on the offending pupil, adjusting the Size slider if necessary to roughly match the size of the eye, and iPhoto will do the rest.

The Retouch tool requires a bit more effort. It's good for removing small blemishes from faces or unwanted specks from clear skies. However, because it smooths out detail it needs to be used with care.

The last and most powerful of iPhoto's editing tools is Adjust. Clicking its icon will open a whole palette of corrections. The multi-coloured chart at the top is called a histogram, and it shows the distribution of colour values. If there's a good spread across the scale, rising in the middle and falling gently away at the left and right, your image's tonal range is probably okay. If the values drop to zero some way from the left and/or right, leaving empty areas at the ends, then drag the left and/or right markers inwards to where the values start to rise, and you'll see an immediate improvement. You can

> ## "The most basic edits are rotation, croppng and straightening, and these are the first three options in iPhoto's edit toolbar"

Use the Eyedropper tool
One of the hardest problems to correct can be when your camera's white balance has been fooled by tricky lighting and the whole image has an odd-looking colour cast. Open the Adjust palette and click the Eyedropper icon. Now find a spot in your photo that should be pure white, or failing that a neutral grey (for example, an object that's white usually but it's in shadow). Click here to rebalance the whole photo. If it doesn't work well, try a different spot.

Before   *After*

⊞ Effects window
All of the available effects in iPhoto's Effects pane

✎ The Edit interface

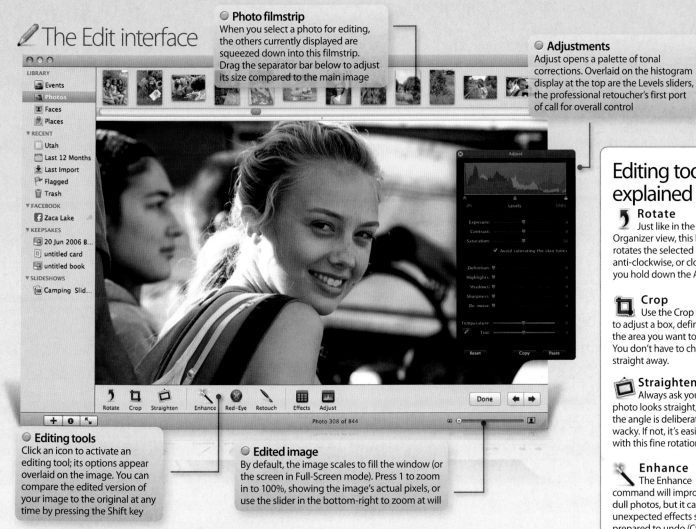

Photo 308 of 844

● Photo filmstrip
When you select a photo for editing, the others currently displayed are squeezed down into this filmstrip. Drag the separator bar below to adjust its size compared to the main image

● Adjustments
Adjust opens a palette of tonal corrections. Overlaid on the histogram display at the top are the Levels sliders, the professional retoucher's first port of call for overall control

● Editing tools
Click an icon to activate an editing tool; its options appear overlaid on the image. You can compare the edited version of your image to the original at any time by pressing the Shift key

● Edited image
By default, the image scales to fill the window (or the screen in Full-Screen mode). Press 1 to zoom in to 100%, showing the image's actual pixels, or use the slider in the bottom-right to zoom at will

Editing tools explained

↰ Rotate
Just like in the Organizer view, this button rotates the selected image anti-clockwise, or clockwise if you hold down the Alt key.

▢ Crop
Use the Crop tool to adjust a box, defining the area you want to keep. You don't have to change it straight away.

▢ Straighten
Always ask yourself if a photo looks straight, unless the angle is deliberately wacky. If not, it's easily fixed with this fine rotation tool.

✎ Enhance
The Enhance command will improve many dull photos, but it can have unexpected effects so be prepared to undo (Ctrl+Z).

⊘ Red-Eye
Flash bouncing off the eye can turn a portrait into a horror show. Best avoid or diffuse it, but if it's too late, click each eye with this tool.

✎ Retouch
Use this to smooth colour and texture from the surrounding area, covering blemishes. Using it effectively will take some practice.

▦ Effects
This Effects icon will open up a palette of nine special effects. Just click on one to apply it to your chosen shot.

▦ Adjust
When a picture looks washed-out, too bright, too dark, or a funny colour, and Enhance won't fix it, it's time to try some adjustments.

"Sharpening is an important trick for making a reasonably well-focused shot look pin-sharp… don't go past the point where things start to look speckly though"

also move the centre marker to adjust the midpoint or gamma, which will ensure that the picture isn't too light or too muddy.

If that all sounds a bit technical, then you'll probably find the sliders more straightforward. The first slider can help if your picture is over or under-exposed. Increasing contrast and saturation will give more punch, as long as you don't overdo it. Tick 'Avoid saturating the skin tones' to whack up the background colours without causing red faces. The Definition slider selectively boosts contrast to make detail look clearer. Highlights and Shadows are also smart contrast adjustments; use Shadows to rescue excessively dark areas, while Highlights can find texture and colour in an overexposed sky.

Sharpening is an important trick for making a reasonably well-focused shot look pin-sharp, but first be sure to press 1 to zoom to 100% magnification or you

won't see the effect properly (press 0 to make the photo fill the window again). Don't go past the point where things start to look speckly though – the De-noise slider can help stave this off, but too much will erase texture and leave an unnaturally smooth image.

Finally, you can play with the Temperature and Tint sliders to make a dull day warmer or to correct unwanted colour casts, aided and abetted by the Eyedropper, which we explain in the box on p34. With so many new editing features available in iPhoto, from the simple one-click effects through to more detailed precision adjustments using the Adjust pane, applications like Adobe's Photoshop Elements are becoming increasingly less of a requirement. With all the tools available in iPhoto's Edit screen you're well equipped to deal with any issues that may crop up when you import your pictures, and a little experimentation will usually provide decent results. ▶

The complete guide: Sharing

There's little point amassing a neatly organised collection of finely tuned photos if you keep them all to yourself. Fortunately, iPhoto makes it easy to get your pictures out into the world and do whatever you want with them.

To transfer photos to another storage location, such as a USB drive, select them and go to File>Export. You can select any combination of individual photos, events, albums, or whatever you want to include. In the Export Photos box, choose a file format, JPEG compression quality setting, output size (so you can reduce the resolution if the files are to email or store on a smaller device), file naming structure, and whether title and keyword metadata are included.

The Export Photos box also includes tabs for creating a standalone webpage, QuickTime video or slideshow. You can quickly create slideshows suitable for viewing on a Mac, AppleTV, iPhone or iPod. If tinkering with video settings is your idea of fun, click Custom Export in the Slideshow tab, then click the Options button to tailor the output to your exact requirements.

Burning selected photos to CD or DVD is easy, too. To create a disc for other iPhoto users, select some pictures and go to Share>Burn. For a multi-purpose disc that PC users can view too, export your images first, as above, then drag them to a blank disc in the Finder and burn it.

To share images with other Macs on your own network, go to iPhoto>Preferences>Sharing. Remember to set the other Mac's iPhoto to 'Look for shared photos'. You can even copy your whole iPhoto library to another Mac. However, you may need to create an identical user

"Fortunately, iPhoto makes it easy to get your pictures out into the world and do whatever you want with them"

account on that computer before you can use it, and you can't use more than one library at a time. If you need multiple libraries, try the third-party app iPhoto Library Manager, from www.fatcatsoftware.com/iplm.

Want to share pictures through your Facebook or Flickr account? There are buttons for that in iPhoto, plus one to attach photos to a new Mail message. If you use a different email, select it in iPhoto>Preferences>General> Email Photos Using, then select your email program.

Got a MobileMe account? You can publish photos to your Public Gallery, which anyone can view in their web browser. Select the photos you want, then click the plus icon and choose MobileMe in the box. Give your online album a name, select who can view it and click Publish. Your online album will be listed under the new heading MobileMe Gallery in iPhoto's Source list. Click it to see the pictures it contains and the web address where others can find it. If you want to take the album down from the web, just select it here and press Delete.

Finally, if the occasion demands something more substantial, check out the Book, Calendar and Card options. Simply select some photos and you'll be led through the process of constructing a product that you can buy online or print yourself.

Slideshow settings explained

Perfect your settings to show off your images in style with new slideshows

Themes
When you begin a slideshow you will see this menu. The first tab allows you to pick from one of six themes to show off your pictures. See all of the great new slideshow themes in iPhoto '09 in the box below (left).

Music
The next tab lets you pick some music to play behind the slideshow. Select a source and then search for the perfect song from the list. You can also use the search box to hunt down and preview your audio choices.

Settings
Now choose the specifics of your slideshow from a variety of settings. Set the length of time each image is shown for, whether music should play and the titles to be shown. You can set these choices as your default slideshow style.

▦ Slideshow themes

New in iPhoto '09: Classic, Ken Burns, Scrapbook, Shatter, Sliding Panels and Snapshots

iCandy
MacBook Air

MacBook Air The supermodel of the MacBook lineup, the Air is thin, sexy and, unlike its catwalk-based counterparts, has the brains to back up its beauty.

Tutorial: Use Faces in iPhoto to pinpoint friends

Faces is an interesting feature in iPhoto '09 that identifies and recognises familiar faces. We give you the lowdown…

Task: Use Faces to organise who's who in your shots

Difficulty: Beginner

Time needed: Depends on how many people you have images of

After an update, iPhoto now has an extremely handy function known as Faces. This allows you to organise your images based on the people within them. This fun feature uses face detection to identify the faces within an image, and face recognition technology to match and recommend other faces that look like the same person.

This feature is set to dramatically reduce the amount of time on admin, as previously users would have had to track through images and add this data into the information associated with each picture accordingly. So take five minutes to study this nine-step session to learn how it is done.

Step-by-step | iPhoto Put a name to a face with Faces

1: Put a face to a name
To begin adding names to your friend's and family's faces open up an image then select the icon in the bottom-left labelled Name.

2: Type here
A little white frame will now appear around the subject's face and iPhoto will prompt you to add the name of the individual. Type this in and hit Done.

3: Remember me?
The software will begin to remember faces and asks whether the person is someone you've already catalogued. Hit the tick for yes and the cross for no.

4: DIY
If for some reason you hit Name and a box doesn't frame a face, use the Add Missing Face button. Drag the box to fit around the person's face. Hit Done.

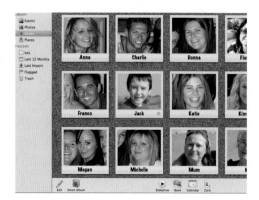

5: Pin up
By hitting Faces in the Source List your images are added to a funky pin board. To delve into the individual's collection just select the snapshot.

6: Move around
The app arranges the snapshots in alphabetical order. To re-arrange this simply select and drag the snapshots around the pin board.

Use Faces in iPhoto

Faces
Hit this folder to discover the funky and fun Faces pin board. Scroll down to see all your faces and use the scale bar to enlarge or reduce the size of the snapshots

Knowledge base

Get smart
Another neat feature of Faces is that users can create Smart Albums. Drag one or more snapshots to the source list or hit the appropriate icon and the app will produce the corresponding Smart Album. Now every time you update your collection and confirm the name of a subject, the image can be filed away accordingly.

Smart Album
Hit this helpful icon to organise a Smart Album, taking all of the hard work out of organisation. See our Knowledge Box for more info

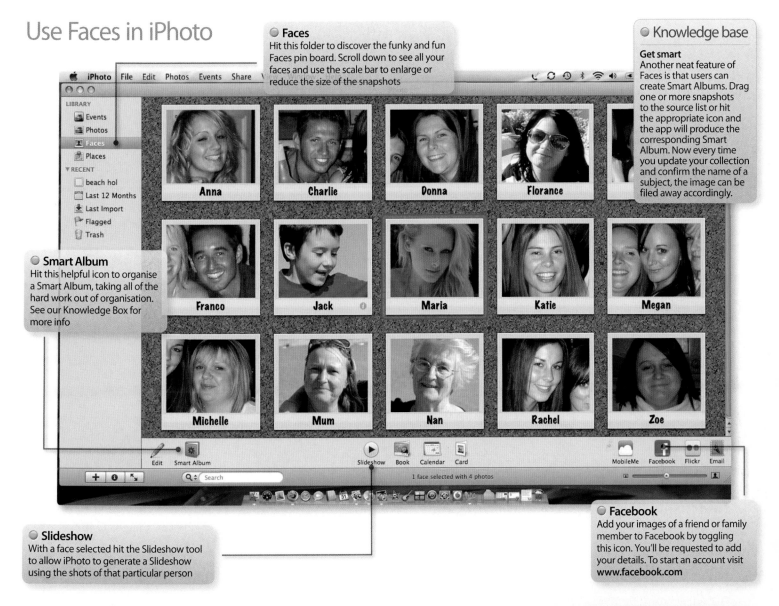

Slideshow
With a face selected hit the Slideshow tool to allow iPhoto to generate a Slideshow using the shots of that particular person

Facebook
Add your images of a friend or family member to Facebook by toggling this icon. You'll be requested to add your details. To start an account visit **www.facebook.com**

7: Can I make a suggestion?
To find suggestions of more matches click on a snapshot and you'll be given suggestions of new matches. Click to accept the right ones.

8: Good but not perfect
Although the feature is good it isn't fool-proof, and often confuses similar looking subjects. If iPhoto incorrectly groups a face, click on it to correct it.

9: More information
Flip the snapshot over by pressing the Information icon and add the person's surname and Facebook ID or email address.

Tutorial: Add missing faces in iPhoto

iPhoto is great but it's not perfect. It may not be able to recognise every face in your collection, so it pays to know how to add a missing face the manual way

Task: Input a missing face into iPhoto's Faces

Difficulty: Beginner

Time needed: 15 minutes

So you love the latest iPhoto and are thrilled with its neat new feature Faces, but hate it when it misses certain images out from your portrait collection. These inconsistencies can be very annoying, especially if you are tracking down an image. You have it in your mind's eye, but then you dip into Faces to find it it's not there.

iPhoto is priceless in our eyes, but we know it's not perfect. Every now and then it just needs help. The reason why some faces aren't recognised and grouped with others could be because the portrait is obscured with a hat or shades, or because it's a side-on view, or perhaps there's issues like the face being out of focus.

So, what can we do? Well, we can input the faces ourselves the good old-fashioned DIY way. Follow our quick four-step workshop to find out how.

Step-by-step | iPhoto Add a missing face in Faces

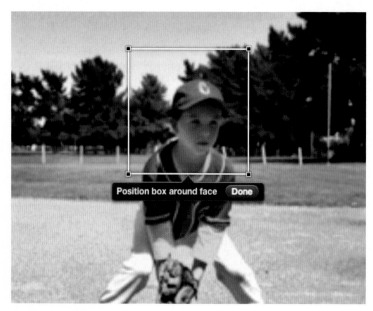

1: Find a face
Isolate an image and hit the Name icon. If there is no name box around the subject, click Add Missing Face. Pull the box into position around the facial area, resizing it to fit, and finalise this by hitting Done.

2: Give it a name
Next type in the name of the person and hit Return. You may find that as you type iPhoto will suggest other names that begin with the letters you are typing. This will speed things along.

Add missing faces in Faces

Add a missing face the manual way in iPhoto

Knowledge base

Click to confirm

Once you have inputted a fresh face into the Faces folder, iPhoto may suggest new matches. Simply click on the image and choose the Confirm Name icon. Then click the correct matches once and the incorrect matches twice. A coloured tag underneath the image will explain which you have actioned. Finalise the decision by opting for Done.

Suggestion

Once you start collecting Faces, iPhoto will be able to suggest people stored in your Faces folder who begin with the same letter as you type in a name

Unknown face

Sometimes iPhoto will recognise that there is a face in the picture, but not be able to ascertain who it is. Simply add the name of the person into the space 'Unknown face'

Add missing face

Hit this button to add missing faces to the image. A box will appear on screen and it will be your task to move it to fit around the subject's face and give it the correct name

Arrow

By punching the arrow to the right of the nametag, users can transport themselves into the Faces folder where other images of this person will be stored, as well as possible suggestions of new matches

3: Faces collection

Look to the Source List and hit the Faces folder. On this corkboard all your Faces will lie in wait. Source your newly added face and hit it to see other images of the same person.

4: Add more information

Why not take this one step further and add the new Faces photo to Places? Spin the image around by actioning the 'i' button and enter the relevant event, date and location details. Once complete choose Done.

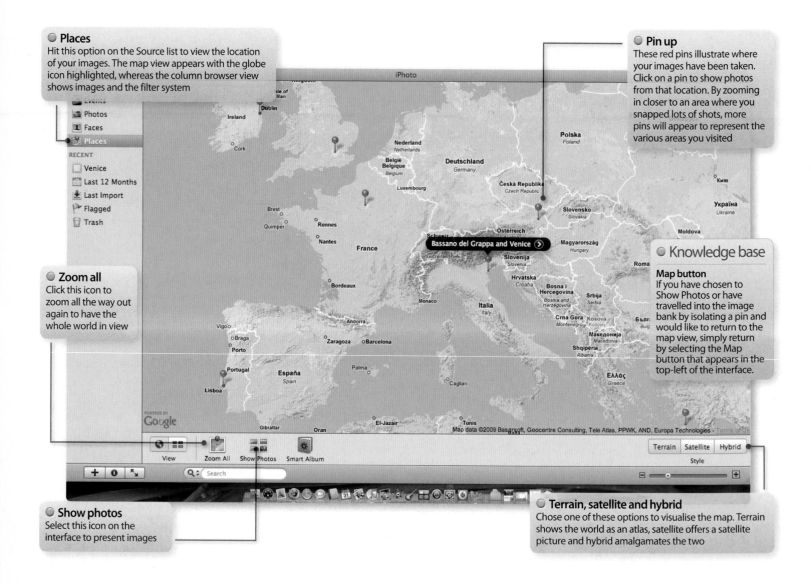

Places
Hit this option on the Source list to view the location of your images. The map view appears with the globe icon highlighted, whereas the column browser view shows images and the filter system

Pin up
These red pins illustrate where your images have been taken. Click on a pin to show photos from that location. By zooming in closer to an area where you snapped lots of shots, more pins will appear to represent the various areas you visited

Zoom all
Click this icon to zoom all the way out again to have the whole world in view

Knowledge base

Map button
If you have chosen to Show Photos or have travelled into the image bank by isolating a pin and would like to return to the map view, simply return by selecting the Map button that appears in the top-left of the interface.

Show photos
Select this icon on the interface to present images

Terrain, satellite and hybrid
Chose one of these options to visualise the map. Terrain shows the world as an atlas, satellite offers a satellite picture and hybrid amalgamates the two

Tutorial: Use Places to sort your images in iPhoto

iPhoto '09 offers photographers the opportunity to store shots in the area they were snapped. Follow this handy tutorial to discover all you need to know

Task: Separate shots into the location they were taken with Places
Difficulty: Beginner
Time needed: Varies depending on the number of images and wealth or lack of GPS data

iPhoto '09 offers users a plethora of new and exciting features for organising and viewing your sacred magic moments. One facet sure to delight those bitten by the travel bug is Apple's new Places facility.

With this version, iPhoto delivers the ability to explore, store and view your snaps by the place where they were captured. The technology uses data from a GPS-enabled camera (or the camera on an iPhone) to filter shots by location and convert GPS location tags to recognisable names. This means if you took a holiday picture of the Taj Mahal, iPhoto can label it with searchable names such as 'Agra', 'India' and 'Taj Mahal'.

iPhoto '09 doesn't discriminate against those not blessed with GPS-enabled cameras or camera-integrated telephonic equipment, as users can add the location themselves by typing the name of the place and setting the pin on the interactive map.

1: Get started
Go to your Events folder and hit the information icon in the bottom-right. iPhoto will illustrate the location the image was taken with a red pin.

2: Several snaps
If you have taken several shots in the same area and have stored these together as an Event the app will display several red pins in the flip out window.

3: DIY
If your camera hasn't stored the GPS data add the location yourself. Open an image and select the information icon. Type in the location and hit Done.

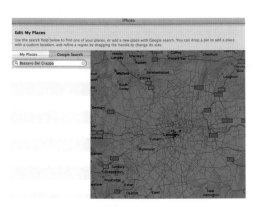

4: DIY some more
The list is US-centric, so span down to find more options. If your place isn't listed hit New Place. Type the name into the Google plug-in to find it.

5: Span out
A blue pin will appear in the location you have entered. Select and drag the pin to the correct part of the map. Hit Assign To Photo when you're ready.

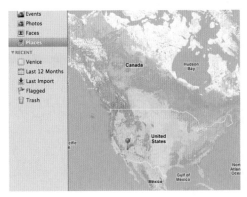

6: Map it out
To view your images, track to the Places folder on the Source list and a map will appear. The red pins illustrate where your images have been taken.

7: Show me the photos
To view photos simply pick a pin. Zoom in to differentiate between close lying pins or to find an individual photo. Or you can hit the Show Photos tab.

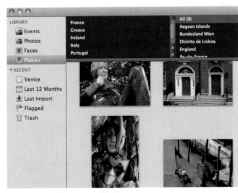

8: Column browser
Another way to find images is to hit the Column browser. Travel through the columns to filter through locations and isolate photos.

9: A new view
You can also use the app as an interactive map: terrain shows an atlas, satellite presents a 'Google Earth' view and hybrid offers a combination of both.

iPhoto '09

Tutorial: Use Places without a GPS-enabled camera

No GPS on your camera? No problem – you can still use iPhoto's Places by tagging a selection of images from your trip

Task: Tag photos without GPS data for Places
Difficulty: Beginner
Time needed: 10 minutes

Places is a brilliant new feature in iPhoto, but one that won't appeal to those importing images from a camera that doesn't tag pictures with GPS data. That doesn't have to be the case, however, as there are ways to add the information about where you took a photo from right within iPhoto. While it's much easier to simply import your pictures and watch them appear on the Places map, it's a fairly painless process to add the GPS information required to a bunch of images in a matter of clicks. Obviously, you're free to fine-tune the process and add a location for each individual image you add to your library but, to keep things simple, we're going to show you how to select a bunch of photos and place them all in one location so you can get some use out of the Places feature. Imagine you've just come back from vacation and want to use Places to show off your trip. With this guide you'll be able to add a location to each event and use Places to put them on the map.

Step-by-step | iPhoto Add GPS data

1: Select your event

● Open up an Event or selection of photos you would like to provide location data for and select them by dragging over them, or hit Cmd+A to highlight all of the images on the screen.

2: Get info

● Click the 'i' button on one of the selected images to bring up the info window for your selection of pictures. Now click 'Enter location of photos' and click the New Place button to bring up the map.

Tag photos for Places

Move around the map
You can click and drag to move around the map view and use the plus and minus buttons to zoom in and out. You can view the map in terrain, satellite or hybrid views

Local area
For a selection of photos you can use the handle to enlarge the area the photos were taken in to cover more ground

My places
Locations you have already added will appear under this tab and you can add more by using the Google Search option to find a specific location for your pictures

Drop Pin
When you have found the exact spot where your photos were taken, click the Drop Pin button to add that place to your My Places section and add the GPS data to your chosen pictures

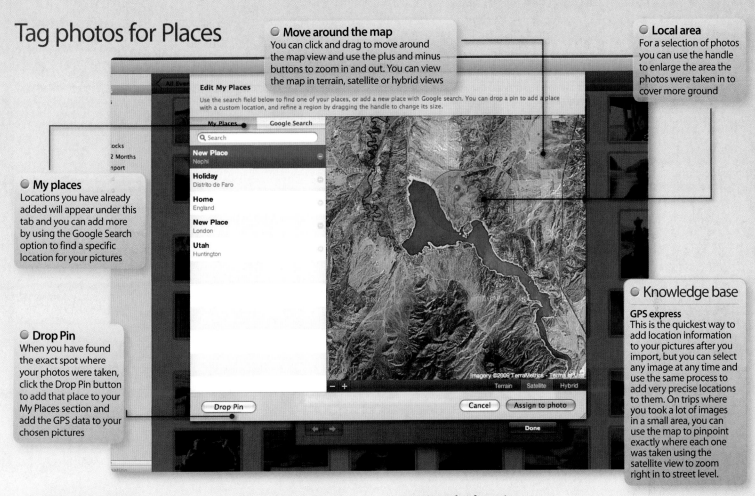

Knowledge base

GPS express
This is the quickest way to add location information to your pictures after you import, but you can select any image at any time and use the same process to add very precise locations to them. On trips where you took a lot of images in a small area, you can use the map to pinpoint exactly where each one was taken using the satellite view to zoom right in to street level.

3: Find your location

Start by typing the location you wish to add into the search field to bring up the rough area. You are now free to scroll across the map to find the exact location you're after and drop a pin to show where the photos were taken.

4: Assign the location

Click 'Assign to photo' and the location information will now be added to all of your images. Head over to the Places view by clicking Places in the Source pane to see your images on the map.

The complete guide: Tutorial

iPhoto '09

Tutorial: Enrich colours and define your photos

Make your digital images come alive with a few simple tweaks from iPhoto's Adjustment pane and this guide

Task: Enrich colours and define your images
Difficulty: Beginner
Time needed: 10 minutes

There a number of reasons for images to turn out dull, dark or out of focus when you come to look at them in iPhoto. Anything from the settings on your camera to the absence (or presence) of a flash will change the way things turn out and won't necessarily look as good as they did in the flesh or on the LCD screen of your camera. Fortunately, iPhoto has a wealth of tools available to counter some of these issues, including the magical Enhance tool that, more often than not, will be able to make all the changes you need. Should your pictures need a little extra help then this guide to adjusting saturation and definition should be one of the first places you look. In iPhoto '09 the Saturation slider becomes all the more important as you can now tell it to ignore skin tones to keep people looking normal while enriching the surrounding colours. Definition also does a great job of creating crisp images without adding unwanted noise. Here's how…

Step-by-step | iPhoto Enrich & define

1: Original image

● Here we have a beach scene that appears a little washed out. There are colours present but they're flat, such as the bright clothing and the sea in the background. Start by hitting Edit and then choose the Adjust pane.

2: Check the box and we're off

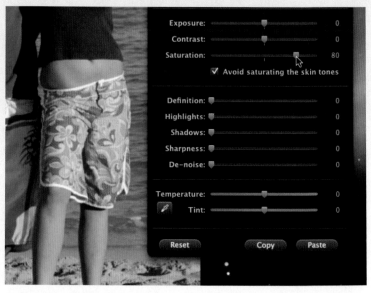

● Begin by ensuring that the 'Avoid saturating skin tones' check box is selected and then drag the Saturation slider to the right. This will begin to boost all of the colours in your image, but leave your subjects skin tone alone.

Brighten and boost

Saturation
Adjusting an image's saturation will boost the colours and add a richer feel to your photo if it appears washed out initially

Definition
Careful use of this slider will bring out the edges of objects and clean up blurry areas without adding any noise

Avoid skin tones
By checking this box you can make sure that the skin of the people in your photos isn't saturated, which can cause odd 'fake tan' effects

Adjust pane
Access iPhoto's wide range of adjustment sliders by clicking this button once you have entered the Edit mode for a selected image

Knowledge base

Experimentation ease
Don't worry about messing around with the sliders on the iPhoto Adjust pane, if you make a mistake you can click the Reset button to revert all changes back to normal and, even if you save your changes, Ctrl+Click on an image in your library and select Revert To Original to undo any adjustments you have made to it.

3: Make the definition

Now your colours look richer you can make the image stand out more by adding some definition. At present the skin tones near the sand in our picture are a little blurry. Slide the Definition slider to the right to adjust it.

4: Copy the changes

If this image is part of a set of images affected by washed-out colour or a lack of definition, make sure to hit the Copy button once you've made your changes. You can then Paste these changes onto the rest of your photos.

Tutorial: Create a themed slideshow in iPhoto

In iPhoto '09's box of new tricks lies the facility to create dynamic and fun-filled themed slideshows. The new format is sure to tempt you

Task: Build a themed slideshow with your images in iPhoto
Difficulty: Beginner
Time needed: 20-40 minutes

The word 'slideshow' carries the connotation of boredom, but how times have changed! You will be ecstatic to hear that there is nothing boring about sharing your images with iPhoto '09, and the stack of new themes give us even more to enjoy and exploit!

In the same fashion to iPhoto's books, calendar and card options, the Slideshow function has had a makeover to offer the choice of six template designs. Furthermore, the software has been designed to detect faces and so maintain the focus and position of images accordingly. A sleek new filmstrip has been incorporated at the bottom of your slideshow and helpful pop-up icons offer you the ability to alter themes, music, speed, effects and presentation at any point during the show.

Step-by-step | iPhoto Produce a themed slideshow

1: Start by selecting
Sometimes viewing images in a slideshow is more fun, so select the snaps you want to see then hit the Slideshow icon.

2: Choose a theme
Choose which of the six themes you would like to utilise. Click each of the boxes to see a mini preview of the slideshow. Select one and hit Play.

3: Filmstrip
Move your cursor to the bottom of the screen to bring up the filmstrip. Here you can navigate the show by dragging the playhead at will.

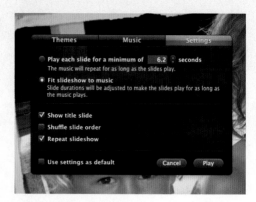

4: Change settings
Why not mix things up and change the settings? You can alter the theme, music, length of time and whether to include image titles.

5: Create a project
If you crave more control create a Slideshow project. Select the Event, the person in Faces or a location in Places and hit the Add icon.

6: Choose an order
The new project will pop up in the Source List. Travel through the images using the arrow buttons. You can drag and drop at will in the Photo Browser.

Make a themed slideshow in iPhoto

● Photo browser
To re-arrange the order of your images select an image or set from the Photo browser and drop them into the new desired slot. If leave the order as you find it, the slideshow will run in the order your images are stored within the album (unless you hit Shuffle Images in the Settings box)

● Theme it up
Hit the Theme icon at the bottom of the interface to click between Themes. Template themes include: Classic, Ken Burns, Scrapbook, Sliding Panels, Snapshots and Shatter

● Knowledge base

New themes
The new themes are as creatively charged as they are easy to utilise, but what is each one like? Classic offers a simple, straightforward show with a black backdrop and images placed neatly on the page. Shatter shows the image break apart in components, pulled apart and then rebuilt into the next slide. Snapshot offers slides that appear as if a Polaroid photograph is developing before your very eyes and is complete with a realistic shutter noise. Scrapbook shows as a quirky, creative way of displaying shots, offering jaunty angles set within a faux scrapbook backdrop. Finally Ken Burns and Sliding Panels operate as their names suggest.

● Create a new project
As soon as you decide to create a Slideshow project, iPhoto will stack it here on the Source List. Simply hit the Add button and opt for the Slideshow tab, give it a name and Bob's your uncle!

● Export
Once you've constructed your new slideshow press this Export button and opt for the desired share options. iPhoto '09 allows users to export the show as a movie into iTunes. From here users can download it on iPods, iPhones and more

7: Adjust settings
When you're ready to get creative and manipulate things, choose one of the appropriate icons at the bottom edge of the panel.

8: Preview
To test how your mini creation is coming along, hit the Preview icon. The icon will turn Blue to indicate it's in use. To return to editing the strip hit Preview.

9: End and export
When you're happy, click Export and select how you wish to save and share the file. You can view the file on iPods, iPhones, Apple TV and on your computer.

Tutorial: Share your photos on Facebook

Embrace the convenience of the new and improved iPhoto '09 and sync your newly added images to Facebook with the greatest of ease. We'll walk you through the process…

Task: Upload and tag your images using Faces in iPhoto '09 to Facebook

Difficulty: Beginner

Time needed: 30 minutes

Love it or loathe it, you're probably on it. That's right, we're talking about Facebook. It's conquering the popularity of MySpace and facilitating the online community to be as nosey and voyeuristic as their hearts desire.

So where does iPhoto come in? Well, no longer do we have to painstakingly upload images to the Facebook website one at a (mind-numbing) time. With iPhoto '09 you can simply select a bunch of images to upload to the website and hit the Facebook icon. Once you've entered your login details all you need to do is travel to your brand new Facebook folder, hit the link and fly forward through the realms of the information super highway and marvel as your picture-perfect portraits are embedded in your online picture gallery. What's more, combined with the power of iPhoto Faces, the integration means that the people in your pictures are automatically tagged! Cast your eyes over our easy four-step guide below.

Step-by-step | iPhoto Upload to Facebook

1: Select, log in and upload

● Select a bubbling batch of images or an Event and hit the Facebook button. Enter your account details, which you'll only need to do on your debut, and watch as iPhoto uploads your images. As soon as this is complete a new folder will appear in the Source List.

2: Tagging

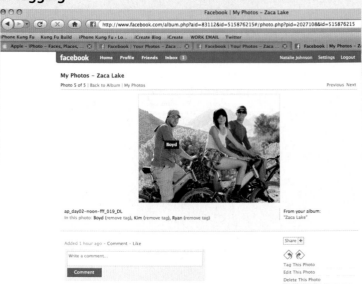

● The uploaded snaps will be stashed in this new folder. Travel straight to the page containing them in Facebook by hitting the link at the top of the interface. If you've used the Faces feature to name your friends then their tags will automatically appear on the webpage.

Sync iPhoto with Facebook

New Facebook folder
iPhoto's Source List will now contain a new folder – identifiable with the Facebook icon positioned to the left-hand side of it

Link
This is the link that, when actioned, will open up the Facebook page where your images are stored. This may take a few seconds

View album
The images you upload to Facebook will be presented in an album matching the title of the album in your iPhoto application. To change the name in iPhoto just hit the folder's title bar once and input a new name. Hit the Publish icon to sync the update

Publish
This little icon to the right of the folder's name is the button to press for publishing or sending your new images or edited information to the website. Hit it to sync changes. This will also bring back data on new tags added to your images by your friends

Knowledge base

Make new friends
Once you upload your images to Facebook your friends can tag new names on the shots. These names are then sent back to your iPhoto library the next time the app syncs with the website, automatically dropping the new names into your photos. Simply confirm these names online by hitting the Facebook icon on the website. Once accepted, a new polaroid with the new friend's face will appear on your Faces corkboard.

3: Notify your friends

Let your Facebook friends know you've uploaded an image of them by dipping into iPhoto's Faces and locate a pal's Polaroid. Spin it around and input their name and Facebook ID. The next time you add another shot containing their portrait, Facebook will alert them to the new addition.

4: Housekeeping

Once you've set up this neat feature you can add more images (by dragging and dropping onto the Facebook folder) or remove shots (by dragging to the trash) at any time. To refresh the changes in your Facebook account, hit the Publish icon to automatically sync the changes.

Tutorial: Remove red eye in iPhoto

Thanks to the tweaks Apple has made in iPhoto, it can now automatically detect and correct red eye. We take a look at how it's done

Task: Detect and remove red eye in iPhoto

Difficulty: Beginner

Time needed: 10 minutes

Red eye is the result of several factors. First, the image would have been taken in an ambient level of light, causing the subject's pupils to open wider to allow more light into the retina. The younger the subject the wider the response. The light from the camera's flash then bounces off the subject's retinas because the human eye isn't quick enough to process the invasion of light and reflects this back to the camera lens. The closer the proximity of light bulb to lens on compact cameras, the greater the reflection angle of the flash, which will strengthen the effect as the light recoils back to the camera.

To stop this from happening when you take a shot read this tutorial's Knowledge Base, but for a one-click fix check out iPhoto's new and improved Red-Eye removal feature, thanks to the app's new intuitive and innovative Face Detection technology.

Step-by-step | iPhoto Red eye removal

1: Ridding red eye

Start by selecting an image where the subjects appear to have red eyes. Activate the Red-Eye icon then hit the Auto button on the pop-up bar. The colour of the eyes in your frame should now be more normal.

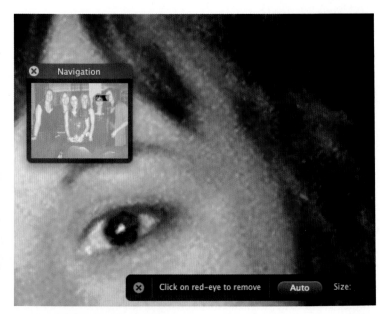

2: Close but no cigar

You can zoom into the image by keying 1 or 2 for greater magnification. By doing this you'll notice that the app sometimes fails to cover the pupil. When this happens you'll need to do it the old-fashioned way.

Detect and correct red eye in iPhoto
iPhoto can now automatically remove red eye in your snaps

● Red eye at work
This is an example of red eye at work. The unsettling red eyes are not only demonic, but they distract the image as a whole. Make sure you banish them with iPhoto's one-click fix

● Compare and contrast
To compare the results of the red eye adjustment hit Shift for an automatic comparison. For a more studied approach duplicate the image (Cmd+D) and transform one back to its original state then compare them in the Edit screen

● Knowledge base
Photography tip
To avoid red eye in the first place set your camera's flash to the red-eye option (check you camera's manual to identify which setting this is). The camera will then fire a succession of flashes preparing the subject's pupils for when the shot is actually captured. Alternately, buy an external flash head and position this flash further from the lens.

● Red-Eye icon
This is the icon you are looking for. Hit it once to retrieve the pop-up red eye bar. Use the Size slider to control the circumference of the brush

● Auto
iPhoto's Face Detection technology will isolate and remove the problem when Auto is keyed

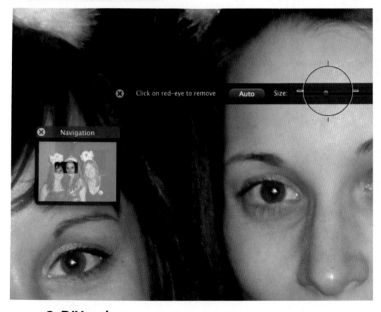

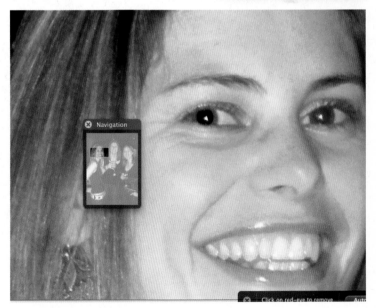

3: DIY red eye
To correct red eye yourself zoom in as close as possible to the frame and select a brush size that will be large enough to cover the pupil. Hover over the iris to measure the circumference accurately.

4: Dot away
When you're happy with the size of the dot, simply click over the red pupil to apply it and hit Done to finish. If the results are unsatisfactory open the Photos menu and opt for Revert To Previous.

Tutorial: Remove blemishes in iPhoto

Dust spots, moles, runny noses… there are a million reasons why you would need to use the Retouch tool

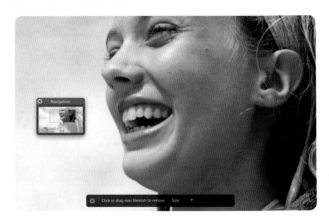

Task: Harness the brilliance of the Retouch tool

Difficulty: Beginner

Time needed: 20 minutes

"What the hell is that?" You exclaim as you load up a fresh batch of images. You've noticed your beautiful smooth shots are blighted with a random dappling of brown marks – and they're in the same place for every frame. UFOs? No, it's dust spots. When articles collect on the image sensor or when smears stain the lens these pesky pimples will pop up on your photos. In the long term you'll need to invest in a gutsy lens spray, and consider having the sensor professionally cleaned. In the short term there is hope in the form of iPhoto's Retouch tool, which gives you a one-click solution to rid frames from unsightly blots.

Step-by-step | iPhoto Remove unwanted spots and marks from your pictures

1: Pick a pic
Let's begin this tutorial by isolating a frame with an offending blemish you wish to remove. Select it from your Library, Event, Faces or Places and hit Edit.

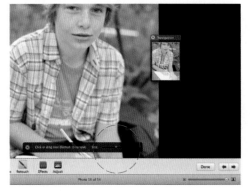

2: Size matters
Now select the icon labelled Retouch and the Retouch bar will pop up on your screen. To increase or decrease the size of the brush, drag the slider.

3: Click away
Hover over the offending blemish with the circular tool and click once to remove the blemish. The mark should now be removed completely.

4: Add a second shot
Thanks to improvements in iPhoto's latest face lift, the app automatically detects hard edges and tries to keep these intact while removing the blemish.

5: Precision Editor
iPhoto also allows users to zoom in closer to the blemish for greater control when attacking a blemish. Hit 1 or 2 to zoom in and 0 to zoom out.

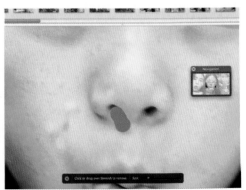

6: Edit point
Some blemishes may be larger or more stubborn to rid. When you come across a situation like this click and drag across the blemish.

Use the Retouch tool in iPhoto
Remove unwanted dust spots from your shots

● In action
When the Retouch tool is in action a beige-brown mark will be seen. If you click once the blemish should be removed but, should it be larger than the size of the brush you chose, click and drag across the area to ensure it has completely vanished

● Navigate
Grab the clear rectangular portion of the Navigation box and drag it to the area of the image you want to see. To zoom in this close and have the panel pop up, hit 1 or 2 for greater detail. Select 0 to zoom all the way out

● Knowledge base

Dust spots
It's incredibly common, especially for images taken in dusty or sandy environments, for particles to collect on the camera's image sensor or for spots to cover the lens. When this happens spots like this can appear on your images. You may notice them in the same place in a series of images, especially when shown on an image with a block colour such as this. An easy and effective way to remove them in post processing is with a tool like the Retouch brush, but to cure the problem you'll need to have the sensor cleaned professionally and use a specific lens cleaner and cloth on the glass.

● Drag me
Drag this slider to the left to decrease the size of the brush's circumference and the right to enlarge it

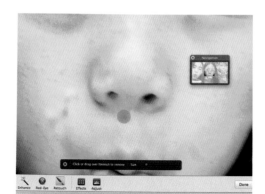

7: Trim the clips
To tidy up any parts of the blemish you may have missed click around the area to remove them from the picture.

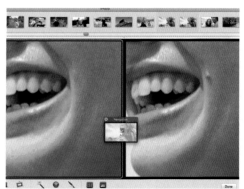

8: Preview the edit
To compare the before and after key Shift. For a more conclusive comparison duplicate the image before editing and compare in the Edit screen.

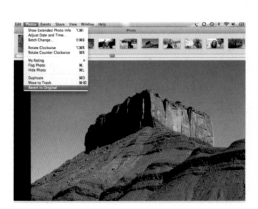

9: Trim final shot
Should you be unhappy with the last retouch hit Cmd+Z. If the whole image is a disappointment head to the Photos menu and hit Revert To Original.

Get to Know iPhoto

New to the Mac or just got yourself a new digital camera? This guide will show you what you can achieve with iPhoto '08

O f all the applications in the iLife suite, iPhoto is probably the one most people use on a regular basis. Its main purpose is to catalogue your digital stills so that they are all available in one space. But iPhoto is much more than a digital shoebox: you can label your shots, add keywords to them to make it easier to find them in the future, enhance their colour and perform all manner of improvements to turn a dull shot into something a lot more memorable. iPhoto also makes it easy to share your shots with others in many ways: you can order traditional prints, create books to print yourself or have them delivered to your door, you can burn them to a CD and send them to loved ones or – better yet – upload them to the web using your .Mac membership so they can be enjoyed instantly by all your friends and family.

Since its launch seven years ago, iPhoto has become a very rich application capable of handling most of your needs. However, some new users may well become intimidated when faced with so many options, even if the outcome is a lot easier than they originally thought.

Because of this, we thought we'd produce a guide to iPhoto '08 to help you get acquainted with an application you will probably spend a lot of time in – especially if you've just got a new camera or a new Mac. We will cover every major aspect of the application and guide you through the process of importing, cataloguing, editing and sharing your photos. This will hopefully give you enough knowledge to feel comfortable with the application and maybe even lead you to go out on your own and discover new features.

Importing photos

iPhoto tries to be as versatile as possible, and its import process shows just how flexible it can be. The most obvious way to import your stills into iPhoto is by connecting your camera to your Mac via a USB cable. Depending on its make and model, you either have to set it to View or PC mode, or the simple act of connecting to a computer will initiate the export process.

When this happens, a new section appears in iPhoto's sidebar, called 'Devices'. In it lies your camera, which should have been selected automatically (if it hasn't, click on it). All pictures contained in your camera can be seen as thumbnails. Clicking on Import All will bring all those pictures into your library. However, with iPhoto '08, you also have the option of only selecting specific shots. Click on the ones you want (Cmd-clicking lets you select multiple shots at the same time) and then click on the Import Selected button. Once the import process is complete, iPhoto offers you the option of either leaving the shots in your camera's Flash card or erasing them. You can choose whichever one suits your needs best.

But this isn't the only means you have of importing photos. You could, for instance, get them from a small USB flash drive, a CD and so on – anything that contains data can be used to transfer photographs. You can in fact drag a picture straight from a webpage into iPhoto's library, but the quality of such shots isn't very high, so printing them may not yield very good results. However, places like .Mac's Web Gallery (more on that later) let you download high-quality versions of the thumbnail it displays, making them as good as any shot you took yourself.

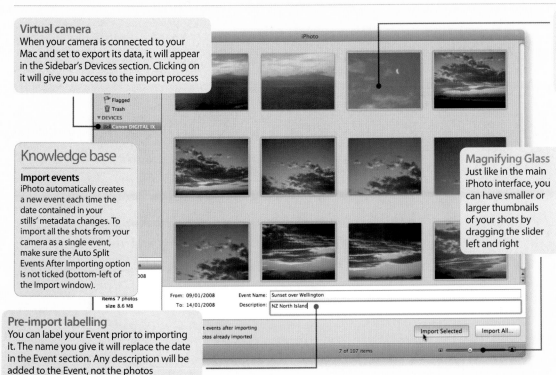

Virtual camera
When your camera is connected to your Mac and set to export its data, it will appear in the Sidebar's Devices section. Clicking on it will give you access to the import process

Import selection
You don't have to import the entire content of your flash card – you can just highlight the ones you need by selecting them individually. When done, click on Import Selected

Knowledge base

Import events
iPhoto automatically creates a new event each time the date contained in your stills' metadata changes. To import all the shots from your camera as a single event, make sure the Auto Split Events After Importing option is not ticked (bottom-left of the Import window).

Magnifying Glass
Just like in the main iPhoto interface, you can have smaller or larger thumbnails of your shots by dragging the slider left and right

⚠ Troubleshoot

When iPhoto won't import
Sometimes a camera won't appear in iPhoto, but that doesn't mean you can't import your shots: it may have appeared on the desktop as an external drive. If so, browse through it and add the photos manually.

ⓧ Top tip

Hide imports
If, when connecting to a camera, you notice that some shots have already been imported previously, tick the Hide Photos Already Imported options to only focus on the new shots.

Pre-import labelling
You can label your Event prior to importing it. The name you give it will replace the date in the Event section. Any description will be added to the Event, not the photos

---

Step-by-step | Import from CD or HD

It's happened to us all: relatives or friends send you CDs (or lend you a flash drive) full of their photos. Here's how to get them into iPhoto…

1 Connect the drive or insert the disc. In iPhoto, go to File>Import to Library. A window appears, designed to help you locate the files you need.

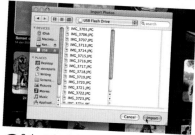

2 Select the folder of photos and click on Import to copy to iPhoto's library. You could use this to import them individually, but there's a better alternative.

3 Highlight a pic in the Finder. Hitting the Spacebar launches Quick Look. If you like it, click the Add To iPhoto button. If not, use the arrow keys to go to the next shot.

Organising photos

Getting stills into iPhoto's library is the easy part. Once there, you may wish to start organising them. This is not by any means compulsory, but the bigger your library grows, the harder it will be to find the exact picture you are looking for.

Thankfully, Apple has tried to make this process easy to achieve. There are, in fact, various ways to sort your pictures, from the quick to the meticulous. You're free to use whichever one works best for you.

The first one that you'll notice is in the library itself. Left of the interface is a sidebar. Top of the sidebar is the library, with two categories: Events

and Photos. Photos is set to show you each of your pictures, usually sorted chronologically (although this can be changed by going to View>Sort Photos). If you only have a few hundred pictures, this display is fine. Any more and it might become difficult to find the right photos. This is where Events come in: you can group your shots by events like 'Summer Holiday 2006' or 'Lionel's Birthday' and put all the pictures related to that moment in it. This shrinks your library considerably, letting you focus your search on only dozens of events rather than thousands of photos.

You can also create albums to organise your shots. At the bottom of the interface is a 'plus' button; clicking it lets you create a standard album (you drag pictures into it manually), or a smart album (you add pictures automatically based on certain parameters).

You can use the Information button to add a description to shots, and, if you go to Window>Show Keywords you will see all available keywords that can be added to a shot: drag one and drop it onto an image. Although this can take time, it makes it easy to find the exact picture you need.

Library views
The default view is now set to Events. However, if you prefer to see your pictures chronologically without any other visual organisation, click on Photos

Albums
You may wish to further organise your photos by using albums and folders. With them you can catalogue shots that span events, such as pictures of a child growing up or stills taken in America

Organisation tools
Create and merge events straight from the toolbar with these two buttons. If you'd rather use the Menu bar, those commands are in the Events menu

Skimming
Mouse over an event and you get a preview of all photos contained within it. To replace the main photo, hit the Spacebar when the cursor is over the desired one

Knowledge base

Albums and libraries
Don't think that if the image is in an album, it can be deleted from the main library: the library keeps track of all your photos. Those in albums merely point to the originals stored in the library. Deleting a shot from the library will also delete it from all albums that contain it.

⚠ Troubleshoot

Multiple libraries
Sometimes, a camera won't appear in iPhoto, but that doesn't mean you can't import your shots: it may have appeared on the desktop as an external drive. If so, browse through it and add the photos manually.

✕ Top tip

Hiding images
Some pictures are so bad, you delete them right away. You may wish to keep others but not see them all the time. To do this, select them and go to Photos>Hide Photos.

| Step-by-step | Edit and merge Events |

**Using Events is the quickest way to organise your shots.
Editing Events is almost as easy as dragging and dropping**

1 If you wish to turn multiple events into a single one, select them all (click on the first and Cmd-click on the others). Go to Events>Merge Events.

2 Double-click on an event to open it. To split it into two, select the last picture to be part of an event and click on the Split icon, bottom-left of the interface.

3 You can then move shots from one event to another by dragging and dropping them. You can also name your event by clicking on its title.

Edit photos

Getting the perfect shot is never easy, so it's a good thing that iPhoto comes with many editing tools to help you turn an average image into something more spectacular.

The first editing tool is used so often that it shouldn't even be considered as editing, but more along the lines of organising – the Rotate tool. As the name implies, it's used to rotate pictures from landscape to portrait and vice versa. As it's used so often, it has its own icon on the main toolbar, bottom-left of the interface when viewing the library as photos.

The other tools can be found by clicking on the Edit button, to the left of the Rotate tool – just make sure you select a picture first, otherwise iPhoto will either choose the first picture in its library or use the last shot you selected.

In the edit toolbar you'll notice the Rotate tool again – it's the first on the left. To its right is the Crop and Straighten tools, which can be used to cut out unwanted parts of an image or make sure the horizon is as horizontal as it should be, or not – nothing is stopping you from using these tools to be a little bit creative.

The next three options are designed to help fix an image very quickly. The first one is called 'Enhance' and plays with the colour balance and contrast to help create a better, richer image. Using the next tool – Red-Eye – will remove those devilish effects that often occur when doing flash photography. Retouch is there to make reality look better by removing unwanted blemishes. The Effects buttons give you a series of eight special colour effects to apply to your image. Finally, Adjust lets you manually alter a photo's levels from exposure to saturation to sharpness.

Floating windows
The Adjust tool is the most complex but offers the most flexibility. You can alter your image drastically with it; press the Shift key to see your changes

Mini thumbnails
Choose a shot to edit from within an Event and the other pictures are still visible at the top of the interface. This saves you time when you are editing multiple photos

Knowledge base

Working with other image editors
If iPhoto's tools aren't enough, you can easily use another image editor. To set this up, go to iPhoto's Preferences. Middle of the Edit section is an Edit Photo pop-up menu; click on it and choose In Application. Locate what you need and click Choose.

Greater detail
When editing a shot, you sometimes need to get up close to your subject. This slider lets you zoom into the image to help you be as precise as possible

⚠ Troubleshoot

Rotate image preferences
By default, the Rotate tool is set to turn the image counter-clockwise. You can change it to clockwise by going to the Preference's General tab. Also, holding down the Option key temporarily changes the rotation's direction.

⊗ Top tip

Non-destructive editing
iPhoto never overwrites your original shot, but creates a new copy when changes are made. Should you wish to undo all alterations, you can go to Photos>Revert To Original.

Editing toolbar
All editing tools are available at the bottom of the interface. They're designed to be easy to use. When your editing is complete, click on Done to return to the library

Step-by-step | Remove red eye

Aside from Rotate, the tool you'll be using most often is the one designed to remove red eyes. Here's how it works

1 Select your picture and click on the Edit tool to enter iPhoto's Edit mode (if this launches another app, set the Edit Photo preference to In Main Window).

2 Click on the Red-Eye tool and a small window appears. You can change the tool's radius from Automatic to Manual, but Automatic usually works best.

3 Now, click near the middle of each eye… and that's it. The effect should be instantaneous and as close to perfect as digital photography allows.

Share photos

Storing pictures, cataloguing them and editing them is great, but none of this would be worth much if you couldn't share your shots with others. In this respect, iPhoto excels as it offers a myriad of ways to distribute your photographs.

Like iMovie and GarageBand, iPhoto has a Share menu where most options are located to distribute your stills to others. One of these lets you set a picture as a desktop background where you – and others peering over your shoulder – can enjoy them. As a nice touch, if you select more than one picture and choose this option, you will be sent to

the desktop System Preference where you will be able to select how long the background should remain on one shot before moving to another.

Should you wish to share your pictures over the web, you can either email them, send them to iWeb for further processing or create a Web Gallery. The latter replaces photocasting, introduced with iPhoto '06. This lets you upload images to .Mac where others who know the address can view them. The advantage of the gallery is that you can password protect those pages and choose whether or not to allow your viewers to download your images.

Perhaps even better, you can even let your viewers upload their own photos, making the gallery extremely interactive.

.Mac slides are also available (as long as you're a .Mac member) and lets other Mac OS X users view your photos as slideshows. They can even use them as a screensaver.

You can choose to order prints online, although this option isn't available worldwide. If you're building a DVD with iDVD, you can send shots straight from the Share menu. You can also burn a CD to archive your library or share with friends.

An Event for a backdrop
You can set an Event as a desktop background. When you do so, your Mac will cycle through the stills. You also get to choose how long it stays on the same picture

.Mac and the web
Use your .Mac account to upload pictures onto the web – the interface makes it easy to browse and enjoy. Viewers can download shots or even upload their own

Knowledge base

QuickTime Export
iPhoto has a secret feature. With it, you can export a series of images as a QuickTime movie in the form of a very basic slideshow. To access it, select your shots or album and go to File>Export. Click on the QuickTime tab and choose from the options.

⚠ Troubleshoot

Email photo sizes
When emailing pictures, iPhoto offers to shrink the image so it won't take much space in the recipient's mailbox. Anything between 100-250KB is good. However, you can always send full-size stills if you so wish.

❌ Top tip

Share on Facebook
One way to upload photos to Facebook is to drag them from iPhoto to the desktop. It's then easier for find them using Facebook's Java interface.

Webpage insertion
Sending an event to iWeb saves you a lot of work: for example, the new page takes the Event's name and any name given to a shot is automatically added to its thumbnails

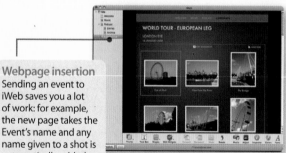

DVD slideshows
To add a slideshow to a DVD, choose an event and it will be automatically imported into iDVD with a link on the main menu (named after the event) leading to a pre-configured slideshow

---

Step-by-step | Set up a Web Gallery

iPhoto's Web Gallery is an excellent way of sharing your photos with friends and families, as long as you have a .Mac account

1 Select the images to upload from the library. You could also choose an entire album from the sidebar. When ready, click on the toolbar's Web Gallery icon.

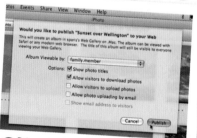

2 Prior to publishing, you can determine who can view your photos, or if people can download your shots or upload theirs. You can even set up a password.

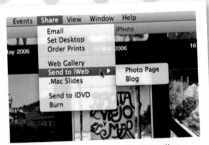

3 Click Publish to upload your stills to .Mac. A new gallery heading will appear containing the uploading album; the web address will then be displayed at the top.

Print photos

The internet is a fantastic tool to share your photos with friends and family instantly, but sometimes you may wish to create something more traditional. You may want something that will commemorate an important event, something that you can physically hold in your hands.

This is why you can design books straight from within iPhoto. There are many options available to you, from soft to hard covers. You can even set the number of pages you wish to have.

Creating these books is a breeze: select an event or album and click on the Book button, bottom of

the screen. Find the right template and drag your photos into it. If the default layout for a page isn't to your liking, you can also modify it by clicking on the Layout button and choosing a more appropriate display. The same goes for background colours and fonts, letting you create truly unique designs.

Hardcover books

Large (double-sided)
Size: 21.5 x 28 cm, 20 pages (ten sheets)
Price: £19.96 (UK) / €30.24 (Ireland)
Additional pages: £0.76 (UK) 100 max

Large (single-sided)
Size: 21.5 x 28 cm, ten pages (ten sheets)
Price: £19.96
Additional pages: £1.05

Softcover books

Large (double-sided)
Size: 21.5 x 28 cm, 20 pages (10 sheets)
Price: £14.09
Additional pages: £0.53

Medium (double-sided)
Size: 15 x 20 cm, 20 pages (10 sheets)
Price: £7.39
Additional pages: £0.34

Small (double-sided, three-pack only)
Size: 6.7 x 8.9 cm, 20 pages (ten sheets)
Price: £8.78
Additional pages: £0.22

Wire-bound books

Large (double-sided)
Size: 21.5 x 28 cm, 20 pages (ten sheets)
Price: £14.09
Additional pages: £0.53

Medium (double-sided)
Size: 15 x 20 cm, 20 pages (ten sheets)
Price: £7.39
Additional pages: £0.34

Calendar

Large (double-sided)
Size: 33 x 26.4 cm
Price: £14.09 12 months
Additional months: (24 max) £1.05

Cards

Size: 13 x 18 cm
Price: 1-24 cards £1.35
25-49 cards £1.23
50+ cards £1.12

Postcards

Size: 10 x 15 cm
Price: 1-24 cards £1.05 each
25-49 cards £0.93 each
50+ cards £0.69 each

Prints

Size: 10 x 15 cm
Price: £0.18 each
Size: 13 x 18 cm
Price: £0.58 each
Size: wallet
Price: £1.35 for 4
15 x 20 cm £1.35 each
20 x 25 cm £1.63 each
20 x 30 cm £1.99 each

THE MAC USER'S GUIDE TO
PHOTOGRAPHY

Create photos that the pros would be jealous of with this hands-on guide to shooting, editing and sharing your images…

S o, you own a pretty good camera and enjoy going out and about at every given opportunity to take some snaps. But how do you go about turning those snapshots into something a little more professional looking? How do you turn so-so holiday shots into the stunning travelogue photography you see in magazines and books?

Wonder no more, as over the next nine pages we're going to show you how to take full manual control of your camera, as well as giving you some essential buying advice to create the perfect kit. We'll then be stepping into the digital darkroom and explaining how to put the 'wow' factor into your photos. From buying through to shooting, we'll show you how to capture amazing landscapes, portraits, architecture, wildlife and more. There's never been a better time to start shooting!

Over the last decade, digital photography has broken free of the stigma of being only for the rich or pro-level shooters. Ever-plummeting prices coupled with more user-friendly controls now mean that more and more households own a digital camera of some sort or another. Just like film cameras before them, DSLRs, bridge and compacts have become affordable enough to be the choice of the amateur enthusiast. What's more, the well-known benefits of shooting digitally can now be enjoyed by even more people thanks to programs such as iPhoto coming complete with your new Mac.

But it's just not enough nowadays to create a great image, and that's why we've dedicated a whole section to looking at ways to share your images with other people. From uploading them to an online gallery site such as **Digital Photographer** magazine's online forum (**www.dphotographer.co.uk**) to getting your images printed on canvas and Perspex or books and posters for friends, family or just your wall at home. Everything's covered.

Whether you're already a crack shot with the camera and want to know more about the post-production side of photography, or you're simply looking to pick up some buying tips on the best camera to suit your needs, this feature will set you up to start composing, editing and sharing your digital images with ease.

"We'll show you how to capture amazing landscapes, portraits, architecture, wildlife and more. There's never been a better time to start shooting!"

Jargon buster
If you're new to photography, the jargon surrounding the genre can make you feel like you're learning a whole new language. We reveal the meaning behind the speak…

Aperture
Located behind the lens of your camera (or in the lens in some compacts) is a circular iris that opens and closes to determine the light falling on the sensor. This is measured in f-stops.

Shutter speed
Measured in fractions of a second, shutter speed is the amount of time your shutter stays open, which again determines how much light falls on your sensor. Long shutter speeds can be used for night or low-light photography.

ISO (ASA in America)
In film photography this would have demonstrated the light sensitivity of a film. It's now used to express the light sensitivity of your sensor at shooting.

Exposure
To get correct exposure, your camera will meter the light that's bounced off your subject and determine how wide the aperture and how long the shutter speed is (in auto). Underexposed images are dark, overexposed shots are too light.

Depth of field
The amount of your image that's in sharp focus, determined by the aperture you choose. A shallow depth of field will have only your subject in focus, while a large depth of field will help to keep everything in sharp detail.

Dynamic range
HDR (high dynamic range) images are very popular at the moment and are created by combining images to produce a photo with very bright highlights, dark shadows and everything in between.

Distortion
Comes in all shapes and sizes: barrel distortion and pincushion distortion will distort horizontal lines, chromatic aberrations may cause purple fringing around objects and converging verticals occur when shooting up a straight building, for example.

P, A, S, M
Most DSLR cameras, as well as the higher-end compact, will feature these modes: Program, Aperture Priority, Shutter Priority and Manual, as well as automatic and scene modes (on all but a pro-spec DSLR).

Feature: Mac photography

"The deciding factor for most people at an enthusiast level is cost"

There's a wealth of gizmos and gadgets, practical and peripheral, that you can buy once you decide you want to invest in digital photography.

First, you'll obviously need a camera. Whether you opt for a DSLR (Digital Single Lens Reflex camera), bridge or compact is going to come down to what you want, as well as your budget.

For ease of use, there's nothing as simple as a basic compact. Leave this pocket gadget set to Automatic and the camera does all the work for you. The problem comes when you start wanting better image quality. Compacts have sensors a fraction of the size of those found in a DSLR, so when you want to enlarge your images, you're going to start running into trouble. Higher-end compacts can still boast decent image quality though, as well as offering more manual functions. With Panasonic's higher-end compacts the optical quality is very good, although you will pay for this premium technology.

Lying in-between the compacts and the DSLRs are the bridge or prosumer cameras. These offer the look and feel of a DSLR, but with additional scene settings and auto features, making them the ideal camera to 'bridge' between compact and SLR.

While the specific requirements of a camera are extremely important, the deciding factor for most people at an enthusiast level is cost. With the price of low-end DSLRs falling every day, they can be an appealing option. The Nikon D40, for example, is an older DSLR that you can pick up from around £200 with a kit lens, putting it more in the compact camera price bracket with the added feature set of an SLR.

Always go to your local camera store and handle a camera before you buy. Pentax, Canon, Sony and Nikon all have good low-end DSLRs that have been superseded, meaning you can pick up a bargain no matter which manufacturer you prefer.

Once you've decided on the SLR of your choice, it's time to talk accessories. There's no end to what you can buy to accompany your new digital toy, from extra lenses and filter sets to bags, flash guns, memory cards and more.

We'll start by looking at lenses. Your kit DSLR lens is likely to be in the region of 18-55mm, which will cover most photographic situations including landscapes, portraits and travel shots. However, if your fancy trying your hand at sports, wildlife or something you need to zoom in a little more on, then a longer focal length is essential. For our Nikon D40 example, you can look to buy either the manufacturer's own or a third-party lens like Sigma, Tokina or Tamron. Think about investing in 18-200mm length – this means you won't need to keep taking your lenses on and off, therefore minimising the risk of getting dust on your sensor. Make sure you choose a lens with vibration reduction and autofocus if you're just starting out.

Filters can add a great deal to your images, and ones such as a polariser (which boasts your blues and greens and reduces reflections), ND grads (digital cameras can only capture a limited contrast range and the ND grad can extend this range) and UV filters can be lifesavers for the landscape shooter in particular.

When you're out for a day with your camera, make sure you have a large memory card and switch your camera to

Fixed lens vs SLR

With the price of DSLRs coming down every day, what can the compact or bridge camera offer the amateur shooter?

DSLR
A Digital Single Lens Reflect camera can be identified by its removable lens. Opt for telephotos for distant action, fisheye for the obscure or macro for the little things in life.

Bridge
Same build and most of the features of a lower-end SLR, but with simplicity on its side. The extended zoom range and fixed lens means no sensor dust problems like on your DSLR.

Compact
The benefits here are obvious, as you can slip most of these cameras into a pocket and forget about them. However, distortion can be a problem due to the small sensors they use.

shoot either RAW or RAW and JPG. RAW file formats allow more detail to be captured and allow for more flexibility later on in post-production. We'll cover this a little later on. A good, comfy kit bag (like those made by Kata, LowePro and Tamrac) is essential, as is a good lens cloth.

So now you're all kitted out with the camera, lens and filters, it's time to get to the nitty-gritty of actual shooting techniques. We'll be covering these in more depth over the next few pages, but the first thing we want you to do is switch your camera off Automatic mode and learn how shutter speed, aperture and ISO affect your images. We'll start you off with a brief summary, and the various examples on the right should also help to cement the idea of shooting techniques further.

Shutter speed is the most self-explanatory term here and demonstrates the time the shutter is open for. This is measured in fractions of a second. The longer the shutter is open for, the more light enters your lens. Long shutter speeds are great for night-time shots when there's less ambient light around, although you may find you need a tripod for anything approaching a second and certainly for anything over. This is due to camera and hand shake making your picture blurry. Short shutter speeds can freeze time, allowing you to capture pin-sharp images of intricate details, such as water droplets from a wave.

Aperture is the other control you have over the amount of light that comes into your camera, but this time is controlled by how large or small the aperture opening is. Very small apertures (these will vary depending on your lens, but will be around f16/f22) give you a large depth of field, meaning more of your image will be in focus – which is particularly great for landscapes. Large apertures (f2.8) give you a shallow depth of field where just a small section of your images will be in sharp focus. This is a nice effect for portraits and macro work in particular.

ISO refers to the sensitivity of your film (the sensor). High ISO settings are great where you have limited light, but the downside is a lot of digital 'noise' on your images. Ideally you'll be shooting somewhere between ISO 100 and 400, if conditions allow.

►

Experiment for effect

Have a play with your shutter speed, aperture and ISO and you could achieve some creative results...

Long shutter speed

Fast shutter speed

Smaller depth of field, aperture f5.6

Wide depth of field, aperture f16

ISO 400

ISO 1600

Cloning:
Remove unwanted objects
Crop and Straighten:
Level and trim an image
Depth of field:
Imply depth in a 2D image
Boosting a sunset:
Enhance colours for dramatic results
Exposure correction:
Fix poorly shot, dark images

As well as understanding how aperture, shutter speed and ISO can work together to create a better picture, you should also understand the pitfalls each genre of photography can bring and how you can avoid, correct or embrace them.

Cityscapes are a good example where a lot can go 'wrong' in your technically perfect image. The narrow streets, traffic and sheer volume of other people mean the only way to shoot that jaw-dropping piece of architecture is straight up. Trying to fit a tall structure into your picture frame and shooting from below means you will end up with converging verticals at the top or barrel distortion, where any horizontal beams look bowed towards the edge of the frame. You'll probably also find yourself best friends with the Clone tool as you remove all those random rubbish bags, pieces of litter or the people that become distracting elements in your shots.

Landscapes may appear easy, but they can be tricky too, especially when it comes to keeping a straight horizon! Gadgets like the new Action Level by Seculine (**www.intro2020.com**) can

> "Landscapes may appear easy, but they can be tricky"

level uses a traffic light system to tell you if your camera is level or not, and can be seen even when shooting through the viewfinder. There are also lots that can be done in the digital darkroom about this little flaw, which we'll be covering a bit later on.

Portraits can also cause the novice photographer problems. Shooting with a wide-angle lens for instance may cause your subject to appear wider, especially in the centre of the frame, so expect their nose to get a lot bigger! Opt for a telephoto lens and stand well back when shooting your subject. Try and use a large aperture (f5.6) to focus on the face and blur out some of the background to avoid distractions.

If all these tips aren't possible, then fear not. Computer technology and digital camera design is progressing at an incredible rate. Not only do computers help craft images to perfection, but the corrections and manipulation they are capable of has made great imagery available to all in our modern world. Search the internet for some before and after images that transform so-so snaps into photos to be proud of, all with just a few simple

The following techniques are described using Photoshop CS2, but c be done in any image-editing app, suc as iPhoto or Aperture.

To straighten that wonky horizon start by copying your background laye then work on your newly created laye and turn your Rulers on (Apple+R). These will appear at the edge of your work area. Drag a horizontal guide across your image using these rulers a a guide. Apple+T calls up the Transform command, where you'll be able to twi your image until it is straight. Crop the photo's edges to finish.

Depth of field is just as easy to fake to create a pro feel to your image. Fake a shallow depth of field on your flowe shots by cutting the main subject out and pasting this onto its own layer. Th apply a Gaussian, or for a more realisti look, a Lens Blur. Use the Preview opti to monitor your progress.

To remove distracting objects, the aptly named Clone tool is best. Select your source start point by pressing Al and clicking your mouse. Then select the object you wish to clone out. Easy Keep your brush size small for a more authentic finish and take source spots

Fix converging verticals by heading to the Edit menu, where within the Transform tools you'll find Warp. Click on this option and a basic nine-section grid will appear over your image. Push and pull the corners and midpoints until you've corrected the distorted perspective. This will take a bit of time, patience and practise!

Another common problem is having images that are affected by over and underexposure. If this is the case for you, select Image>Adjustments> Exposure. You'll be faced with three options: Exposure (left darker/right lighter), Offset (this effects the shadow tones) and Gamma (this helps your midtones). For basic adjustments you only need worry about the Exposure slider. Simply drag the slider until you are happy with the preview image. This will only be done if the image is in RGB.

There are lots of other great quick photo fixes that can be performed. We've covered some of them over the page, but for a more complete guide to Photoshop visit **www.imagineshop. co.uk** where you can buy all the back issues of **Photoshop Creative** and **Advanced Photoshop**, on super-searchable eMags.

▶

"If all these tips aren't possible, then fear not. Computer technology and digital camera design is progressing at an incredible rate"

Step-by-step | Photoshop Elements 6
Create your very own best shot

Photoshop Elements offers a quick way to perfect any image. As this three-stepper shows, you can correct underexposed areas at the post-shoot stage quickly and easily

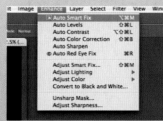

1: Browse with Bridge
When you first load Elements you'll be asked what you want to do: search with Bridge, start a clean document or import direct from your scanner or camera.

2: Load up your image
We've loaded our image direct from a Nikon D40 in its native RAW format, .NEF. Select Open Image to open your photo as a shot. It's now time to make it perfect.

3: Smart Fix
Go to Enhance, and from the drop-down menu select Auto Smart Fix to watch those underexposed areas ping back to life! Remember to Save As to preserve the original.

Understanding how your camera works is vitally important when you want to become a better photographer, but composition is also key to your success.

The rules of composition should be learnt and considered, but not necessarily used in every photo. As you become a better photographer you'll be able to find creative ways to stretch or break the rules, but that doesn't mean that they aren't worth knowing. The more you understand, the better you'll be at knowing when to follow the rules and when not to.

The rule of thirds is probably the best known and easiest to understand guide. The rule suggests that your picture frame can be divided into three vertical and three horizontal sections, and wherever these lines connect is the ideal spot for positioning your subject or point of interest.

Leading lines can be powerful composition tools and can lead your viewer's eye through your image. If there are strong lines in the scene, try to get them to disappear into the corner. If the lines break into the centre or the edge it tends to divide the photo, but disappearing into a corner seems to make composition stronger. This is true of straight lines, but also S-shaped lines. Apparently, the eye enjoys following 'S' curves. This seems to apply mostly to water, roads and the silhouettes of people. It doesn't strictly need to be an 'S', either; you could reverse it or use a strong zig-zag.

Try also 'framing' your subject using things like tree branches in the top and side of your composition. Think about the colours and how they work together and keep things simple. Identify your subject and make sure your image leads the eye to this point.

Once you've learnt the rules, you'll be able to understand when it's best to conform or rebel against them. As famed photographer Ansel Adams once said: "There are no rules for good photographs, there are only good photographs." This is certainly true, but doesn't rule out the ability to fake them with your image-editing app of choice.

If you've ever looked at the work of a pro shooter and wondered why their shot of the same subject looks better than yours, these editing tips are for you. Using image-editing programs isn't 'cheating', although you should aim to do as much in camera as possible. Use iPhoto or the like to finish your photos, not to fix them.

We've already covered some of the basic correction techniques on the previous spread, so here we're going to cover some typical finishing techniques. You can see some of them in action in the annotated image on the right. So let's have a look at using iPhoto to correct any mistakes.

Get rid of any signs of red-eye by simply selecting the Red-Eye button and then placing the crosshairs over the eye that is affected. It's best to zoom in quite close (using the slider on the bottom right), as you'll be able to be more accurate and see iPhoto work its magic.

Next, select the Adjust button and within the pop-up menu you'll find the tools to adjust your exposure. As before, this requires you to push and pull the slider and will correct both under and overexposed images.

Straighten can also be found here, and again works on a sliding system, allowing you to quickly sort out any tilt. Sharpness, which is also found here, is great for a low-light image like the one we're working on here. In low light you'll find your digital camera creates more noise due to the higher ISO used. By adjusting the Sharpness slider you can create a sharper-looking image. Use sparingly though, or you could make things worse!

In wedding images in particular it's important to get your white balance right, or your subject's dress will look off-white. Correct it in iPhoto using the Temperature and Tint sliders. Again, experiment is key but, as with most things, the old adage 'less is more' is a good rule of thumb.

Vignette
Add a slight vignette around the edge in order to give a rounded finish to the image. It will also serve to remove more distractions

Straighten
Correct the slight slant you can see at the top of the image by selecting the Straighten slider in the Adjust palette

"The rules of composition should be learnt and considered, but not necessarily used in every photo"

Proud prints
Inspiration for your photos

iPhoto PhotoBooks
URL: www.apple.com/ilife/iphoto/#prints
Print photobooks direct from your iPhoto library on your Mac for a quick and easy way to display your images. You'll need a .Mac/MobileMe account in order to create any of the iPhoto products.

Foto Cube
URL: www.fotocube.co.uk
Offers images to be printed directly onto premium-quality acrylic freestanding blocks and wall-hanging panels, ideal for displaying that family portrait or stunning landscape from your last holiday.

Photobox
URL: www.photobox.co.uk
From mugs and cushions to calendars and diaries, sites such as Photobox offer a range of ways to display your images about your home. Our personal favourite is the large poster collage.

Tesco
URL: www.tesco.com
On a budget? Surf over to the Tesco site and discover the supermarket giant's online storing and printing site – ideal for cheap prints, both large and small, as well as other media.

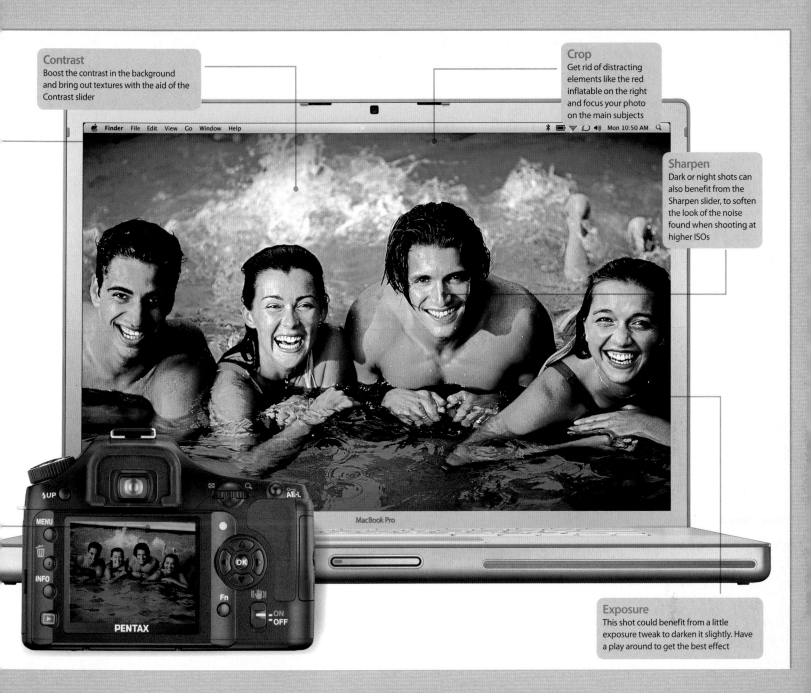

Contrast
Boost the contrast in the background and bring out textures with the aid of the Contrast slider

Crop
Get rid of distracting elements like the red inflatable on the right and focus your photo on the main subjects

Sharpen
Dark or night shots can also benefit from the Sharpen slider, to soften the look of the noise found when shooting at higher ISOs

Exposure
This shot could benefit from a little exposure tweak to darken it slightly. Have a play around to get the best effect

MacBook Pro

PENTAX

Online portfolios
Share your photos with the world!

Flickr
URL: www.flickr.com
Possibly the best-known image-sharing site on the web, flickr gets around 5,000 images uploaded a minute! A great way to back up your image collection and share with the world at the same time.

photoSIG
URL: www.photosig.com
Rate, review and comment on other users' images, then upload your own for some constructive critiques from fellow photographers. A great way of getting inspiration and feedback.

ePhotozine
URL: www.ephotozine.com
With daily news updates, regular reviews, an active online community and nearly half a million visitors a month, this site is one of the biggest for all things photography, and it's definitely worthy of a look.

Digital Photographer
URL: www.dphotographer.co.uk
Share your images online with a free gallery on this website. Here you can rate and comment on other people's images, as well as getting essential reviews on your own efforts.

Head-to-head

We compare the essential specs of three top image-editing softwares

	Formats supported	Management of photos	Output	Performance	Cost	Overall ratings
iLife	JPEG, TIFF and RAW. Other formats will work, but are not fully supported	Albums, Smart Albums and more	Connects direct to MobileMe for books, prints, etc	Great for quick editing and organising	Free	A good, simple solution to your photo-editing and cataloguing needs, but one that you might grow out of as a photographer
Aperture 2	JPEG, GIF, TIFF, PNG, PDF, PSD and Native RAW import and editing of images from leading digital cameras and camera backs	Projects, Albums, Smart Albums and more	Order colour-managed prints online, publish to a MobileMe gallery, author books, etc	Pro-level power and performance	£120	Pro-level software that will take a bit of experimentation to master, but it's good-looking, powerful and offers every tool you need
ADOBE PHOTOSHOP ELEMENTS 7	JPEG, TIFF and RAW. Other formats will work, but are not fully supported	Built in Organizer. Easy to find and view all your photos	This easily prints directly to your home printer	All the best bits of Photoshop but easier to use	£76	Cost-effective, mid-level app that is particularly suited to those who are looking to take a step up without the complications of pro-spec software. A good all-rounder

"The boom in digital camera sales has brought about a host of more modern ways to share your images"

Now you've mastered the art of seeing, composing and shooting stunning images, not to mention the art of post-production, it seems like a waste to leave your digital works of art festering on your hard drive or merely adorning the computer monitor as a background. Why not share your images?

Friends and family will love getting bespoke gifts that you have created just for them – Christening albums of images you've shot of your new niece, for example, will be a much more personal and thoughtful gift than a voucher for the local book shop. For other inspirational ideas or the kind of media you can print your images to, have a look at *Photoshop Creative* or *Advanced Photoshop* magazines.

But sharing your images is not just about novelty items such as mugs, coasters and cushions adorned with your art. The boom in digital camera sales has brought about a host of cooler and altogether more modern ways to share your images.

HD-compatible cameras, like the new releases from Kodak and Panasonic, can link up to your high-def TV for a 21st century take on Grandad's slideshow. You can add music, captions and even a voiceover, and you can create these in your image-editing app or a program like iMovie. This compatibility means your camera will fit into your home entertainment system like never before, giving you full integration. Check your camera specs for HD compatibility.

Then there's the really fabulous range of digital picture frames now available from many different manufacturers. These can be wall-mounted or sit atop of your mantlepiece where they'll scroll through your memory card full of images, which guests can then view at their leisure. Make sure you invest in a 10" frame, as some of the smaller offerings can fade into obscurity in a larger room. Also be careful about how long you leave these items on for, as they can get very warm.

To reach a larger audience, why not upload your images to one of the plethora of sites online? There's so many to choose from.

However you decide to share your images, make sure all the hard work and effort you put in to creating the perfect picture gets displayed for all the world to see!

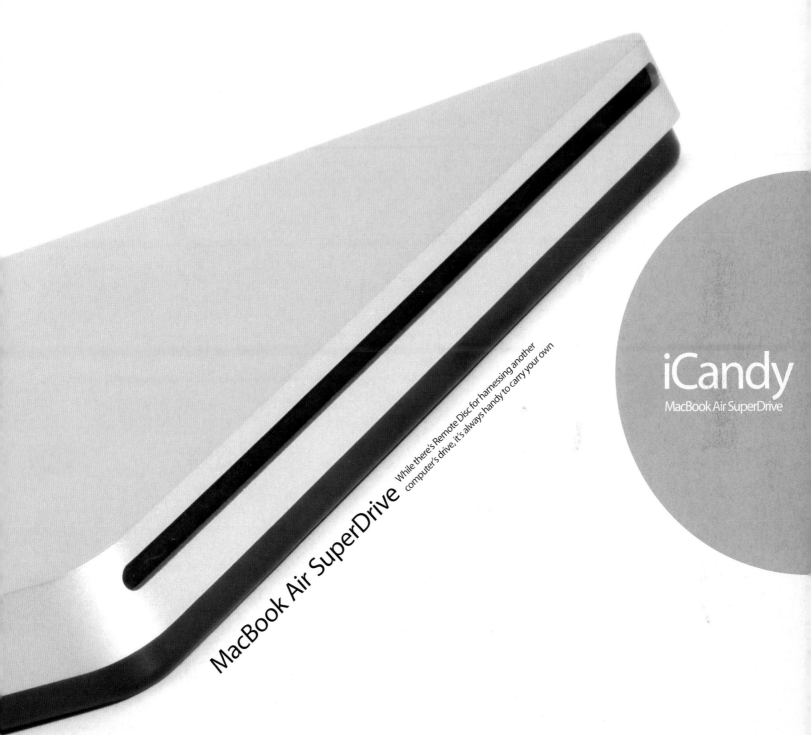

iCandy
MacBook Air SuperDrive

MacBook Air SuperDrive While there's Remote Disc for harnessing another computer's drive, it's always handy to carry your own

Tutorial: Flag and unflag images in iPhoto

If your photo library is busting at the seams and could do with an overdue spring clean, it's time to use the Flag tool and make your Mac tidy!

Task: Use the Flag feature to organise images and prepare them for projects
Difficulty: Beginner
Time needed: 20 minutes

The best thing about the digital medium is the fact you can be as snap-happy with your photos as you want and the only thing it will cost is a few extra bytes of memory. However, the flip side is that your iPhoto library becomes chocked full of images. The app starts taking an age to load and your finger begins to ache from the RSI of scrolling down reams and reams of images.

Fortunately for all of you image lovers, one of the most handy iPhoto mechanisms for the job is Flag. By flagging together images there is so much you can do. Photo fans could flag poor, out-of-focus or repeated images into a group and bin them en masse. You can also flag images and make a Smart Folder comprising of snaps taken on a certain date, with a certain camera at a certain ISO. And you can even collate images that you wish to use for a book or clump together into an Event. Flag really is an underrated tool, so let's show you just what it can do for you and your picture collection.

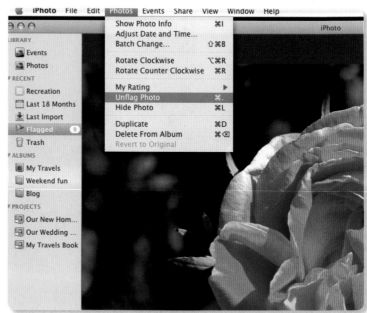

Step-by-step | iPhoto Use iPhoto's Flag tool

1: Flag it up

● With an image or group of pictures selected, travel to the Menu bar and from Photos hit the Flag Photo option. Alternatively, you can use the shortcut Cmd+. or keystroke the Flag icon on the toolbar.

2: Take it back

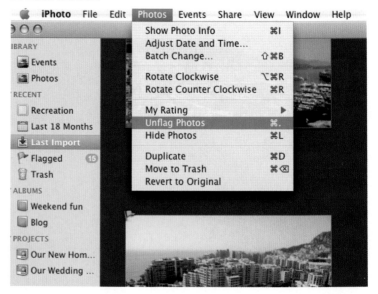

● Once an image has been flagged, it is possible to remove the tag. Simply select the offending snap and use the relevant option in the Photos menu, the shortcut (Cmd+.) or the Toolbar icon.

Flag up your photos

Create an Event
To create an Event that contains solely flagged images from other Events, select Events and Create Event From Flagged Photos. Be warned – this will remove the images from their original Event

Knowledge base

Move to trash
Obviously your motives for flagging photos may not be to separate them as masterpieces or because you have a desire to construct a glorious book or calendar. Instead, you may just wish to flag offending photos and bin them. If this is the case, flag your sad snaps, hold down the Ctrl key, hit the Photos menu and execute by choosing Move Flagged Photos to Trash.

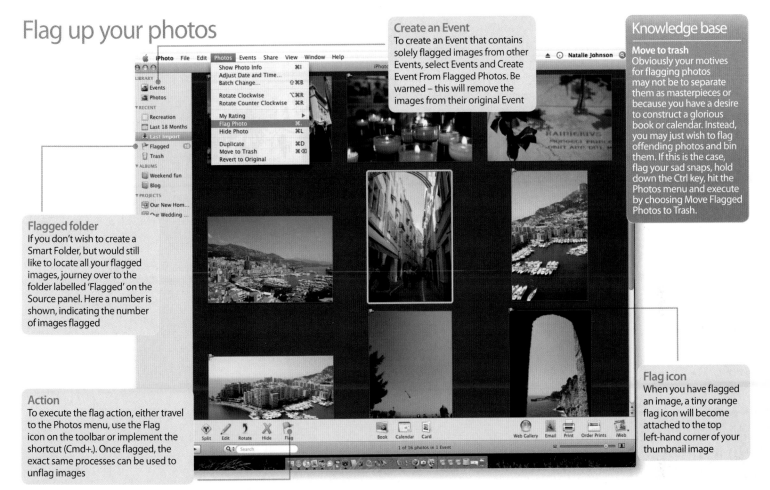

Flagged folder
If you don't wish to create a Smart Folder, but would still like to locate all your flagged images, journey over to the folder labelled 'Flagged' on the Source panel. Here a number is shown, indicating the number of images flagged

Action
To execute the flag action, either travel to the Photos menu, use the Flag icon on the toolbar or implement the shortcut (Cmd+.). Once flagged, the exact same processes can be used to unflag images

Flag icon
When you have flagged an image, a tiny orange flag icon will become attached to the top left-hand corner of your thumbnail image

3: Get smart

● You may wish to collate all the flagged images that meet a certain criteria into a Smart Album. Travel to File, opt for New Smart Album and add in the options you wish to cater for. We want to find all five-star flagged images.

4: Booked

● A neat way to make a book, calendar or card is to collect all the desired images together using the Flag mechanism. With your Smart Album, Event or Flagged photos folder selected from the Source panel, hit the Book icon.

Tutorial: Learn how to reverse an image in iPhoto

Do you wish the subjects of your photo had been facing in the other direction? iPhoto can make this happen…

Task: Use iPhoto to flip and reverse an image
Difficulty: Beginner
Time needed: 10 minutes

 How many times have you looked at an image and wish you'd shot it from a different direction? Well, there is a handy feature in iPhoto that can solve this problem: Mirror Image.

Mirror Image flips the image horizontally so your models are facing to the left instead of the right, or vice versa. This is particularly useful for situations where you may be generating a creative project, and want to arrange the snaps in a particular way. You may decide to have the people in all of the images face each other, or have the subjects in one shot look away from those in the neighbouring frame.

But what if the mirrored image isn't as good as the original? Easy – just flip it back by carrying out the same process as before. A tick next to Mirror Image in the pop-up menu indicates when an image has been affected. The original is preserved in the Photo browser, and in your iPhoto library.

Step-by-step | iPhoto Flip a picture

1: Let's get cracking

● Reversing an image will probably be most useful when you're generating a project like a book, card, calendar or web gallery. Here we will begin by selecting a folder of images in Events, and then opting for the Book icon that's displayed.

2: Reverse reverse

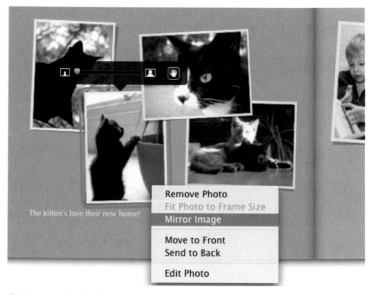

● The key selection for reversing an image is extremely easy when you have the process down. All you need to do is hold down Ctrl and click on the particular image you want to change. From the list of options that appear, select Mirror Image.

Flip-reverse your photos in iPhoto

Originality rules
Regardless of the changes you make while constructing your product, the original image remains in the Photo browser

Knowledge base

Show me more
Creatives can do many more things by Ctrl-clicking an image; reversing a frame is only one facet. In fact, the menu provides iPhoto users with many more options. For example, you can alter the arrangement of your pictures by moving them to the front or back. Alternatively you can access the Edit menu here, as well as removing the snaps altogether.

Enlarge and move
When you select an image you are presented with a Zoom scale and a Move tool. Slide the image to the right to zoom in on your frame, and select the Hand icon to change and adjust its position

Mirror Image
By choosing an image and pressing the Ctrl key, this menu will present you with the ability to mirror an image

3: Don't change everything

Fortunately, making a change in an image on one of your pages will not force the original, or any other copies, to change elsewhere. As you can see, the reversed image is shown on the book, but the original is maintained in the Photo browser.

4: Bulk change

The Mirror Image tool allows you to get really creative with images, as shown in this example. Change more than one image at once by holding down Shift and clicking on the frames you want to affect. When you've done this, Ctrl-click and then choose Mirror Image.

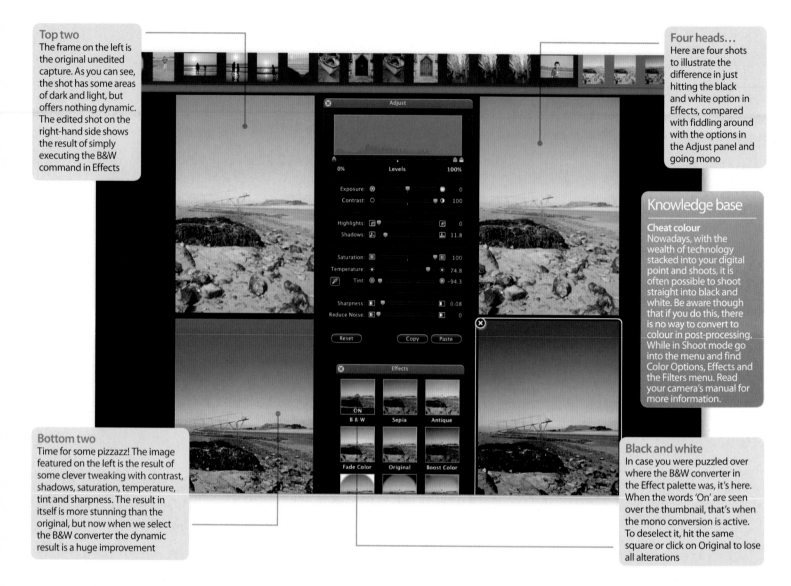

Top two
The frame on the left is the original unedited capture. As you can see, the shot has some areas of dark and light, but offers nothing dynamic. The edited shot on the right-hand side shows the result of simply executing the B&W command in Effects

Four heads…
Here are four shots to illustrate the difference in just hitting the black and white option in Effects, compared with fiddling around with the options in the Adjust panel and going mono

Knowledge base

Cheat colour
Nowadays, with the wealth of technology stacked into your digital point and shoots, it is often possible to shoot straight into black and white. Be aware though that if you do this, there is no way to convert to colour in post-processing. While in Shoot mode go into the menu and find Color Options, Effects and the Filters menu. Read your camera's manual for more information.

Bottom two
Time for some pizzazz! The image featured on the left is the result of some clever tweaking with contrast, shadows, saturation, temperature, tint and sharpness. The result in itself is more stunning than the original, but now when we select the B&W converter the dynamic result is a huge improvement

Black and white
In case you were puzzled over where the B&W converter in the Effect palette was, it's here. When the words 'On' are seen over the thumbnail, that's when the mono conversion is active. To deselect it, hit the same square or click on Original to lose all alterations

Tutorial: Get more from black and white images

Many iPhoto users seem happy to stop the creative train at the B&W effect, but why make them passable when you can make prints dazzle?

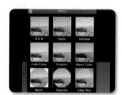

Task: Transform your images into a mono masterpiece
Difficulty: Beginner
Time needed: 45 minutes

Black and white images have the potential to wield an enigmatic power that somehow doesn't transcend from a colour image. But many users of the iPhoto Edit palette are satisfied to simply hit the Black and White conversion option in Effects, or Desaturate Color in the Adjust panel. While both these options are valid routes, they only offer the very basic visual effects of conversion. To really squeeze more into the frame, you'll need to fiddle with other options, including: exposure, contrast, highlights, shadows, white balance, temperature and tint. The most important tool we will look at is Contrast, which is especially excellent for shots featuring a great difference in light and dark tones.

There are several routes and achievable effects on offer, so follow this quick guide to establish what your next monochromatic move will be.

Step-by-step | iPhoto Creative juices at the ready? Let's make mono magic!

1: Where to start?
Once you've located your images, open them in Full Screen Edit (Control-click an image and choose Option). Now activate the Effects and Adjust panel.

2: Trial and error
Hit the B&W option in Effects, or drag the Contrast cursor to the right to make a larger difference in the dark and light tones.

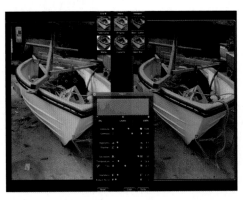

3: Compare and contrast
iPhoto has a handy Compare tool. Select the image and key Cmd+D to duplicate. Highlight both copies and travel to the Compare feature on the dock.

4: Cheat and boost
If your image has a highly saturated element, you can achieve a stronger effect by boosting colour in the Effects Tray, then resorting to the B&W effect.

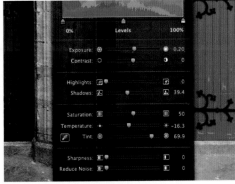

5: Lost but not gone
Sometimes areas become too dark, which can lose detail. But simply drag the Shadows cursor to the right to regain any detail lost in the shadows.

6: Moody monochrome
Altering a shot's colour tint, and warming and cooling its temperature can play a large part in the ultimate mood of the frame.

7: White balance
Convert to mono and, with White Balance selected, hit various areas of the screen. The inaccurate readings will offer a choice of subtle differences.

8: Portrait passion
Portraits look fantastic in black and white, but distracting backgrounds will steal focus. Use the Crop tool to cut it away and focus on the face.

9: Great light
If the portrait has been captured in great light, playing with the Contrast and Shadow will enable you to create a really dynamic black and white shot.

iPhoto

Knowledge base

Camera control
To go that extra mile with sunset shots, here's a good cheat for when you shoot the sunscape. If you use Scene modes, switch the dial to overcast or cloudy (commonly a sun and cloud icon). This tells the camera to boost colour and add vivid tones, which increases the colour drama in your frame.

Effects
Use the Effects box to drench your image with intensity. Keep in mind that you want to keep it realistic and if you boost the tones too much you could end up with a migraine!

At the controls
Use the Adjust panel to administer the changes needed in this tutorial. Remember to keep it warm and recover detail with the Highlights scale

Compare
Compare your work of art to the original by hitting this button on the toolbar, or alternatively drag the original from the Photo browser above

Enhance
If you don't have time for the nitty-gritty of this tutorial, you can cheat by hitting the all-encompassing Enhance tool. Although this won't be as precise, it will help you on your way

Tutorial: Create stunning sunscapes in iPhoto

The summer is perfect for sizzling sunsets, but do your summer snaps look more sad than stunning? Here's a few iPhoto tricks to perk them up

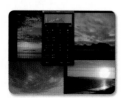

Task: Use iPhoto's Adjust palette to vamp up sunrise and sunset images
Difficulty: Beginner
Time needed: 30 minutes

At some point during these sun-drenched hazy days of summer, it is inevitable you're going to want to grab your digital camera and head out looking for a luscious landscape to capture a still of the setting sun. But has the beautiful vista you witnessed before your eyes translated onto the screen upon your return? If the answer is no, you may want to check into the iPhoto editing suite for some helpful tips.

The idea here is to add warmth, enhance tones and deepen the drama. Thankfully iPhoto's Adjust palette offers keen photographers a quick and easy feature set to spruce up those scenes in comprehensive and accessible steps. Use the sliders to gradually affect change and exploit our nine-step guide to find the key areas to hit. Once you've improved the colour, don't forget to hit the other tools on offer in the edit suite. Straighten those wonky horizons, crop out distracting foregrounds, retouch unwanted elements, blur the edge to fake that sizzling sensation and generally experiment to the ends of your imagination. Just don't forget to make a duplicate before you begin!

Step-by-step | iPhoto Transform washed-out sunsets into colour-drenched sunscapes

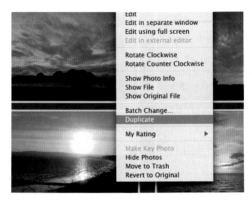

1: Learn from our mistakes
How often have you edited an image and wished you'd kept the original? If it's more than once, Ctrl-click on the sunset snap and choose Duplicate.

2: Go large
Sunset shots tend to be on the dark side, so opt for full-screen editing. Ctrl-click the shots and hit 'Edit using full screen'.

3: Warming up
Open the Adjust palette and notch up the degrees by dragging the Temperature control to the right and Tint to the left for a rosy afterglow.

4: Exposed
Reducing the exposure enhances silhouettes. To ensure you don't lose details, notch up the Shadows, Highlight and Contrast features.

5: Give it a boost
To really up the anti, drag the Saturation control to the right just a little. Alternatively, boost colour in the Effects palette.

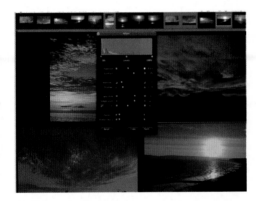

6: Copy and paste
Apply the effects you've administered on this sunset onto others by choosing the Copy button. With each one selected, hit the Paste button.

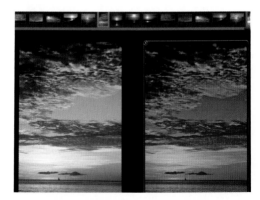

7: Compare and contrast
If you're apprehensive about veering too far away from the original, bring it up as a guide. Simply drag it onto the Editing page from the Photo browser.

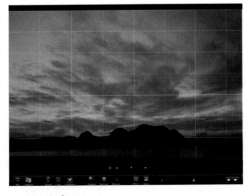

8: Straighten up
Other tools can also help. The Straighten feature improves wonky horizons, so drag the scale to align the grid to match a horizontal landline.

9: Come a cropper
Crop allows you to cut away distracting areas and focus attention. Set the option to Custom and drag the length and width to suit your preference.

Tutorial: Personalise iPhoto using Preferences

Tune up your iPhoto operation as we guide you through the possibilities that Preferences offers you…

Task: Explore iPhoto's Preference options to personalise its appearance and performance
Difficulty: Beginner
Time needed: 30 minutes

As much as we know you love iPhoto, there may come a time when you wished it would do something differently. Well, chances are it can. Preferences features loads of design and operation choices for you to customise.

Find it in the iPhoto menu on the Menu bar, or use the Command+, shortcut. Choose from six sections: General, Appearance, Events, Sharing, Web Gallery and Advanced. General offers options for click control function, email, camera connection and sources. Appearance enables you to get creative with the layout of iPhoto's interface, while Events offers control over the Events co-ordination. Sharing works in the same way as shared music in iPhoto and Web Gallery showcases .Mac galleries. Finally, the Advanced section extends colour profile, RAW and import options to the user.

So whether you want to set up a shortcut or discover how much room your .Mac web galleries are consuming, Preferences is your port of call for control. Read on as we guide you through the options at your fingertips.

Step-by-step | iPhoto Preferences explained

1: Generally speaking

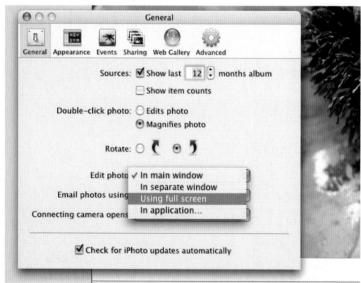

● The first set of options is labelled 'General'. Here users can tell iPhoto to display images added in a particular time frame, add up the total photo count, define what variation of mouse clicks should activate which command, alter how the Edit screen is presented and tweak camera connection options.

2: Appearance is everything

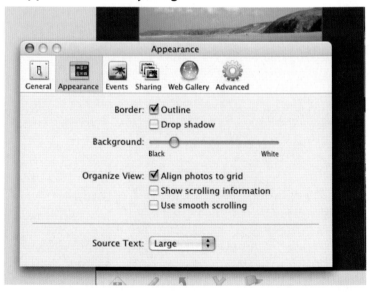

● Click on the Appearance icon to alter iPhoto's appearance. Users can decide to include an outline and drop shadow to thumbnails, as well as how images are aligned and information is presented. The background scale offers the options of black, white or a shade in between.

Custom iPhoto views

Menu bar
To get cracking on this you'll need to open up the Preferences toolbox by going to iPhoto on the menu bar and selecting Preferences. To trigger the shortcut type Command+,

Knowledge base

Animated scrolling explained
In Appearance users have the option to use animated scrolling. This essentially refers to how the page looks when you key up and down the app's interface or hit an empty spot on the scroll bar. If the option is off then the window will move to the next lot of images down or up the page. When it is on, the thumbnails slide before your eyes.

Backdrop
To change iPhoto's backdrop from black to white or any shade of grey, all you need to do is venture into Preference's Appearance panel and move the Backdrop slider from left to right until you discover a shade to suit your taste

Reflections
If you decide to select the Show Event Reflections in the Appearance tab of Preferences your thumbnails will display an attractive reflection. Having this activated doesn't take up extra space

Splitting up
The Autosplit Into Events feature grants users the power to decide how iPhoto separates imported snaps into time-grouped batches. This is particularly handy if you have images from two events taken on the same day

3: Share and share alike

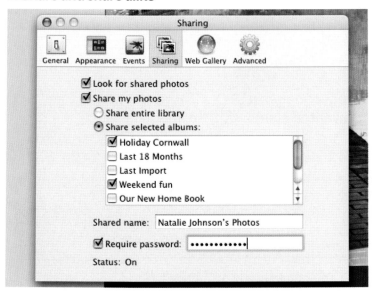

○ Use this panel to discover sharing options for your iPhoto library. This works in the same principle as shared music in iTunes and photographers are given the choice of what albums to share, and whether to look for shared photos. A password can be included if necessary.

4: Advance to the next level

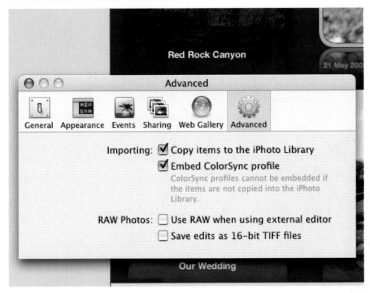

○ iPhoto stacks its importing and RAW photo selections in the Advanced section. Copy Items To The iPhoto Library works as an On/Off switch, while Embed ColorSync Profile attempts to make the images you see consistent with those you later print or publish.

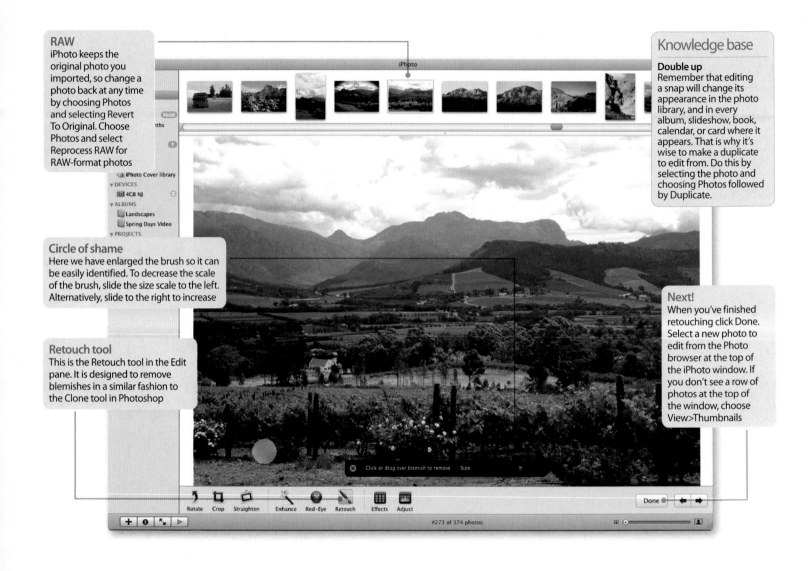

Tutorial: Removing objects in iPhoto

What's that in the photo? A bit of dirt, a rogue jogger, a UFO… There will always be an occasion to 'remove' unwanted elements of an image

Task: Clean up your images and remove elements with the Retouch tool

Difficulty: Beginner

Time needed: 10-30 minutes – depending on the size of removal

What a lovely photo of granny blowing out the candles on her 80th birthday cake. But what's that? Little Johnny is making bunny ears behind the birthday girl's blue-rinse barnet! Luck would have it that iPhoto makes allowances for these scenarios and offers you relief in a creative outlet.

iPhoto has an excellent tool for disposing of naughty children's fingers (not literally), or any other unwanted element degrading the overall impact of a sacred snap. The Retouch tool, stocked in iPhoto's handy Edit panel, can help users blend away just about anything in the background of what would otherwise be a wonderful image.

Once activated, Mac-lovers can click on the offending pixels and watch as they magically disappear. If it's a stubborn or larger mark, simply zoom in and execute a few gentle strokes, or increase the size of the brush by dragging the slider. We show you how…

Step-by-step | iPhoto Perfect your photos with the Retouch tool

1: Isolate offending elements
When you have isolated an image that needs cleaning up, select it, and open the picture in iPhoto's Edit screen.

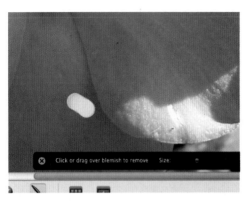

2: Clean it up
To activate the Retouch tool, key stroke the icon and hit the offending mark on your image. Drag the Size scale to increase or decrease the size of the brush.

3: Stubborn stains
Depending on the extent of the mark it may take a few attempts to retouch. Position the brush over the mark, and drag the brush to remove it.

4: Larger lumps
If it's a small mark, chances are a few clicks will do the trick. However, to remove larger objects use short strokes to blend it into its surrounding colours.

5: Compare and contrast
It is a good idea to monitor progress, so hit the Shift key to quickly compare the edited photo to its original version.

6: Get a closer look
To make sure the blemish is fully removed, zoom in to the area to retouch all offences. Simply drag the zoom scroll in the Edit panel to the right.

7: Before and after
To decipher how improved the new image is, try comparing it to the original. Select both new and old versions in the Photo browser and click Edit.

8: Too far gone
The Retouch tool may take some time to get used to. In this image we intended to remove a boat, but the offending area has just become blurred.

9: All is not lost
If this should happen, or you are unsatisfied with the result, all you need to do to alter the most recent change is choose Edit>Undo from the menu bar.

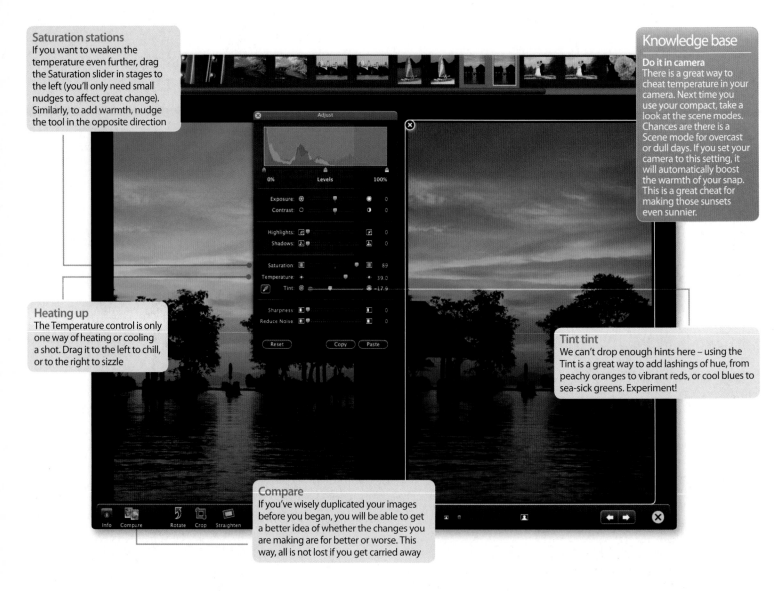

Saturation stations
If you want to weaken the temperature even further, drag the Saturation slider in stages to the left (you'll only need small nudges to affect great change). Similarly, to add warmth, nudge the tool in the opposite direction

Knowledge base

Do it in camera
There is a great way to cheat temperature in your camera. Next time you use your compact, take a look at the scene modes. Chances are there is a Scene mode for overcast or dull days. If you set your camera to this setting, it will automatically boost the warmth of your snap. This is a great cheat for making those sunsets even sunnier.

Heating up
The Temperature control is only one way of heating or cooling a shot. Drag it to the left to chill, or to the right to sizzle

Tint tint
We can't drop enough hints here – using the Tint is a great way to add lashings of hue, from peachy oranges to vibrant reds, or cool blues to sea-sick greens. Experiment!

Compare
If you've wisely duplicated your images before you began, you will be able to get a better idea of whether the changes you are making are for better or worse. This way, all is not lost if you get carried away

Tutorial: Change a photo's temperature in iPhoto

Your images should be exploding with colour! Use iPhoto's Temperature controls to cheat what the camera left out, with the help of our nine-step guide…

Task: Use iPhoto's Temperature controls to alter your shots
Difficulty: Beginner
Time needed: 30 minutes

iPhoto's editing suite is fantastic for correcting all manner of imaging sins. Whether it's cloning out splodges or straightening the horizon, you can bet that there will be a way of cheating everything in iPhoto.

For this sneaky session of iPhoto exploration we will show you how to cheat the temperature of a photo, meaning you don't have to jet off to the Med to capture that sunset! It's as simple as opening the image in the Edit screen, taking the lid off the Adjust toolbox and tweaking a set of variables.

The controls you'll need to heat up or cool down will mainly revolve around temperature, tint and saturation. But you'll also need to control the highlights, shadows and exposure. We'll show you how to incorporate iPhoto's effects to really make your images pop. And the fun doesn't have to stop there, as you turn green grass purple or blue oceans red. What to do first..?

Step-by-step | iPhoto Learn how to inject warmth or coolness in to your collection

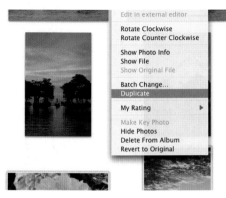

1: Prevention is better than a cure
To prevent your precious photos being altered forever, start by creating a duplicate. Simply Ctrl-click on the images in question and hit Duplicate.

2: Add warmth
Now locate an image that is in dire need of some warmth. Select Full Screen Editing, hit Ctrl and opt for the appropriate action from the menu.

3: Sunshine on a rainy day
Sunset shots are great for boosting. Open the Adjust panel, drag the Temperature slider to the right, and take the Tint to the left to add a peachy-red hue.

4: Dark and mysterious
Make images sinister or arty by 'cooling' them. We took the Temperature to the left, used a green hue, and faded the colour with the Effects option.

5: Colour cast remedy
Correct a colour cast by counteracting the hue with the opposite temperature (ie add warmth for a blue cast, and cool for an orange).

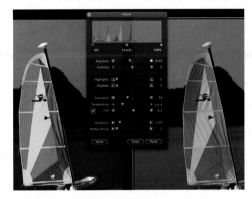

6: Compare and contrast
If you can't decide whether to heat up or simmer down the tonal values, why not compare them side-by-side? Action the icon marked 'Compare'.

7: Old-school rules
Use Temperature controls with the Effects options; turn a landscape sepia, add a red hue, drag Temperature to the left and increase the Highlights.

8: Art attack
Get into the swing of it and they'll be no stopping you. Cool temperatures and add hues to play with people's perceptions – is that really purple grass?!

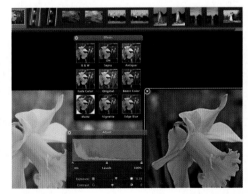

9: Effect it
Also strengthen or weaken the temperature by using the Effect options of Boost/Fade colour. Adjust the intensity by altering the values.

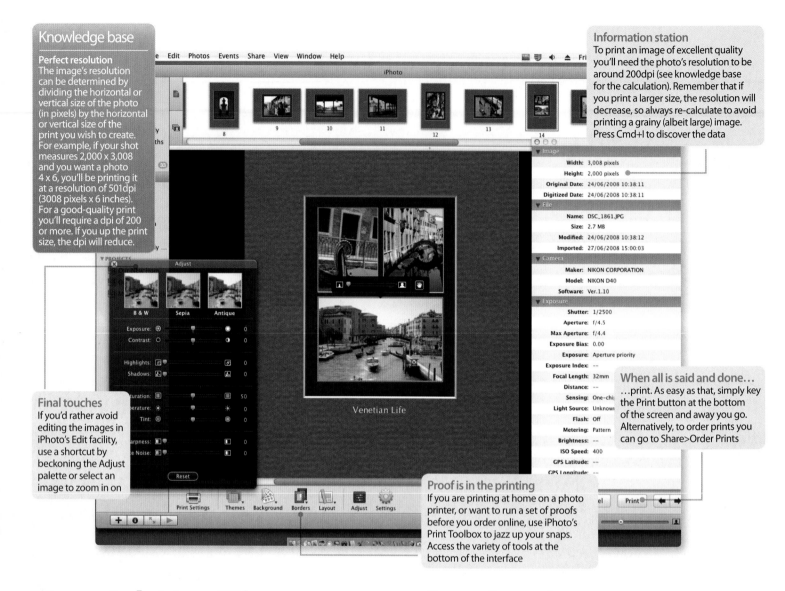

Tutorial: Use iPhoto to proof and order prints

If you want to free your frames from their iPhoto prison, come with us as we show you how to proof, print and order prints online…

Task: Produce printed images with iPhoto's range of printing options
Difficulty: Beginner
Time needed: 40 minutes

Before the big switch over to digital photography, printing images went hand in hand with taking images. Nowadays, the majority of people are happy enough to simply hoard their shots as soon as the shutter has been released, filed away into iPhoto's organised bank of memories, maybe to never see the light of day again. With that in mind, we've decided to explore iPhoto's bevy of printing options to reignite our passion for the printed form.

As with everything Apple-made, the decision to print is not a question of black and white, but in fact all manner of colours and creativity. Users have the option to proof images, turn them into PDFs, or print them at home as individual shots. There are options to add frames and graduated borders of varying colours and designs. Photo enthusiasts can print at home on a tidy desk printer, or churn them out in the office as simple black-and-white previews. We'll even cover iPhoto's integrated online ordering system, which allows photographers to send their images off to the printers in one easy step.

Step-by-step | iPhoto Printing and proofing

1: Cherry picking
Cherry pick the images you wish to print by using iPhoto's Flag tool. Track through your library, event or album, isolate an image and hit the Flag icon.

2: Calculated success
To ensure images will appear clear when printed, call up the information by pressing Cmd+I. See the knowledge base to calculate how well it will print.

3: Final touches
Your snaps may look fab, but under the microscope or in Full Edit, they may need a few tweaks. Ctrl-click on a frame and select Edit using Full Screen.

4: Preview please
Before you whiz your pics off to the printer it's wise to implement a trial run using your own printer. Hit the Print icon and adjust the settings accordingly.

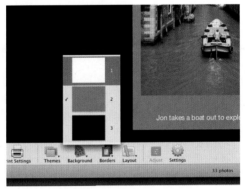

5: Have some fun
iPhoto's Print feature set extends a creative hand here; play around with the variety of backgrounds, borders and layouts to inject some pizzazz.

6: Colour happy
If you have a home printer that embraces the world of Technicolor, top up your snaps with splashes of colour to make your prints more than just proofs.

7: PDF power
Hit the button labelled Print to bring up the Option box. It's wise to save the finished frames as PDFs, to keep a digital record of your completed creations.

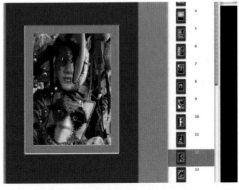

8: Preview prints
Opt to preview your pictures onscreen before you run the Print command – if you see an error it is better to correct it this way than waste paper.

9: And finally…
Once you are satisfied, head to Share>Order Prints. Fill in your .Mac account details and select the prints you wish to order at the relevant sizes.

iMovie

Features

Tutorials

Having two different versions of iMovie available to you means that you can get the best of two brilliant worlds. In iMovie '08 you can organise and edit movies with the greatest of ease, and in iMovie '06 you can get more involved and create some truly amazing effects.

Introducing

Forget the troubles of the last version and usher in a new era of Mac movie making with the latest and best release of Apple's consumer editing suite...

W hen iMovie '08 made its debut back in 2007, its dramatically different looking interface alienated many die-hard iMovie '06 users. To many the totally re-designed iMovie '08 was a big step backwards as it lacked many of the features boasted by the old-school iMovie '06 – like the ability to add special effects and themed animated graphics to your footage, for example. iMovie '08 couldn't even change the speed of footage, which is something iMovie '06 could do with ease. Such was the resistance to the new kid on the block that Apple made iMovie '06 available as a free download for those who couldn't (or wouldn't) adapt to iMovie '08. With the recent release of iMovie '09 there's a genuine reason to get excited. The new package rocks! If you're an iMovie '06 fan it's time to come out with your hands up as iMovie '09 outguns iMovie '06 in many ways. At first glance it's true

"If you're an editing expert you'd probably think twice about using iMovie, but as it can now perform video edits with ease, you can produce slickly edited programmes"

that your newly installed iMovie '09 looks remarkably similar to iMovie '08, but don't let that put you off. The new package addresses many of its immediate predecessor's problems and can now proudly hold its head up high due to its effective organising and editing powers.

The great thing about iMovie '09 is the fact that it's really easy to use if you're a video-editing novice. It'll even add an animated title and transitions to your footage automatically if you ask it nicely. If you're an editing expert you'd probably think twice about using iMovie to make your videos, but as it can now perform split sound and video edits with ease, you can produce slickly edited programmes in a jiffy. You could, in theory, re-arrange sound and video independently in older versions of iMovie, but this was a cumbersome

your first movie

and long-winded process. iMovie '09 lets you insert cutaways into your main footage in a click and adjust the position of the sound track with ease thanks to a powerful new set of editing tools, like the Precision Editor. More of that later!

Although iMovie '09 is capable of producing slickly edited video with high production values, it can only work with the footage you give it. Think of the acronym GIGO (Garbage In, Garbage Out). It was coined to describe the behaviour of computers, but it also applies to video production. If your footage is badly shot, badly lit and out of focus, then the edited video will be tricky to edit and not much fun to watch. iMovie '09 does have some clever tools designed to remove problems like camera shake, but we'll kick off this feature by showing you how to shoot high-quality footage that you

can import into iMovie and turn into a slick video sequence.

By the end of this feature you'll be familiar with all the new features in iMovie '09 and be able to raise the bar when it comes to organising, editing and sharing your own videos. You'll finally be able to move on from iMovie '06 and enjoy a fulfilling, productive and exciting relationship with iMovie '09.

▶

Essential kit

Sony Handycam DCR-HC37
£200 www.sony.co.uk
This highly portable Mini-DV camcorder has a Carl Zeiss lens that lets you zoom in very close.

Adjustable mini tripod £3.50
www.jessops.com
A tiny tripod like this will dramatically improve the quality of your footage.

Head cleaner £20
www.jessops.com
Jessops will throw in a head cleaner when you buy five Mini-DV tapes. What a bargain!

Camera bag £27.50
www.jessops.com
Keep your camcorder, tapes and mini tripod safe using Lowepro's Apex 100 AW camera bag.

Travel adaptor £8.99 for two
www.dixons.co.uk
Keep your camcorder battery topped up even while abroad by buying a travel adaptor.

Essential Technique
1: Shoot yourself
A tripod helps you to avoid 'hose piping' your camera aimlessly around the location in search of interesting sights. Short well-framed shots captured on a tripod are easier to edit together in iMovie than long rambling handheld epics. You could also pop the tripod on a flat surface and film you and your family enjoying their holiday as you walk through an exotic location. Just don't walk too far away from your unattended camcorder in case it gets stolen!

Shooting Tip   Editing Tip   Sharing Tip

If you buy a photographer's bag to store your video shooting kit in go for an unbranded bag as it makes your kit less of a target for opportunistic thieves

Your camcorder may have sat on the shelf all winter due to the short days and dull weather, so an impending summer holiday is a great time to start shooting again as new locations provide you with plenty of colourful videogenic sights to capture. You'll want to share your holiday experiences with friends and family at home so here's a few tips to help you capture good quality footage that you can edit into slick sequences, thanks to iMovie '09 and its video editing powers. The shooting tips, tricks and techniques we'll describe don't just apply to holiday videos – you can use our advice to get better results from any shoot!

Choose your weapon
By investing in a relatively cheap camcorder you can capture the highlights of your holiday as raw footage and use the greatly improved iMovie '09 to edit your video memories into mini documentaries. Then, when summer wanes, you can re-visit your holiday courtesy of your iMovie edited productions and keep the winter blues at bay. While preparing to buy provisions for your summer holiday you may have a checklist that includes flip flops and suntan lotion. Give yourself a video kit checklist too so you can start shooing as soon as you hit the beach. It's well worth

investing in a compact camcorder. You can carry a small camcorder in your hand luggage so it won't get bashed about by the luggage handlers. Buy a photographer's kit bag so you can carry your camcorder around with you wherever you go on location. You can also use the bag to store tapes, batteries and even your suntan lotion.

When it comes to camcorders there are many different recording formats that you can buy, including camcorders that shoot straight to DVD or flash disc. iMovie '09 can digitise video with ease, or you can drag and drop movies from a compact flash card into the Event browser in seconds. For our regular iCreate iMovie tutorials we use Mini-DV (digital video) to capture our raw footage. Mini-DV produces decent quality footage that you can import (or digitise) with ease. You can pick up a pack of Mini-DV tapes for bargain prices at the airport departure lounge (tape can be cheaper and store more footage than a flash card). While you're shopping in the airport make sure that you buy a power adaptor for the country you're flying to. Then you can recharge your camcorder's batteries from the comfort of your hotel room. It's also a good idea to keep a pen handy to label your tapes. There's nothing more tedious than wading through a batch

of unlabelled tapes looking for a specific shot, so get into the good habit of labelling them on location.

Quality control
iMovie '09 can stabilise wobbly handheld footage – as you'll see in our tutorial. However, the stabilisation process increases the work you have to do in the editing stage and it crops the image too. One of the best ways to improve the quality of the footage you shoot is to use a tripod. You can pick up tiny tripods that are big enough to support a compact Mini-DV camcorder and small enough to fit inside your camera bag. A tripod enables you to compose your shots with care to capture well-framed holiday landmarks, for example.

On location
Although iMovie '09 can help you tweak your footage's colour and exposure and iron out wobbles in your handheld footage, it's well worth doing all you can to capture high-quality footage in the first place. Your tripod should

Skimming clips
Once you import a clip you will see it displayed as a filmstrip in the Event browser. To find a specific moment simply skim the cursor across the filmstrip. The filmstrip thumbnails will play back as mini clips.

alleviate the need to stabilise wobbly footage, but it can still be a challenge to capture well-exposed shots with accurate colours. Many camcorders have a flip-out LCD monitor that lets you see your location's colours and tones.

Amateur videographers tend to leave the camcorder set to auto-focus. This can produce good results most of the time, but if you have a scene with constantly moving subjects (like soaring seagulls) then the camera will constantly 'hunt' for a focal point. This will cause the footage to become sharp, then blurred, then sharp again! Cameras like those in the Sony Handycam range let you focus on a specific object by tapping on it on the LCD. Once you've used the LCD to set up exposure and colour, flip it shut and use the rear monochrome viewfinder. This will dramatically prolong your battery life and let you shoot for longer, so you won't miss an important or interesting subject.

Importing footage

Once you've returned from the shoot it's time to take iMovie '09 for a test-drive and import your footage. If you've shot on Mini-DV format then you'll need to plug your camcorder into your Mac (via USB or FireWire) and import (or digitise) the relevant clips in real-time. You can access and control your camcorder from iMovie by clicking on the Camera Import button. Rewind, fast forward and play the tape, then click Import when you see any raw footage that you fancy using in your film. Like iMovie '08, version '09 enables you to store footage in

chronological order in named Events, allowing you to organise and access your clips with ease. iMovie '09 also allows you to import video files from hard drive or flash-based memory cameras. If you have a memory-based camera then the browser will change to display thumbnails of all your clips. You can import the contents of the camcorder in a single click without having to play the clips in real-time. If you set the Import window to Manual you can tick which clips you want to import and leave the unwanted clips stored on the camera.

Storage
Video footage demands hard drive space. If you have an external hard drive you can browse to it and save valuable space on your Mac

Events
By storing your imported footage in a named Event you can access it with ease. This type of housekeeping is an area where iMovie excels

Automatic
If you select Automatic and click Import, iMovie will rewind the tape and import everything. It'll import the contents of a memory-based camera too

Import
When you see a clip or a section of footage that you like, click Import and iMovie will copy it to your designated drive and store it in an Event

Shooting Tip	Editing Tip	Sharing Tip

If you have dozens of clips in the Event browser you may not be able to see them all. Drag the Zoom slider to scale down the filmstrips so that they all fit

"Like iMovie '08, version '09 enables you to store footage in chronological order"

Essential Technique
2: Energy saver
You may be tempted to watch your footage while still on location, but this will make your batteries run out of juice quicker, which could cause you to miss something interesting. You also run the risk of taping over your footage if you forget to fast forward the tape. Instead of watching footage on location, have a screening of your holiday rushes from the comfort of your hotel room at the end of each day instead.

Supported formats
As technology advances there are a variety on non-tape-based camcorders on the market that can record straight to a hard drive, DVD or even to flash memory. iMovie '09 supports all of these formats.

Shooting and importing

Tutorial: Edit in iMovie '09 – Part 01

Get to grips with the powerful new editing tools in iMovie '09 by importing, editing and adding transitions to your raw video footage

Task: Import and edit footage
Difficulty: Beginner
Time needed: 20 minutes

Let's dive straight in and use iMovie '09 to edit some raw holiday footage into a slick video souvenir that can be shared with friends and family. All the clips that you'll need to follow this walkthrough are on this the free disc (in Holiday Footage).

In part one of this iMovie '09 editing tutorial you'll test-drive some of the enhanced editing tools and add a transition to give your video more professional-looking production values. You'll even be able to salvage shots ruined by a shaking camera thanks to the exciting new Image Stabilization feature. In part two you'll enhance the video with graphics, music and themes.

Step-by-step | iMovie Import footage, stabilise it then edit and add transitions

1: Create new project
Go to File>New Project and label it Holiday. Choose Standard 4:3 as the Aspect Ratio. Leave the Theme option set to None. Now click Create.

2: Import footage
Choose File>Import>Movies. Tick Create New Event. and label it Holiday. Browse to the Raw Holiday Footage folder (on the disc). Click OK.

3: Analyse camera shake
The zoomed lamppost shot shakes. Select the clip's Gear icon and choose Clip Adjustments to open the Inspector. Click Analyze Entire Clip.

4: Stabilise footage
Click Done when the camera shake has been analysed. Drag the clip into the Project window to view the dramatically stabilised version

5: Add clips
Drag the close-up of the hands breaking up bread into the Project window. Then add the wide shot of the girl throwing bread to the gulls.

6: Fine-tune the edit
By cutting on repetitive movements you can make the action flow smoothly. Click on the last clip's Gear icon and open the Precision Editor.

92

Add smooth transitions in iMovie '09

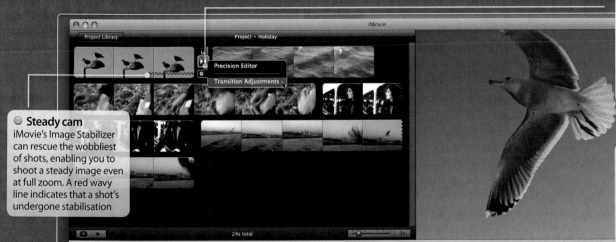

○ Tweak transitions
For a longer dissolve between clips click on the Gear icon below a transition and choose Transition Adjustments. A longer duration creates a gentle jump forward in time from a static seagull to the birds in flight

○ Steady cam
iMovie's Image Stabilizer can rescue the wobbliest of shots, enabling you to shoot a steady image even at full zoom. A red wavy line indicates that a shot's undergone stabilisation

○ Knowledge base

Save space
Video can take up huge chunks of hard drive space. Once you've finished editing your project go to File>Space Saver. Tick the option to reject an Event's clip if it hasn't been added to your project. Click Reject and Review. All clips destined for destruction will appear in the Rejected Clips window. Click Move Rejected To Trash.

○ Precision editing
The iMovie 09 Precision Editor enables you to fine tune where one clip ends and the next begins, letting you match repetitive actions and produce smooth flowing cuts from one shot to the next

○ Thin blue line
The blue line indicates the point where we cut from the previous clip to the next clip. Click on the grey bar between the top and bottom clips and hit the Spacebar to preview the cut in the main Viewer

7: Precision editing
Drag the top clip so that the arm begins to fall. Drag the bottom clip to place the arm in the same position. Click Done. Hit Space to play the sequence.

8: Quick trim
Add the next clip. Click its Gear icon and choose Clip Trimmer. Drag the trim handle so that the clip starts with her arm in mid throw.

9: Transitions
Place the flying seagulls clip ('Swoop.mov') after the first shot. Click the Transitions browser icon. Drag a Cross Dissolve between the first two clips.

▶

Editing, themes and transitions

Tool Guide

Tool: Crop tool
The Crop tool will enable you to improve composition and remove unwanted objects at the edge of the screen. Just click the Fit option to undo a crop.

Tool: Picture in picture
This cool new feature lets you use the main Viewer to slide the inserted picture anywhere you like and even resize it by dragging its corner handles.

Tool: Beat marker
Add music to a new project then choose Clip Trimmer from the clip's Gear icon. Press the M key whenever you want iMovie to cut to a new clip.

Tool: Keywords
By using the View Keywords tool you can assign keywords to a selection in the Event browser. You can then hunt for specific clips via keywords.

Theme gallery

The Transitions browser boasts a wide range of themed graphics that you can drop your clips into, from the colourful animated Scrapbook theme to the rather cool Filmstrip theme. When you choose a new theme from the Transitions browser then additional themed graphics will appear in the Titles browser.

"In iMovie '09 you can take sound from a clip and add it to existing video footage with ease"

Slick Transitions

Each theme provides you with a different but graphically similar animated transition, so you can create a varied but unified transition style for the project.

Once you've imported your raw footage into iMovie '09 you can access the chronological list of events in the Event library. This is a great way of storing and organising video clips, especially as we're generating more and more footage thanks to cheaper camcorders, phones with video functions, and so on. By default iMovie checks the metadata stored in your clips and automatically creates a new event for each day. If you've come back with footage from a long holiday then the Event library can become cluttered with dozens of events. To merge multiple events into one simply drag one day onto another and re-label the merged event. The footage inside the merged event will still be stored in chronological order so you can find clips quickly.

Before you can share your holiday memories with family and friends (or the entire world if you're planning to upload the footage online)

then it makes sense to edit it. No one wants to sit through hours of unedited rushes when they're used to a diet of fast moving, well-edited programmes with high production values. Fortunately iMovie '09 has all the tools you need to produce slickly edited programmes that come complete with animated title sequences, transitions and music. Later in this feature we'll walk you step-by-step through importing, organising and editing footage in iMovie '09 in our double bill iMovie tutorial. But first we'll have a closer look at some of the new features that will make editing a pleasure.

Closer look
To work out which bits of raw footage will make it into your edited programme, skim the pointer over the filmstrips in the Event browser and watch quick previews of the footage in the Viewer. If the Viewer window is too small go to Window>Viewer and choose Large. For an even better look at your unedited clips click the Play Selected Events Full Screen button at the bottom of the interface (or press Cmd+G). When you click this button iMovie '09 lets you use Cover Flow to skim through your footage in full-screen mode. You can also use Cover Flow to access other events in the Event browser without leaving full-screen.

Insert editing
Earlier versions of iMovie did a good job of allowing you to run a series of clips together to create an edited

programme, but they lacked the sophistication of high-end packages like Final Cut Pro. Experienced video editors like to drop cutaway shots into existing footage or extend sound from one clip over another to create a split-sound edit that links the two clips together. To take sound from one clip and add it to another in iMovie '08 you had to use a fiddly keyboard shortcut. In iMovie '09 you can take sound from a clip in the Event browser and add it to existing video footage in the Project window with ease. Simply drag a yellow selection border over the clip that you want to steal sound from in the Event browser. Drag the selection onto a clip in the Project window. A new pop-up menu will appear in the Project window offering you three editing choices. Replace will remove the current clip in the Project window and replace it with the selection from the Event Browser. The Insert option will drop

Credit Crunch

To maintain visual continuity you can 'top and tail' your programme with animated credits that match the theme of your transitions.

Shooting Tip | **Editing Tip** | Sharing Tip

Once you've imported and viewed your footage it's good practice to drag a yellow border around bits that you don't need and clicking Reject Selection

Terrific Titles

Organic Main
There are a wide variety of animated titles to browse through, so you can find a style that suits your video's subject.

the selected sound and video from the Event browser into the clip in the Project window. This is a fast and effective way of dropping in cutaways. The Audio Only option allows you to take the sound from the selected clip and overlay it onto the main footage. The ability to insert audio footage with ease is a massive boon to iMovie '09. When it comes to editing, iMovie '09 caters for both the expert and the novice.

Terrific transitions
Once you've refined your raw footage into a structured programme you can make it flow more smoothly with a variety of transitions. When you click on the Transitions browser you'll find the usual suspects (like Cross Dissolve) present and correct. There are also a few new transitions, like the flashy Mosaic and Spin In (though we think these showy transitions will date your footage, whereas a classy Cross Dissolve will be around forever). If you really want to show off then you can unleash extra editing functions by going to iMovie>Preferences and turning on Show Advanced Tools. Now when you drag a selection from the Event browser onto a clip in the Project window you'll see nine options appear in the pop-up menu. One of these is Picture In Picture, which lets you view the inserted clip as a picture alongside the footage.

Themes
One of the things people missed when iMovie '06 was replaced by iMovie '08 was the library of themes that allowed you to present your footage in a more professional way, thanks to the animated graphics. Themes are back with a vengeance in iMovie '09, and you can access them from the Transitions browser. Once you click on the Set Theme button you can choose from a variety of animated graphics that will help you present your clips in an entertaining and eye-catching way.

Travel maps
To add a travelogue style graphic that shows where in the world your holiday video was filmed click on the new Maps And Backgrounds browser. Choose a globe from a range of graphic templates and drag it to your Project window. After choosing a start and end point, an animated line will illustrate your journey. You can also add maps to your video and use the Ken Burns effect to zoom in to a specific country.

Adjust clips

Clip
To fine-tune a clip in the Project window, double-click on it to open the Inspector. In the Clip section of the Inspector you can change the duration and speed of the clip and even add Image Stabilization to it. You can also choose a video effect.

Video
The Video tab in the Inspector is great when it comes to correcting colour and tone. You can warm or cool colour casts using the White Point colour wheel. The Exposure and Contrast sliders produce a range of shadows and highlights.

Audio
This tab enables you to tweak the clip's volume levels. You can remove unwanted sound by dragging the Volume slider to the left. You can then insert audio from another clip or offset sound from the next clip in the Project window.

Tutorial: Edit in iMovie '09 – Part 02

In part two of our iMovie '09 editing double bill you'll create a more polished production by adding music, captions and even slick animated graphics courtesy of iMovie's new Themes browser

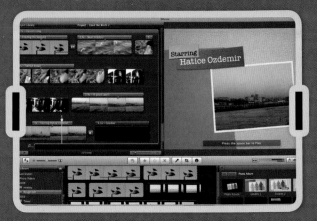

Once you've used tools like the new Precision Editor to cut a slick sequence together you can raid iMovie's large selection of post-production assets to add the icing to your cake! When watching professionally produced programmes we take it for granted that they'll have a title sequence designed to hook the viewer into watching the show, as well as the usual bells and whistles like captions and music.

The iMovie '09 Themes browser enables us to 'top and tail' our video sequence with animated graphics that we can personalise to introduce our edited video in a more professional-looking way.

Task: Add music and graphics to create a professional-looking production
Difficulty: Intermediate
Time needed: 20 minutes

Step-by-step | **iMovie** Add music, captions and animated titles to add polish to your production

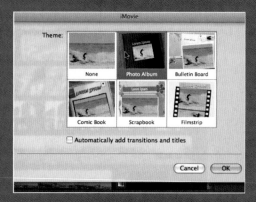

1: Choose a theme
Click on the Titles browser. Click Set Theme and choose Photo Album. Untick Automatically Add Transitions And Titles. Click OK.

2: Add opening title graphic
Drag the Photo Album title to the first shot in the Edit Project window. Extend the title to 1.8 seconds. Type text into the text field in the Viewer.

3: Add an animated caption
In the Titles browser scroll down and drag Lower Third 1 to the second shot in the Edit Project window. Extend it and type in some text.

4: Add more graphics
Add Upper Third to the third shot in the sequence and place Lower Third 2 at the start of the final shot. The captions fly in and out of the screen.

5: Closing titles
Pop Credits 1 over the end of the last shot and type in the name of your movie's star. The video will shrink to fit inside the animated graphic.

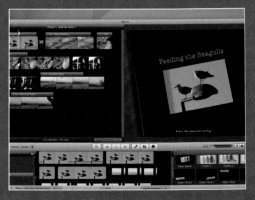

6: Test your titles
Drag the cursor to the start of the movie and hit the Spacebar to play the footage. Fine-tune the duration of the graphics if necessary.

Polish off your iMovie masterpiece

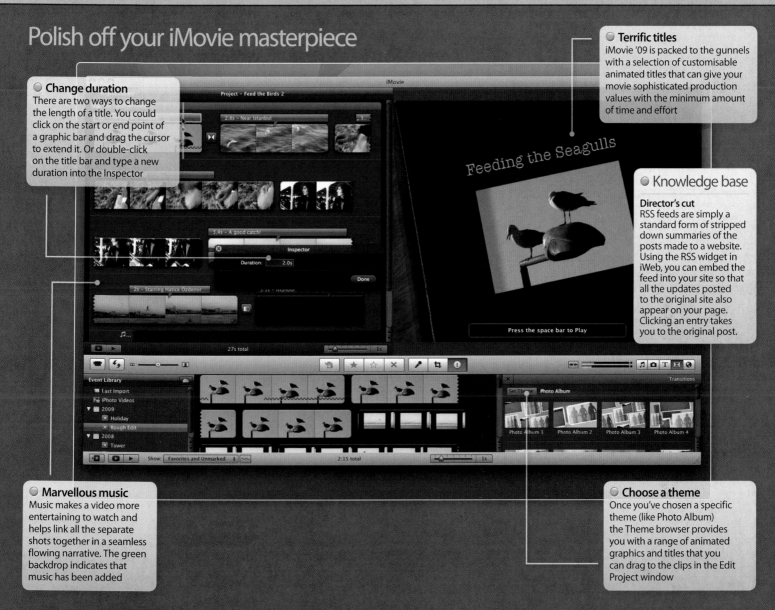

○ Change duration
There are two ways to change the length of a title. You could click on the start or end point of a graphic bar and drag the cursor to extend it. Or double-click on the title bar and type a new duration into the Inspector

○ Terrific titles
iMovie '09 is packed to the gunnels with a selection of customisable animated titles that can give your movie sophisticated production values with the minimum amount of time and effort

○ Knowledge base
Director's cut
RSS feeds are simply a standard form of stripped down summaries of the posts made to a website. Using the RSS widget in iWeb, you can embed the feed into your site so that all the updates posted to the original site also appear on your page. Clicking an entry takes you to the original post.

○ Marvellous music
Music makes a video more entertaining to watch and helps link all the separate shots together in a seamless flowing narrative. The green backdrop indicates that music has been added

○ Choose a theme
Once you've chosen a specific theme (like Photo Album) the Theme browser provides you with a range of animated graphics and titles that you can drag to the clips in the Edit Project window

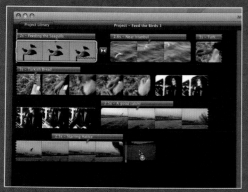

7: Fade to black
In the Transitions browser scroll down to Fade To Black and drag it over the end of the movie. Shorten the Credits 1 bar so it doesn't overlap the transition.

8: Create closing credits
Place the Centered title after the last clip. You could use a colourful animated background, but a classy black backdrop should suffice on this occasion.

9: Finishing touch
Click on the Music browser icon and navigate to Jingles. Drag a music track onto the project's grey background to add music to the whole programme.

▶

▶ Polishing and sharing

Shooting Tip **Editing Tip** **Sharing Tip**

If you spot a spelling mistake after you've published your film online simply correct it in iMovie, then choose Share>Re-publish To MobileMe Gallery

"After you've had fun creating your first slickly edited video in iMovie '09 you'll be keen to share it with friends and family"

Effects gallery

Romantic effect
Instead of smearing the lens with Vaseline, just use the less messy Romantic effect filter to add a soft edge to your footage.

Bleach Bypass
Bleach Bypass crushes the black levels and boosts the highlights to create a high contrast effect that looks great on dramas.

Add music & photos

As an iLife application, iMovie '09 is fully integrated with applications like iPhoto, so you can augment your video edit with stills that you might have taken from the same location. Simply click on the Photos browser and search through your Aperture or iPhoto libraries for shots to drag into your iMovie Project window. You can also add music by searching through your collection via the Music browser.

Once you've cut your raw footage into a tightly edited movie and added transitions and credits, you can then polish it up even further by adding a host of new post-production tools and effects to your iMovie '09 project. Professional filmmakers often tweak colour and tones of their footage to add a distinctive colour palette to their film. This is called grading. You could use the Inspector to change each shot's colours and tones manually, but there is a much

quicker way to add Hollywood-style colour grades and special effects to your clips. One of the reason to be disappointed with iMovie '08 was the fact that it didn't have the video effects that we'd grown to love in iMovie '06. But this problem has been corrected in iMovie '09. Simply double-click on a clip in the Project window to open the Inspector. Go to the Inspector's Clip tab and click on the Video Effect pane. The Inspector will flip to reveal a range of video effect preview thumbnails. These

are designed to mimic a variety of different effects. The Romantic video filter adds a gentle, blurring vignette to the edge of the frame. There's even an aged film effect that fans of iMovie '06 will appreciate. Unlike iMovie '06, the properties of the effects in the latest version of the package don't require rendering, which speeds up your editing workflow. To preview an effect simply skim over the preview thumbnail in the Inspector. Click once to apply it, then click Done to close the Inspector. You can then enjoy the effect instantly by hitting the Spacebar to play the clip.

Share and enjoy
After you've had fun creating your first slickly edited video in iMovie '09 you'll be keen to share it with friends and family. You can do so without leaving your seat thanks

The Export and Share screens
Getting your video online is a piece of cake thanks to iMovie's Share menu. First, type in a description of where and when your video was shot. You can select a variety of sizes to suit the browsing needs of your audience. Click Publish and let iMovie do the rest.

Raster
To make a clip look as though it's being viewed through a CCTV monitor you can simply pop the Raster effect on it.

Aged Film
Turn back time in a click and create a scratched old film effect with this retro-themed filter. See how many people you can trick!

Day Into Night
With this filter you can mimic an old-school technique and shoot by day, then filter the footage to add a nocturnal blue hue.

Cartoon
Turn live action footage into a rotoscoped-style animation with the minimum of effort with this creative Cartoon filter.

"For a wider audience you can make the video viewable by everyone who surfs by, or you can publish directly from iMovie '09 to YouTube"

to a variety of publishing options. To pop it online for your friends to view it in an attractive interface go to Share and choose MobileMe Gallery (check out the Export and Share screens boxout to see how easy it is to publish your programme

online). Once you've clicked Publish, iMovie will create and compress different sized versions of your film and upload them to your MobileMe gallery. You can then send friends the URL (and password if one is required) so that they can enjoy your movie from anywhere in the world.

For a wider audience you can make the video viewable by everyone who surfs by, or you can publish directly from iMovie '09 to YouTube. Alternatively, you can export your footage to iDVD and share your first iMovie '09 film at full PAL (or HD) resolution film on a shiny disc complete with themes and

background music as well as extras and high resolution photos. For viewing on the go use the Share menu to compress the movie for iTunes. You can then pop it on your iPod or iPhone and show off your film, as well as the brilliant new iMovie editing features to anyone you happen to meet, from

colleagues to the guy sat next to you on the bus. Remember, this is just your first iMovie '09 project and we guarantee that you will be thinking about launching into another very soon. As you're likely to have discovered by now, it's not really such a daunting task after all.

Shooting Tip	Editing Tip	Sharing Tip

Not everyone wants to be a movie star for the whole world to see. You can assign a password to your online video to protect your 'actors'

Tutorial: Add a travel map to your iMovie project

Don't just explain where you've been, show your viewers the exact locations with a beautiful travel map in iMovie '09. Follow this simple tutorial as we show you how to make one…

Task: Add a travel map to your movie
Difficulty: Beginner
Time needed: 10 minutes

When you make a movie that includes footage of your travels, you'll probably use titles to set the scene and describe the locations you arrive in. Until now, there hasn't been a facility available to accurately display world travel as you see on TV without knowledge of advanced movie editing or even 3D rendering. But the Maps feature in iMovie makes displaying your travels easier than you could have ever imagined! You simply choose the map style you're after, set a start and end location and you're done. A slick, animated map will then be added to your project with a line charting your journey from start to finish. There is a selection of map styles available, including 2D and 3D variations.

In the following four-step tutorial we will show you just how easy it is to add and edit a travel map to make your holiday footage even more exciting for your viewers (not to mention making your movie look even more professional and impressive!).

Step-by-step | iMovie Add animated maps

1: Add the map

● Start by clicking the 'Maps button (on the far right below the viewing window) and selecting the map style you would like to add to your project. Now simply click and drag it to the point where you want it to appear.

2: Map modification

● The Map Inspector will now appear, allowing you to set the duration of the clip and add effects. For now we're simply going to add the start and end locations by clicking the respective buttons.

Include a travel map in your iMovie project

● Map clip
The map appears just like any other movie clip in your project and can be moved and edited at will

● Map preview
Check your map in the viewing window by skimming or playing the finished clip in your project

● Inspector
From this screen you can select a start and end point for your map, as well as choosing how long you want it to play for. You can also add effects and swap the start and end locations

● Knowledge base

Make the most of maps
At present there's only the option to include a start and end point in your iMovie maps. This doesn't mean you can't show multiple destinations however. Why not add a map for each leg of your travels, with corresponding clips in between?

● Map selection
The map menu offers a selection of map styles for you to choose from. Simply drag them to your project to add them

3: Where in the world?

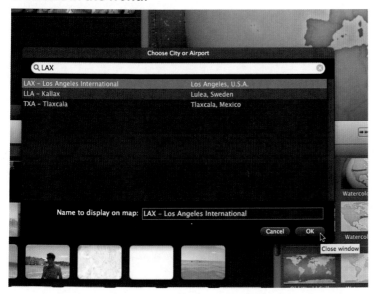

● For both the start and end locations, click the respective buttons and begin typing a location or airport. iMovie will suggest locations which you can then select as a start or end point in your movie.

4: Map action

● With both start and end locations added, your map is now animated to show the route between the two. Your new map will now appear like any other clip in your movie and can be moved and edited in the same way too.

iCreate | Subscriptions Voucher
The creative magazine for Mac users

☑ **YES!** I would like to subscribe to **iCreate**

YOUR DETAILS

Title_____ First name_____

Surname_____

Address_____

_____

_____

Postcode_____Country_____

Telephone number_____

Mobile number_____

Email address_____
Please complete your email address to receive news and special offers from us

DIRECT DEBIT PAYMENT

☐ UK Direct Debit Payment – only £25.20 every 6 issues (Save 30%)

ip IMAGINE PUBLISHING

Instruction to your Bank or Building Society to pay by Direct Debit
Please fill in the form and send it to: Imagine Publishing Ltd : 800 Guillat Avenue, Kent Science Park, Sittingbourne, ME9 8GU

DIRECT Debit

Name and full postal address of your Bank or Building Society

To: The Manager   Bank/Building Society

Address

Postcode

Name(s) of account holder(s)

Branch sort code

Bank/Building Society account number

Originator's Identification Number

| 5 | 0 | 1 | 8 | 8 | 4 |

Reference Number

Instructions to your Bank or Building Society
Please pay Imagine Publishing Limited Direct Debits from the account detailed in this instruction subject to the safeguards assured by the Direct Debit guarantee. I understand that this instruction may remain with Imagine Publishing Limited and, if so, details will be passed on electronically to my Bank/Building Society

Signature(s)

Date

Banks and Building Societies may not accept Direct Debit instructions for some types of account   A6 instruction form

PAYMENT DETAILS

YOUR EXCLUSIVE READER PRICE 1 YEAR (13 ISSUES)

☐ UK £62.40 (Save 20%)   ☐ Europe – £70.00   ☐ World – £80.00

Cheque

☐ I enclose a cheque for £_____
(made payable to Imagine Publishing Ltd)

Credit/Debit Card

☐ Visa   ☐ Mastercard   ☐ Amex   ☐ Maestro

Card number

| | | | | | | | | | | | | | | | | | Expiry date | | | | |

Security number | | | (last three digits on the strip at the back of the card)

Issue number | | | (if Maestro)

Signed _____

Date _____

Code: PAG 069

☐ Tick this box if you do not wish to receive any promotional material from Imagine Publishing Ltd ☐ Tick this box if you do not wish to receive promotional material from other companies. Terms & Conditions apply. We publish 13 issues a year, your subscription will start from the next available issue unless otherwise indicated. Direct Debit guarantee details available on request. This offer expires without notice.

I would like my subscription to start from issue: | | | | |

Return this order form to:
iCreate Subs Department, 800 Guillat Avenue, Kent Science Park, Sittingbourne, ME9 8GU or email it to **iCreate@servicehelpline.co.uk**
To manage your subscription account online visit **www.imaginesubs.co.uk**

EXCLUSIVE SUBSCRIBER BENEFITS

Start a Direct Debit from just £25.20 every six issues and save over £23 per year

- Save 30% on the cover price
- Free postage & packing in the UK
- Free CD every issue
- Delivered to your door

Subscribe and SAVE 30%

iCreate is the creative magazine for Mac users by Mac users. If Apple made a magazine, it would be **iCreate**

Each month **iCreate** delivers the finest Mac tutorials, features, reviews and news. By subscribing, you save money and get **iCreate** delivered pristine to your door

Call Now
0844 848 8401
or subscribe **online**

THREE EASY WAYS TO SUBSCRIBE

1. Telephone
Order by phone, just call:

0844 848 8401
Overseas: +44 (0)1795 592 865

2. Online
Order via credit or debit card, just visit:
www.imaginesubs.co.uk

3. Post or email
Please complete and post the form to:

iCreate Subs Department
800 Guillat Avenue,
Kent Science Park,
Sittingbourne, ME9 8GU

Alternatively, scan and email the form to:
iCreate@servicehelpline.co.uk

 iMovie '09

Get in gear
To tweak the start and end points of two adjacent clips click on the second shot's gear icon and select Precision Editor from the pop-up menu

Knowledge base

In or out?
It can take a while to get your head around the way the Precision Editor includes or excludes footage. The Precision Editor reduces the brightness of parts of a filmstrip when a section is excluded from the edited programme. Included footage remains at full brightness in the filmstrip. Hit the Spacebar to preview your edited footage in real time.

Preview tracks
The top bar previews the previous shots in the sequence. The bottom bar shows us the latest shot. Scrub along the grey bar to preview the edited cut

Change edit point
The blue line marks the spot where the edit occurs. Cut to an earlier or later point in a video clip by dragging it left or right

Added extras
If you want to see how your fine-tuned video clips relate to other elements in the project click here to make extras like music and titles become visible in the Precision Editor

Tutorial: Edit footage with iMovie's Precision Editor

Use iMovie's Precision Editor to fine-tune the start and end points of multiple video clips and make the action flow seamlessly from one shot to the next

Task: Edit with greater precision in iMovie
Difficulty: Intermediate
Time needed: 15 minutes

By repeatedly filming an action clip (like a cyclist flying off a ramp for example) you can make it look like you had multiple camera operators covering the event.

With careful editing you can make the footage look like a single 'live' event instead of multiple takes. iMovie '09's new Precision Editor enables you to tweak the start and end point of each clip with ease so that the action flows seamlessly between each shot. You can use this technique for a number of situations, from cutting between a wide shot and a persons point of view or a close up shot of an event occuring. In this tutorial we've used the example of a mountain biker jumping off a ramp and used shots from different angles to piece together one continuous clip. Check out 'Precision.mov' on the disc to see the end result of this tutorial and then discover the power of the Precision Editor by cutting the raw footage together.

Step-by-step | iMovie Tweak your in and out points with precision

1: Import assets
Go to File>Import>Movies. Browse to 'High Angle. mov' and 'Wide Angle.mov' on the cover CD. Create a new event and click Import.

2: Playback footage
Hit the Spacebar to play the footage in the Event browser. We start off on a high angle shot and then cut to a wide shot.

3: Add first clip
Drag the cursor from the start of the first clip to select 1:20 seconds in the yellow box. Drag the selection to the Project window.

4: Add a second shot
Click on the second clip in the Event browser to select it all. Place it after the first clip in the Project window. Play back the sequence.

5: Precision Editor
At the start of the second clip we wait too long for the bike to appear. Click on the clip's gear icon and choose Precision Editor.

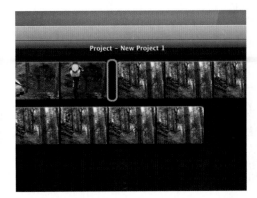

6: Edit point
The blue line indicates when you cut from the first clip to the second. You can change the edit points by sliding the clips left or right.

7: Trim the clips
Drag the top clip right so it cuts while the bike is nearer the camera. Drag the bottom clip left so the bike appears on the cut.

8: Preview the edit
Scrub the cursor along the grey bar between the two clips to preview the new in and out points. The action flows seamlessly between the two shots.

9: Trim final shot
Select the end of the high-angle clip from the Event browser and add it to the sequence. Trim the edit so we cut to the bike as it lands.

Tutorial: Experiment with themes in iMovie

Explore iMovie's wide selection of themes and add sophisticated transitions and graphics to your video projects. Discover how to change a project's themed graphics in an instant

Task: Add animated graphics to your project
Difficulty: Intermediate
Time needed: 20 minutes

A video without titles and transitions is like a cake without icing. Fortunately you can create a more professional looking production with some sophisticated animated graphics. iMovie groups graphics and animated captions together into themed collections. When you choose a specific theme from the Transitions or Titles browsers you're presented with a new selection of themed titles and transitions to play with. These themed graphics give your programme a coherent visual style. You can even change transitions and titles in your project in a single mouse click to find a theme that suits the content of your movie.

Step-by-step | iMovie Experiment with themed graphics to create a suitable style

1: Create new project
Go to File>New Project. Untick the Automatically Add box. As you're going to experiment with various themes choose None and click Create.

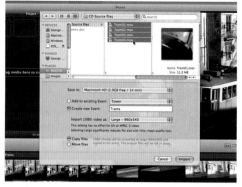

2: Import movies
Choose File>Import. Browse to the footage of trams on your CD and Shift-click to select them. Create a new event called Trams.

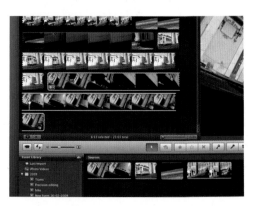

3: Edit project
Drag the cursor along the first clip in the Event browser to select it, then drag it into the project. Add the other three clips to create a sequence.

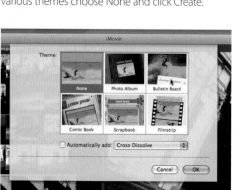

4: Access extra transitions
Go to the Transitions browser. To access extra transitions click Set Theme and choose Bulletin Board. Untick the Automatically Add box.

5: Add a transition
Drag Bulletin Board 2 between the second and third clip. Press the Spacebar to play the animated transition between the two clips.

6: Add another
Place Bulletin Board 4 between the last two clips. Both transitions share a similar style, which adds continuity to the body of your programme.

Add graphics and transitions in iMovie

Groovy graphics
iMovie's collection of animated themes automatically places your video clips into windows within an attractive graphic interface, enabling you to create sophisticated title sequences

Change duration
You can make an animated title run longer or shorter by dragging the start or end point of the title bar. To change the duration of a transition click its gear icon

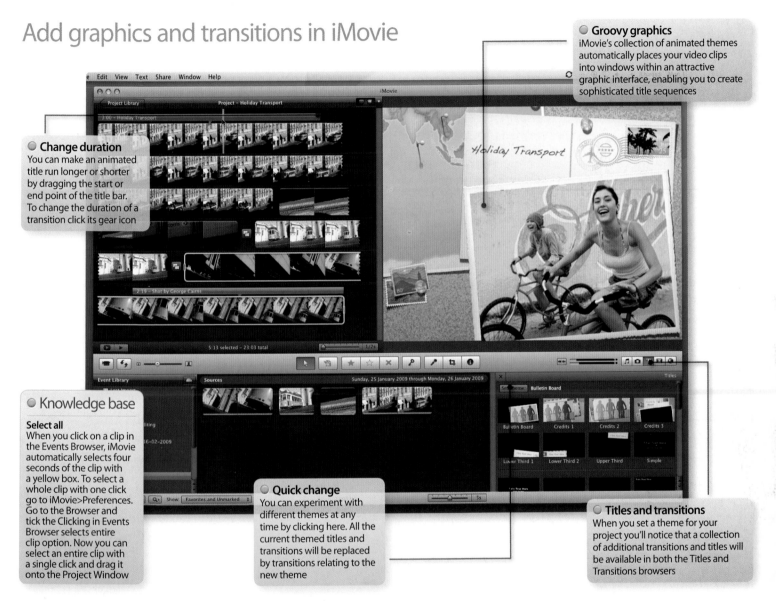

Knowledge base

Select all
When you click on a clip in the Events Browser, iMovie automatically selects four seconds of the clip with a yellow box. To select a whole clip with one click go to iMovie>Preferences. Go to the Browser and tick the Clicking in Events Browser selects entire clip option. Now you can select an entire clip with a single click and drag it onto the Project Window

Quick change
You can experiment with different themes at any time by clicking here. All the current themed titles and transitions will be replaced by transitions relating to the new theme

Titles and transitions
When you set a theme for your project you'll notice that a collection of additional transitions and titles will be available in both the Titles and Transitions browsers

7: Top and tail
Click the Titles browser. Complete your programme by adding animated titles and credits that use the Bulletin Board theme. Drag Bulletin Board to clip 1.

8: End credits
Drag Credits 1 onto the last clip. Double-click on the title bar above the clip in the Project window and type credits into the main viewer.

9: Change the theme
To see how your programme looks with different graphics choose a new theme. All the titles, credits and transitions will instantly update.

 iMovie '09

Tutorial: Edit widescreen footage in iMovie

Shoot and edit footage that will fill the whole screen without distorting, cropping or pillarboxing!

Task: Shoot and edit in widescreen in iMovie

Difficulty: Intermediate

Time needed: 15 minutes

Widescreen TVs have a shape (or a screen aspect ratio) of **16:9.** Old-school TVs have a 4:3 shape. If you show 4:3 footage on a widescreen TV it will be much narrower than the screen, with black bars running vertically on either side of the picture (known as pillarboxing).

Most widescreen TVs will let you stretch a narrow 4:3 image so that it reaches the sides of the screen, but this will distort your footage. You could zoom the 4:3 footage so that it fills the 16:9 screen, but this will crop the top and bottom of your shot. Fortunately, it's a doddle to shoot and edit for playback on widescreen TVs in iMovie '09.

Step-by-step | **iMovie '09** | **Go wide with widescreen editing of your footage in iMovie**

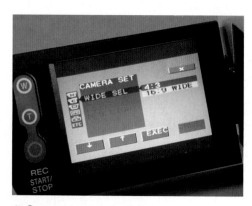

1: Set up your camera
To shoot widescreen footage go into your camera's menu and choose a 16:9 aspect ratio. This will capture a wide 16:9 image instead of a narrow 4:3.

2: Pillarboxing
If your camcorder has a 4:3 LCD monitor you may notice black bars sandwiching the 16:9 frame. This 'pillarboxing' won't be visible on a widescreen TV.

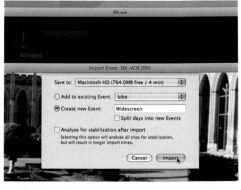

3: Import footage
Click on the camera icon to import your widescreen clips. They will play in a 16:9-sized Import window. Add them to a new event.

4: Pillarboxing
When you play back 16:9 footage in iMovie's Viewer you may notice black bars (pillarboxing) at the top and bottom of the frame.

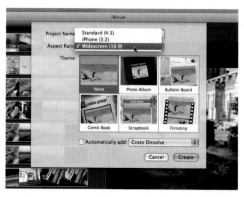

5: Choose an aspect ratio
To remove pillarboxing go to File>New Project. Name the project and choose an aspect ratio of Widescreen (16:9). Now click Create.

6: Add clip to project
Click on a shot in the Event browser to select it. Drag the selection into the Project window and play the clip. The pillarboxing will have disappeared.

Shoot and edit in widescreen with iMovie
Avoid pillarboxing and cropping by editing footage in widescreen

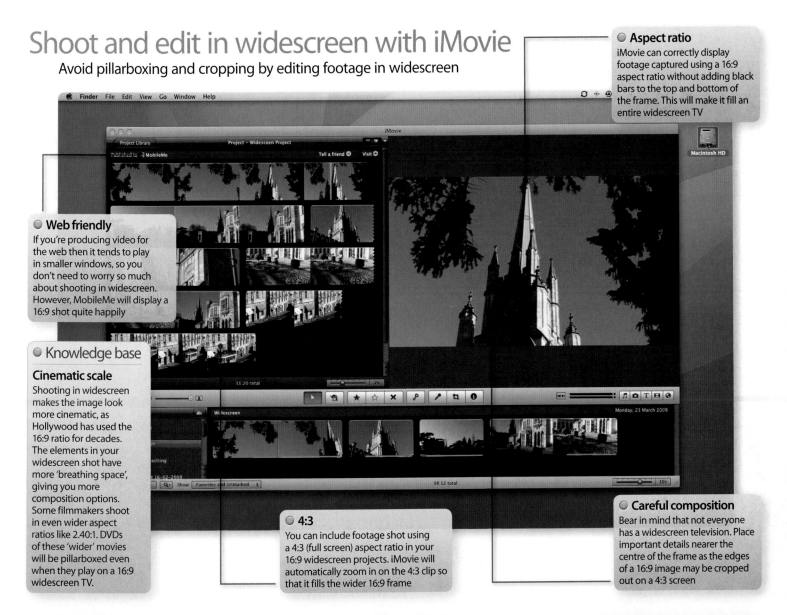

Aspect ratio
iMovie can correctly display footage captured using a 16:9 aspect ratio without adding black bars to the top and bottom of the frame. This will make it fill an entire widescreen TV

Web friendly
If you're producing video for the web then it tends to play in smaller windows, so you don't need to worry so much about shooting in widescreen. However, MobileMe will display a 16:9 shot quite happily

Knowledge base
Cinematic scale
Shooting in widescreen makes the image look more cinematic, as Hollywood has used the 16:9 ratio for decades. The elements in your widescreen shot have more 'breathing space', giving you more composition options. Some filmmakers shoot in even wider aspect ratios like 2.40:1. DVDs of these 'wider' movies will be pillarboxed even when they play on a 16:9 widescreen TV.

4:3
You can include footage shot using a 4:3 (full screen) aspect ratio in your 16:9 widescreen projects. iMovie will automatically zoom in on the 4:3 clip so that it fills the wider 16:9 frame

Careful composition
Bear in mind that not everyone has a widescreen television. Place important details nearer the centre of the frame as the edges of a 16:9 image may be cropped out on a 4:3 screen

7: Mix and match
Although you're editing in the 16:9 aspect ratio, you can add 4:3 shots to the project. A 4:3 shot will have pillarboxed edges when played in the browser.

8: Made to measure
When you drag a 4:3-sized shot into the Project window, iMovie automatically zooms and crops the shot to lose the black edges.

9: Export
To see your 16:9 movie on a widescreen TV go to File>Share and use iDVD to burn it to a shiny disc, or share it in a MobileMe gallery!

Tutorial: Fix shaky footage in iMovie

We all have shaky-handed moments when filming, so here's how to make sure your clips remain useable in iMovie

Task: Use the Video Stabilization tool in iMovie

Difficulty: Beginner

Time needed: 20 minutes

Picture the scenario: you've just come back from your holiday and are desperate to put together your latest iMovie production, but when it comes to importing your clips many of them are just too wobbly to use. Without the option to go back and shoot your footage again, these clips would normally be resigned to the trash. Fortunately, iMovie's new Stabilization feature provides an effective way to fix shaky footage.

By analysing your video, iMovie can cater for shakes such as those found when shooting inside a moving vehicle. You'll need to let iMovie analyse your clip once you add it to the project, so make sure you set some time aside for what can be a time-consuming process. But, given the task it will perform for you, it'll be worth it. Here we'll show you how to import and fix your shaky clips.

Step-by-step | iMovie Stabilise footage

1: Select the shakes
Select the footage from your Library by dragging the cursor across the clip from the start to finish, until the yellow bars are surrounding the area you wish to use. Hit Spacebar to play back your selection.

2: Add your clip
Now drag your selection to the point in your project you wish to add it. If you're looking to simply stabilise the footage but aren't adding it to a project, simply drag it to the Project window. Now press the 'i' button.

Of course, it's always best to cut out the shakes in the first place. Where possible, use a tripod for tracking shots and support the camera.

Fix shaky footage in iMovie
Use the Stabilization tool to keep your clips useable

○ Check it out
You can preview the effect of the stabilisation once the analysis has been applied by playing back the clip from the Project window

○ Thin red line
This red undulating line shows that analysis has been performed on your clip, so you can tell those that have been stabilised

○ Get info
Click this button to bring up a range of options that can be applied to your currently selected clip, including effects, colours and audio adjustments

○ Knowledge base

Less is best
It's often best to use smaller clips with the Video Stabilization feature in iMovie. Not only will it save time during analysis, especially for HD footage, but it will also make it easier for iMovie to detect and fix the problems. There are, of course, times when iMovie may not be able to completely fix the shake, so be prepared if you've got some extreme wobbles.

○ Smooth checkbox
This checkbox will turn the stabilisation off or on for your chosen clip and can be accessed by hitting the Info button on the toolbar

3: Start analysis
From the Inspector window that appears, select the Clip tab and then check the box next to 'Smooth clip motion'. iMovie will now begin to analyse your clip in order to stabilise it.

4: Successfully stable?
Once your clip has been analysed you will notice that a red line appears below the clip in the Project window and the Library. This denotes that stabilisation has been applied. Check your clip by hitting Play.

Master movies
in a weekend

	Friday	Saturday	Sunday
		10.00 - Import clips	10.00 - Design DVD/iWeb interface
		11.00 - Import photos	11.00 - Upload movie to YouTube
		12.00 - Edit movie	12.00 - Publish iWeb site/Burn DVD
	13.00 - Shoot movie	17.00 - Export to iDVD/iWeb	17.00 - Design inlays & labels for DVD

FRI SAT SUN
WEEKEND PROJECT

Plug in your camera and use your time off to create something really special: the ultimate home movie…

So you have a Mac, and you know it's the best platform for media organisation – but you don't know where to start. Fear not, over the next nine pages we're going to provide you with all the information you need to not only shoot and edit a movie, but to take it that step further and make it a memorable, tactile keepsake you can share with friends, or store for that special family reunion.

Apple's iMovie '08 makes the process of sorting your video clips and assembling them into a competent movie a breeze, but you shouldn't leave things there. The aim of this feature is to provide you with all the skills you need to make the ultimate movie that will wow your peers and provide as close to a professional production as is possible. Whether it's adding stylish transitions, music and titles to your movie, or exporting your project to an impressive DVD with its own custom-designed case, we'll show you the essential elements to turn your clips into a cinematic classic.

In the ever-changing digital world, more and more people are accessing content online – and we've not overlooked this aspect of movie production. If you want people to have immediate access to your production there are a number of ways to make them available online, be it on an iWeb site, .Mac Web Gallery or via the very popular YouTube. There are tips for all of the above over the next few pages.

Whether you've shot your footage and want to piece it together well or you're looking to pick up some tips on the best way to capture video before you edit, you'll find all the answers in this feature, which will set you on your way to creating something really special on your Mac.

We all have different cameras and camcorders, but fortunately most of the popular brands and models are compatible with iMovie. Even the new AVCHD format is supported among a set of video types, including DV, MPEG and HDV. Import is normally as simple as connecting your camcorder to your Mac and selecting the Import option in iMovie '08. While some camcorders record to tape, others record clips on a hard drive within the camera. You can also select the Import Movies option, which allows you to copy clips you have downloaded or received via email into your iMovie Event Library.

The Event Library was all-new in iMovie '08, and works in the same way as the iPhoto Event Library (by sorting your clips by date and event). You can easily jump between sets of clips and drag them to your project. When you import clips you are given options, including whether to add them to an existing Event or to create a new one. You can then set the size of the videos to help balance quality with space on your Mac's HD.

You can easily select clips in your Event Library and use click and drag techniques to fine-tune your selection. The Skimming feature means you can use the mouse to scroll across a clip, see each frame and hear the audio. Clips can be adjusted and cropped in iMovie '08, so you can make them look their best before you commit your project to disc or the web. Take a look at the many ways you can import your footage onto your Mac.

Get your movies onto your Mac

There are many formats and many devices you can import movies from. Here's the best route for your movie clips, and the options for your footage once you have imported and edited it on your Mac.

Standard digital camcorders that include HD and Mini-DV models will hook up to your Mac via USB or FireWire, and transfer footage into the iMovie Event Library via the Import screen

Clips on your Mac's HD, or those you have downloaded from another source, can be added to iMovie by using the Import Movies option from iMovie's File menu

Videos from your digital-stills camera are imported into iPhoto along with your photos, and are available in iMovie's Event Library under the iPhoto Videos

"You can make them look their best before you commit your project to disc or the web"

Camcorder movements

Pan
Use a basic horizontal movement so that large environments can be filmed without losing detail. Slow pans are excellent for establishing shots, allowing the entire scope to be captured.

Tilt
Vertical movement can be used in a number of different ways, mostly as an adjustment to find the correct level when shooting fast-moving objects. Shoot from a low or high angle.

Track
Using a combination of both the pan and tilt motions, tracking is an excellent way of following a subject. More of the head's movements need to be used than normally possible, so practise!

Once your movie is complete, the Share menu will allow you to export your project to iDVD to create an interface and burn it to disc. You can then create a unique case for the DVD

Amy's Birthday Party
April 2008
Starring

If you want to share your movie in a hurry, select Export Movie from the Share menu and choose the Tiny size to drop it in an email and fire it out to friends and family

⚠ Do's & Don'ts

Play it safe
To avoid potential corruption of files, always make sure your camera and camcorder are attached to mains power when importing footage. Most cameras, and some camcorders, come with a dock to help you keep them powered while you transfer your media onto your Mac.

You Tube
Broadcast Yourself

As an alternative or accompaniment to your DVD you can share your movie on an iWeb site, or via the popular website YouTube via the iMovie's Share menu

Non-digital media
If you want to edit your old VHS or Hi-8 footage in iMovie you can, with a simple converter device that connects to your Mac and old camcorder or video player. Elgato's EyeTV 250 Plus is a TV tuner and analogue converter, and works via your USB port. See **www.elgato.com** for more details. You can also buy specialist converters, like the Canopus ADVC range, at **www.canopus.com**.

Types of shot

Establishing shot

Setting the scene and the tone for the following action is the main objective of an establishing shot. This also acts as a good opening shot that brings a narrative style to your movie, setting it up for the fast-moving action to follow.

Wide shot

Including as much background as possible gives an overall feeling of the action. Plus, if something is moving fast within the frame then the speed is well-represented because of the distance covered in that time.

Ground-level shot

This is widely used in motor sport, as a low angle denotes a greater degree of speed to the action. If you film down low, especially down to ground level, the objects move past far quicker because of the smaller frame.

High angle

A high-angle view can add depth to the area in which the action is happening, because it provides an overview of what is happening as opposed to focusing on one subject. This adds good variety, as well as acting as a good cutaway.

Tracking shot

Focusing on one subject, you will set up the camcorder on a tripod and pan to follow a piece of action. Following one object can heighten the sense of speed, and also gives a detailed shot of one person instead of a group shot.

Overhead

This is a tricky shot to achieve, but is definitely one that is worth trying if possible. Position yourself and the camcorder higher than the level upon which the action is taking place, and you'll capture great fast-moving action effectively. Look for suitable areas to shoot from as you begin to set up your shot. Be careful though, it's better to be safe than sorry! ▶

The anatomy of an iMovie project
Transitions and titles. Visual and audio effects. Add more to your movie…

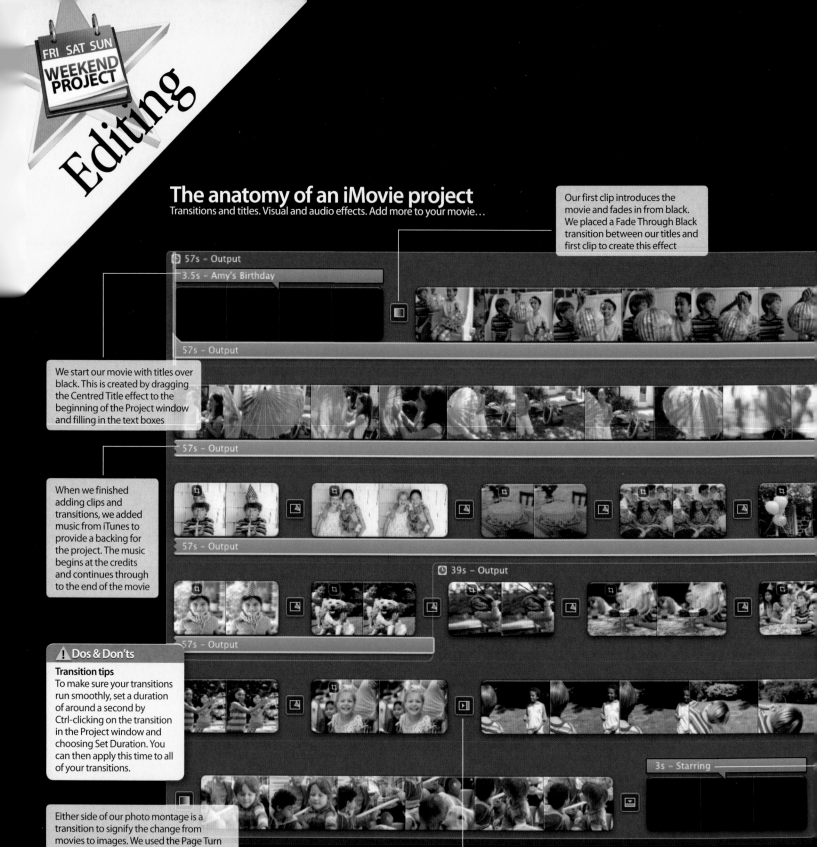

Our first clip introduces the movie and fades in from black. We placed a Fade Through Black transition between our titles and first clip to create this effect

We start our movie with titles over black. This is created by dragging the Centred Title effect to the beginning of the Project window and filling in the text boxes

When we finished adding clips and transitions, we added music from iTunes to provide a backing for the project. The music begins at the credits and continues through to the end of the movie

⚠ Dos & Don'ts

Transition tips
To make sure your transitions run smoothly, set a duration of around a second by Ctrl-clicking on the transition in the Project window and choosing Set Duration. You can then apply this time to all of your transitions.

Either side of our photo montage is a transition to signify the change from movies to images. We used the Page Turn transition between each photo, set to a duration of one second

Luckily there's no dark art to editing a movie in iMovie, as basic common sense will let you put together a great movie in next to no time at all. What you can add to your arsenal is a selection of techniques that will add that professional touch to your project, and enhance the viewers' overall experience of viewing your DVD.

Here we are offering you some useful notes on creating a better movie, and also breaking down the composition of a short iMovie project looking at

elements like transitions and clip narrative, this should stand you in good stead as you go on and edit all of your raw footage.

Of course, you're not limited to only video when putting together in iMovie – you also have a number of options for adding other media, like photos and music, to your movie. With the built-in Media browser in iMovie you can quickly access projects you've created in GarageBand, or music from your iTunes library. Then there's photos, which you can

quickly drop onto the Project window to create an attractive photo montage for your movie.

Picking the right clips and clip lengths is also an essential part of building an effective and exciting movie. Make sure your clips aren't too long or short, and make use of the transitions that are available to break up the action. Using the Skimming feature to scrub across clips is a very handy way to fine-tune your cuts and extract the very best bits from your raw footage.

Midway through our movie we've included a sequence of photographs to sum up events that weren't captured by our camcorder. These were added by selecting the Photo button and picking from our album, before dragging them into the Project window

We end our movie with rolling credits listing all of our actors by dragging the Rolling Credits titles behind the last clip of the movie. We also added a Fade Through Black transition to keep things smooth

⚠ Dos & Don'ts

Less is more
Don't get carried away with adding visual and audio effects, transitions and titles. Too many elements can distract from the most important part of your movie: the footage. Remember, every time you stop recording on your camcorder a clip ends with a new one created when you resume recording.

💡 Inspiration

Creative cutting
Always make sure that your clips flow together nicely, and don't jump erratically from one event to the next. If your footage changes location or shifts forward in time, use a transition to signify the change. When choosing clips in the iMovie Event Library, make sure you add them to the project in sequence to provide a narrative series of clips that follow on nicely from one another.

⚠ Dos & Don'ts

Ditch the defaults
When you're adding a title sequence to your movie, click the Show Fonts button to bring up the Font browser, and select a font that is not only clear but also fits the tone and style of your movie. Very thin fonts don't tend to show up well when you play your movie back on TV, so make sure you choose a heavy font, or the bold variation of a certain font. Aim for a font size above 16pt for best results.

A personal touch
Some of your footage may not contain people talking. To help fill the viewer in on the action onscreen, you can easily record a voiceover once your footage is in iMovie. By clicking the Voiceover button (microphone symbol) you can record audio into your project through your Mac's built-in microphone, or an external device such as an iSight camera or a microphone attached via USB or the Line In port.

Perfect font

Sante Fe
Variations: Plain only
Sante Fe is a stylish font that will need to be displayed quite large to make it clear, but works brilliantly with themes and on plain backgrounds. Experiment with different colours to suit your footage and try a drop shadow for more impact.

Snell Roundhand
Variations: Regular, Bold, Black
To add a classy feel to wedding videos and special events, Snell Roundhand is an exceptional script font that adds a lavish touch to your titles and credits. Best in white over black backgrounds.

Blackoak Std
Variations: Regular
For maximum impact from your titles, go with this fun and striking font at a large point size to hammer home your message.

Party LET
Variations: Plain only
The Party font is a useful addition to your iMovie project, as it works well with iDVD and iWeb.

▶

Amy's Birthday

Amy's Birthday

A stylish case for your stylish movie

Once your project is complete, the obvious route is to send the project straight to iDVD to present it effectively. There's another stage to the presentation of your movie however, and that's the packaging of your disc. What's the point in going to all the effort of building an amazing movie and stylish DVD interface, if you're going to simply write the title of the movie on the disc with a marker pen? There's so much more to be done with a DVD disc, and here we'll point out some of the best options to complete your project. There are a number of applications available that will help you put together a competent CD or DVD case and, with a decent printer, you can show off as much style with the physical product as you have with the media on it. You can also add labels to your discs to add further flair to your project and, if you're feeling really advanced, why not try burning an image or title onto the disc itself with the optical drives we suggest below..?

> "What's the point if you're going to simply write the title of the movie on the disc with a marker pen?"

Inlay software

Disc Cover
Price: $34.95
URL: www.belightsoft.com
BeLight's Disc Cover is an attractive app to help you create stunning artwork for your DVDs and CDs. With over 90 templates and thousands of images, it also offers support for LightScribe and Labelflash technology to burn art onto the surface of CDs and DVDs.

DiscLabel
Price: $35.95
URL: www.smileonmymac.com
DiscLabel is a handy tool for creating CD and DVD inlays and cases. Allowing for imports from iTunes, iPhoto and iDVD, there are a number of templates to choose from – with direct-on-CD printing options. DiscLabel also features .Mac integration.

Magic Mouse Discus
Price: $39.95
URL: www.magicmouse.com
Magic Mouse Discus provides support for many formats of CD and DVD cases, including mini-CD, and is updated regularly to include compatibility for 'now' cases and formats. Graphics can be imported into the templates, of which there are 800MB available.

sunCase
Price: $8
URL: www.sunprotectingfactory.com
The cheapest option; by dragging your artwork into sunCase you can quickly create CD and DVD cases, and print them to standard A4 paper with your printer at home. Brand new international templates are now included to widen compatibility with alternative case formats.

With most homes connected to the internet these days it's important to consider the web for sharing your video projects. Not only is it cheaper and less time-consuming than burning a physical disc, but you can put your creations in front of as many people as you wish in one go. With Apple's iWeb and .Mac Web Gallery you don't compromise on style either, with beautiful themes and templates available. Another benefit of the online delivery method is that you can receive instant feedback that you wouldn't get unless sitting in someone's living room watching a DVD with them. iWeb sites allow for comments and emails, and .Mac Web Galleries offer visitors the chance to download your movie, as well as upload pictures and videos to your gallery to complement the existing media collection. If you're not looking to use .Mac, or you want an even faster way of sharing your movies, head over to YouTube and sign up to upload projects directly from iMovie as soon as you finish editing. These videos can then be embedded on any website, and even on your own blog or movie page in iWeb.

Keep it themed

There are a number of ways to keep a theme running. The first step is to add your film to iMovie '06, and use one of the preset themes as your opening and final credit sequences. You can then export your movie to iDVD, where you can pick a similar theme for the interface. To complete the branding of your project, either take full-screen screen grabs of your interfaces (using Shift+Cmd+4 to select an area of the screen), or find your DVD project in the Documents folder, Ctrl-click on it and select Show Package Contents. Within this folder you will find images of your menu, which you can use.

Amy's Birthday Party
April 2008

Starring

Amy   Jo   Sam   Amber

Inspiration

Advanced CD labels
LightScribe and Labelflash are two technologies that allow printing onto a physical disc. You will need a compatible optical drive like those available from Lacie (**www.lacie.com**) and BenQ (**www.benq.com**), most of which will cost less than a hundred pounds. Once you have burnt your disc with one of these drives you can flip it over and burn a custom image, text or combination onto the surface of the disc. A slightly lower-tech alternative is to use an Inkjet Printable Disc, which can be placed on a special printer tray and printed onto. For more information, see **www.lightscribe.com.**

Inspiration

Print your own inlays
Whether you're sharing your movie on a DVD or CD, you can find printer paper that will allow you to print out a foldable inlay case from your home printer. Available in a variety of quantities, you can pick up inlay printer inserts for as little as a few pence each. An alternative route is to add your own artwork to your iTunes library and print an inlay with iTunes' own print options. Head to the Print screen from the File menu to experiment with CD inlays in iTunes.

Add some colour
If you want to improve the title sequence of your movies, the credits, your DVD interface backing or your DVD case, try searching some Stock Photo sites for any photos that will suit your project. You can buy high-resolution shots from as little as one dollar from a number of online galleries. Check out **www.istockphoto.com**, **www.crestock.com** and **www.fotolia.com** for some excellent pictures to complete your project.

Themes: iMovie & iDVD

Travel: iDVD & iMovie HD, iWeb
Best for: As the name implies, this theme is best for documenting vacations and trips, and is available in iMovie HD and iDVD, and iWeb.

Road Trip: iDVD, iMovie HD, iWeb
Best for: Road Trip is a fun theme that will work for a number of projects, from travel journals to video postcards. It uses a scrapbook style to display your images and video.

Pass Through: iDVD, iMovie HD
Best for: If you have epic, panoramic shots or photos in your project, the Pass Through theme is a top choice for large images, with a smooth scrolling title across the screen.

Reflection White/Black: iDVD, iMovie HD, iWeb
Best for: For a clean interface theme that shows off your photos and movies at their best, try out the black or white reflections. Available in iDVD and iMovie, there is also a black-and-white theme in iWeb, which will complement your movies when added to a site.

Take your project to the next level…

So you thought your DVD inlay was the final stage? Not quite. There are some added extras you can apply to your project to make it that bit more special. As is true of most iLife applications, iMovie, iDVD and iWeb work beautifully together, and there are a number of ways to enhance your project by playing to the strengths of each app. Whether you want to add photos used in your disc to the ROM portion of a DVD, create a companion iPhoto book to give as a gift alongside your movie, or design a custom iWeb page for viewers to enjoy your creativity, there are many ways to take your project to the next level.

> "There are some added extras you can apply to your project to make it that bit more special"

Photo books
To accompany your movie on DVD, why not put together an iPhoto book featuring stills from your movie? The small paperback-style iPhoto book would be a perfect choice. Simply select all the images used in your movie in iPhoto, and select Book to begin creating your bonus gift.

Photos on DVD
If you're sharing your movie on a DVD using iDVD, you can use the free space on the disc to include extras that can be accessed on a Mac or PC. When building your interface in iDVD, head to the Advanced menu and select Edit DVD-ROM contents. Now you can include pictures you used.

iWeb video page
You can share your finished movie directly from iMovie to a .Mac Web Gallery, where others can view it online and even download it or add comments. You can also link to a .Mac Web Gallery from your iWeb site or, if you prefer, add your exported movie to an iWeb video page.

YouTube
YouTube is one of the most popular sites on the web, and hosts thousands of user-submitted videos. If you want to share your movie with the world, or provide an easy way for friends and family to see your creations, select YouTube from the Share menu in iMovie.

PDF booklet
You can quickly create a PDF booklet to accompany your movie. This is simple and can be achieved by exporting an iWeb page as a PDF document, or by using Pages in Apple's iWork. Both options allow you to include photos and, in some cases, video and music, from your project.

Soundtrack CD
Why stop at movies when you can also share some great music? If you've used a selection of songs in your movie you can burn an audio CD complete with inlay straight from iTunes. Make a playlist, label it up and select Burn Playlist to Disc from the File menu.

iCandy
MacBook battery

MacBook battery

No longer do MacBook users need to turn their laptop over to see how much juice they have left

Tutorial: Share your iMovie videos on .Mac

When you've just finished your iMovie masterpiece, get it out into the world in a matter of minutes using your .Mac account

Task: Use .Mac to publish your movies
Difficulty: Beginner
Time needed: 30 minutes

It's all well and good having a library of films that you've made sitting on your hard drive gathering virtual dust and calling yourself a budding director, but what's the use if they're not out there being seen and getting praised? Okay, so there's no guarantee that they're going to get praised, but whether others think your work is good or bad, that's what it's all about – showing the world you have a talent and a creative nature. This is why Macs exist, it's why iMovie exists and it's why .Mac exists. Put the three together and you've got the most simplistic, logical and cool way to get your flicks up online and mingling in cyberspace. With .Mac you can showcase your stuff easily and invite people to pass judgement on your work.

If you're nervous about the reaction you'll get from publishing your efforts, just send the link to your mum first – she's bound give you a glowing report!

Step-by-step | iMovie Publish your movies with .Mac

1: Share and share alike

● Your first step once you've finished editing your movie is to go to the top menu, select Share and then .Mac Web Gallery. iMovie will then begin communicating with the web to get things going.

2: Edit and size it up

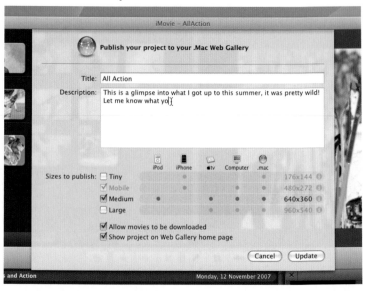

● You can now write a little blurb about the movie you're going to publish and pick the size you want it to be. This will determine the size of the downloaded movie, should you allow viewers to save it.

Widen your audience with .Mac

Gallery options
When you view your .Mac page, you can tell a friend or download the video. You can also play the movie in all its glory

Knowledge base

Catalogue
Now that .Mac has 10GB of storage, you can create an online catalogue of your best work. This is great for making a portfolio that you can get others to view. Use the Tell A Friend option to inform your contacts that you're a filmmaker, and then just wait for the Academy Awards!

Plain and simple
If you want to hide all the buttons and controls, you can just click the Hide Options button

Remember
Bookmark the site address, so you can get straight to the action whenever you want to bask in the glory of having published a superb cinematic project

More options
You can navigate through the video using the Scroll bar; you can also alter volume and screen size

3: **Double-check and click**

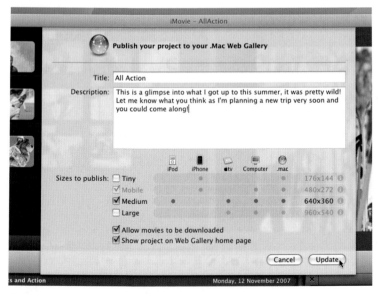

○ The next step is to double-check you've set everything the way you want it. When you're sure it's okay, just click the Update button located at the bottom of the window.

4: **Wait for it**

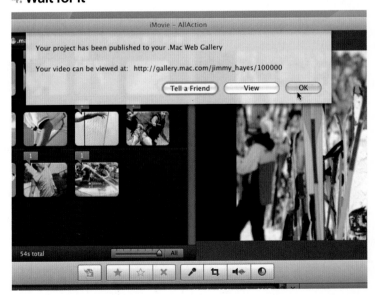

○ It may take a few minutes to upload, so be patient. Once it's complete you can either invite people to view it, see it in all its glory or continue using iMovie for more uploads.

Keep in trim
Fine-tune the start or end point of a shot by clicking on the Trim icon. You can then drag the orange handle to adjust the last few frames of a clip

Bigger picture
To get a better look at your edited clips, go to Window>Viewer>Large (or press [F7]). This displays a larger version of your edited footage

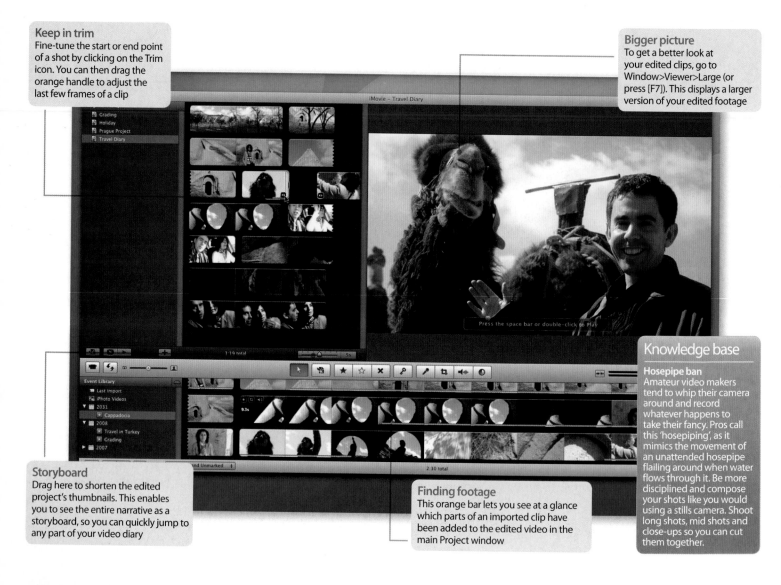

Knowledge base

Hosepipe ban
Amateur video makers tend to whip their camera around and record whatever happens to take their fancy. Pros call this 'hosepiping', as it mimics the movement of an unattended hosepipe flailing around when water flows through it. Be more disciplined and compose your shots like you would using a stills camera. Shoot long shots, mid shots and close-ups so you can cut them together.

Storyboard
Drag here to shorten the edited project's thumbnails. This enables you to see the entire narrative as a storyboard, so you can quickly jump to any part of your video diary

Finding footage
This orange bar lets you see at a glance which parts of an imported clip have been added to the edited video in the main Project window

Tutorial: Create your own travel diary in iMovie

Record holiday adventures in your own video diary, complete with entertaining on-screen narrative that enables viewers to share in your exciting experiences

Task: Create your own video diary in iMovie '08
Difficulty: Intermediate
Time needed: 15 minutes

When filming your holiday experiences, treat your friends and family as the presenters and stars of the programme. Get them to describe where they are going (or what they've seen). A travel diary format lets you link holiday location shots together as an entertaining narrative, rather than a random succession of disjointed shots.

To give you a clearer idea of what you could do with your footage from afar, we've popped a few travel diary-style shots on the CD for you to import and cut together in iMovie '08 (though you could use '06 if you prefer). In our walkthrough we'll talk you through different ways to shoot and edit a travel diary-style programme. Check out 'Travel Diary.m4v' to see our edited version. The tips from our tutorial will allow you to create a more meaningful document of your time away and ensure that those who were left behind feel more involved in your adventures.

Step-by-step | iMovie '08 Shoot and edit a travel diary

1: Set the scene
Film your friend from a distance as they explore ('Diary01.mov'). Pan the camera to reveal more scenery. Cut to a close-up ('Diary02.mov').

2: Dear diary
Get your friend to describe the location to camera ('Diary03.mov'). This docu-style approach lets the viewer learn more about your holiday adventures.

3: Location narration
Describe your experiences while you film cutaway shots of holiday locations ('Diary04.mov'). The on-camera microphone will pick up your every word.

4: Plan ahead
By running ahead, you can film your friend from inside a tourist attraction as they approach it. This adds visual variety to the video ('Diary05.mov').

5: Continuity
Get friends to repeat an action from another camera angle. You can edit shots to make the travel diary unfold like a drama ('Dairy06.mov').

6: Perfect panning
Don't feature people in every shot, or it'll make it difficult to cut scenes together. Pan from a point of interest to re-introduce your friends ('Diary07.mov').

7: Link your shots
A car provides both the time and the space to film 'to camera' diary links, in which you can introduce the next location ('Diary08.mov').

8: Portability
A small palmcorder can go anywhere you can, so you can document experiences like crawling through underground tunnels ('Diary09.mov')!

9: Double act
Use your camcorder's flip-out viewfinder so that you can frame the shot to include yourself. You can then contribute to the diary with friends ('Diary10.mov').

Tutorial: Create a video showreel in iMovie

Show off your video-making skills by collecting the best examples of your work in an iMovie project and linking them together with slick graphics and transitions

Task: Edit your footage into a slick showreel
Difficulty: Intermediate
Time needed: 15 minutes

Thanks to sites like YouTube, video makers can share their work with the world at large. The challenge is to keep people watching your footage when there are thousands of other clips vying for attention. Fortunately, many of these home-grown programmes have terrible production values, so you can use iMovie's high-quality graphics and transitions to give your showreel a professional appearance and make it stand out from the crowd. We've popped a few clips on your disc so you can work through the walkthrough. Check out our finished 'Showreel.m4v' to get a taste of the finished product.

Step-by-step | iMovie Use transitions and graphics

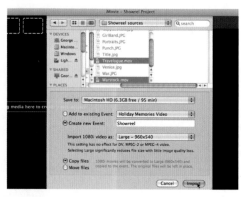

1: Create a new project
Click on the New Project icon and label it Showreel. Go to File>Import Movies. Click Create A New Event and label it Showreel too.

2: Import assets
Import the video clips from the Showreel sources folder into your event. Drag the photo called 'Title.jpg' straight into the project window.

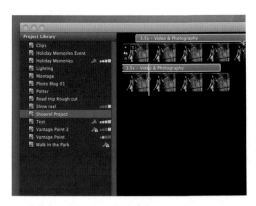

3: Add an intro graphic
Click on the Titles browser icon. Drag the Torn Edge Black graphic onto the still image. Type a caption into the text fields. Click Done.

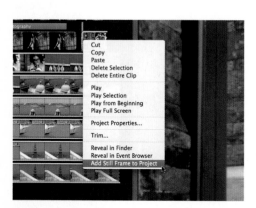

4: Add first clip
Drag the Travelogue clip into the project window. Place the cursor at the first frame. Right-click and choose Add Still Frame To Project.

5: Freeze!
Select the still frame and drag it between the Title and the first video clip. Click the Clock icon and type in a duration of 3.0 seconds.

6: Add new caption
Add the Torn Edge Tan graphic to the frozen frame. Type in a caption to introduce the clip. The caption will fade in and out over the still frame.

Create a showreel in iMovie

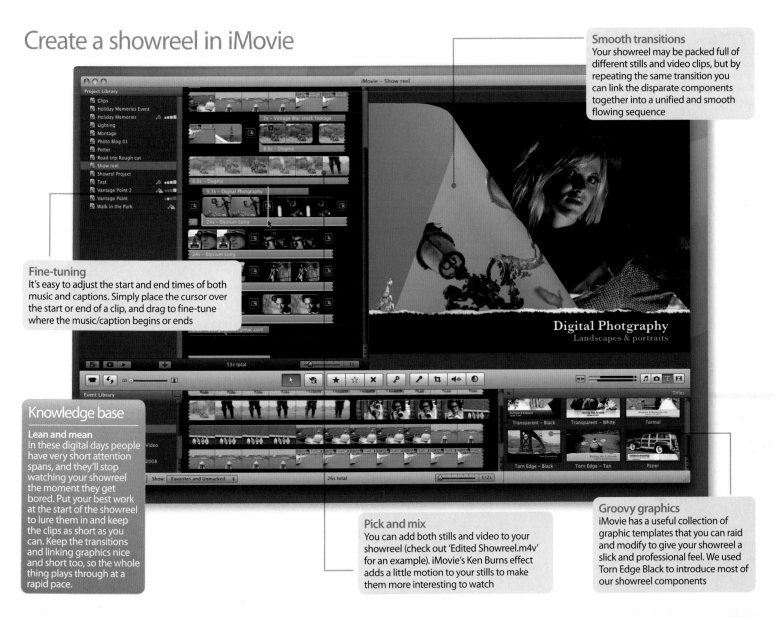

Smooth transitions
Your showreel may be packed full of different stills and video clips, but by repeating the same transition you can link the disparate components together into a unified and smooth flowing sequence

Fine-tuning
It's easy to adjust the start and end times of both music and captions. Simply place the cursor over the start or end of a clip, and drag to fine-tune where the music/caption begins or ends

Digital Photgraphy
Landscapes & portraits

Knowledge base

Lean and mean
In these digital days people have very short attention spans, and they'll stop watching your showreel the moment they get bored. Put your best work at the start of the showreel to lure them in and keep the clips as short as you can. Keep the transitions and linking graphics nice and short too, so the whole thing plays through at a rapid pace.

Pick and mix
You can add both stills and video to your showreel (check out 'Edited Showreel.m4v' for an example). iMovie's Ken Burns effect adds a little motion to your stills to make them more interesting to watch

Groovy graphics
iMovie has a useful collection of graphic templates that you can raid and modify to give your showreel a slick and professional feel. We used Torn Edge Black to introduce most of our showreel components

7: Terrific transitions
Click on the Transitions icon and drag the Page Curl transition between the title and the freeze frame. Right-click and set a duration of 1.48 seconds.

8: Title music
From Jingles, drag Time Lapse onto the first clip. Drag the end of the green bar to the right so the music finishes just after the freeze frame.

9: And repeat…
Add more graphics, freeze frames and page curl transitions to link the other video clips and stills together in a slick showreel sequence.

 iMovie '08

Tutorial: Create an iMovie musical montage

Enhance dramas, holiday travelogues or documentaries with a musical montage sequence that uses a variety of camera and editing techniques

Task: Use music and transitions to create a montage sequence

Difficulty: Beginner

Time needed: 15 minutes

Whatever type of video you produce, from dramas to documentaries, you can enhance it by adding a montage sequence. A montage is a serious of cuts and transitions that adds variety and texture to your programme's narrative, allowing the viewer to sit back and enjoy the mix of sound and vision.

A montage is a great way of condensing hours of footage into a short, easy-to-digest sequence. 'Montage.m4v' on our disc showcases the stunning scenery in Cappadocia, Turkey. We've popped the source files on the CD so you can develop your editing skills and recreate this movie montage from scratch.

<hr>

Step-by-step | **iMovie Create a musical montage sequence**

1: Import footage
Launch iMovie '08 and click on the New Project icon (Cmd+N). Name the project 'Montage'. Choose an Aspect Ratio of Widescreen (16:9) and click Create.

2: Import clips
Go to File>Import Movies and select the clips in your disc's Montage sources folder. Tick the Add To Existing Event option and choose Montage. Import.

3: Make a selection
In the Event library, click and drag to select the first five seconds of the girl entering the tunnel. Drag this section of filmstrip to the Project window.

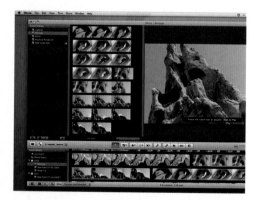

4: Creative camerawork
Add 'ZoomPan.mov' to the project. The shot's combination of zooms, pans and tilts combines variety and movement and spices up the sequence.

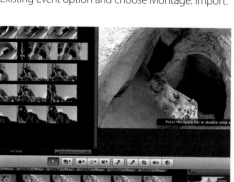

5: Add a transition
In the Transition browser, drag the Circle Open transition between the two clips in the Project window to add a 0.4 sec wipe between the shots.

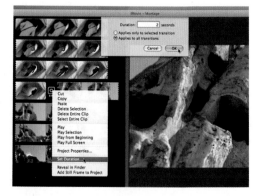

6: Transition duration
To give the transition a slower pace, Alt-click on its icon in the Project window and choose Set Duration. Type in 2 seconds and click OK.

Get musical with iMovie

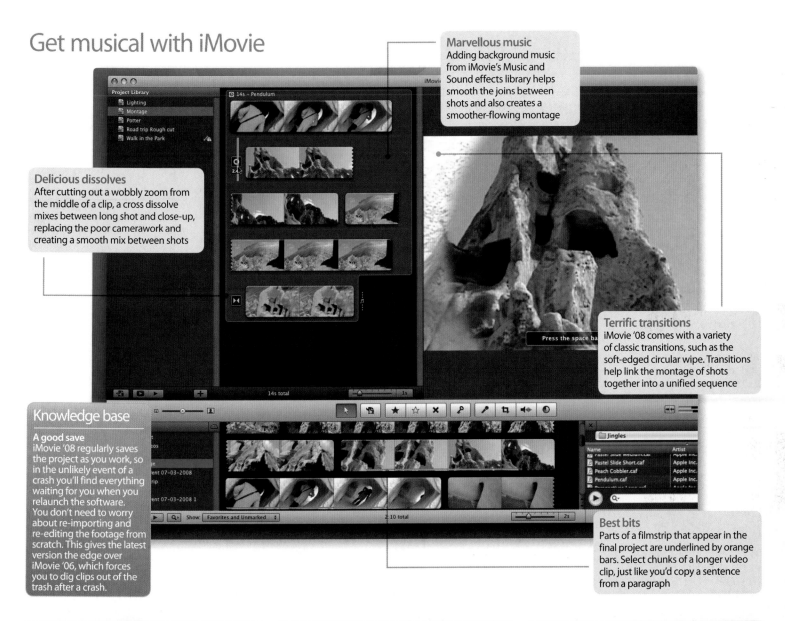

Marvellous music
Adding background music from iMovie's Music and Sound effects library helps smooth the joins between shots and also creates a smoother-flowing montage

Delicious dissolves
After cutting out a wobbly zoom from the middle of a clip, a cross dissolve mixes between long shot and close-up, replacing the poor camerawork and creating a smooth mix between shots

Terrific transitions
iMovie '08 comes with a variety of classic transitions, such as the soft-edged circular wipe. Transitions help link the montage of shots together into a unified sequence

Knowledge base

A good save
iMovie '08 regularly saves the project as you work, so in the unlikely event of a crash you'll find everything waiting for you when you relaunch the software. You don't need to worry about re-importing and re-editing the footage from scratch. This gives the latest version the edge over iMovie '06, which forces you to dig clips out of the trash after a crash.

Best bits
Parts of a filmstrip that appear in the final project are underlined by orange bars. Select chunks of a longer video clip, just like you'd copy a sentence from a paragraph

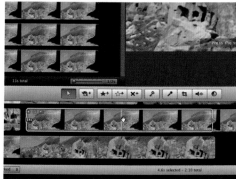

7: Two shots from one
'Landscape.mov' clip is spoiled by a dodgy zoom. Select the first four seconds of the filmstrip and add the wide shot of the landscape to the project.

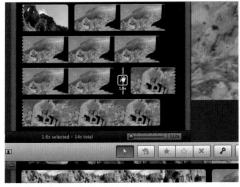

8: Long shot to close-up
Select the static close-up at the end of the Landscape filmstrip. Add this to the project. Use a cross dissolve to mix from wide to close-up.

9: Background music
To link the shots into a single montage sequence, click on the Music browser and drag a track onto the project background. It'll fade automatically.

 iMovie '06

Tutorial: Create animated title sequences

Produce a personalised and professional-looking title sequence by harnessing the power of iMovie's Themes pane. We show you how to mix stills, video clips and text quickly and effectively

Task: Use iMovie's Themes to create a title sequence
Difficulty: Intermediate
Time needed: 15 minutes

One way to make your video productions look more professional is to add a slick animated title sequence to the start of your programme. You could spend time (and money) mastering Apple's Motion 3 software to create an animated mix title sequence, which enables you to have layers of video, stills and graphics flying around the screen. A cheaper and faster alternative, however, is to harness the power of iMovie's Themes. Themes are animated templates that let you turn video and stills into all-singing, all-dancing multi-layered graphical title sequences with the minimum of time and effort.

Step-by-step | iMovie Create a multi-layered animated title sequence in minutes

1: Import source files
File>Import the Venice-related stills and video clips from your disc. You'll use these to make a title sequence for a hypothetical holiday video.

2: Choose a Theme
Click on the Themes button and choose Travel from the drop-down menu. Click on Open in the Theme Elements pane to see an animated preview.

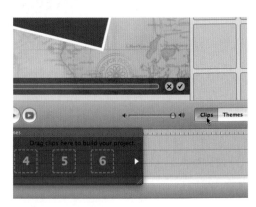

3: Drag and drop
A floating Drop Zone box will also appear. The numbered zones relate to boxes and layers in the Theme's animated video sequence. Click on Clips.

4: Add stills
Drag the Gondola to zone one and Boating to zone three. This ensures that the portrait and landscape-oriented stills fit into a suitably shaped field.

5: Add video
Drag St Marks to zone two. To preview the sequence, click on Themes and then click on the Open Theme. You'll see the video clip playing.

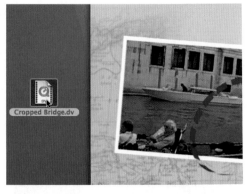

6: Trim a clip
To add an edited video clip to the theme, you'll need to export and then import the clip. Only then will Themes will recognise changes in duration.

Bring sequences to life

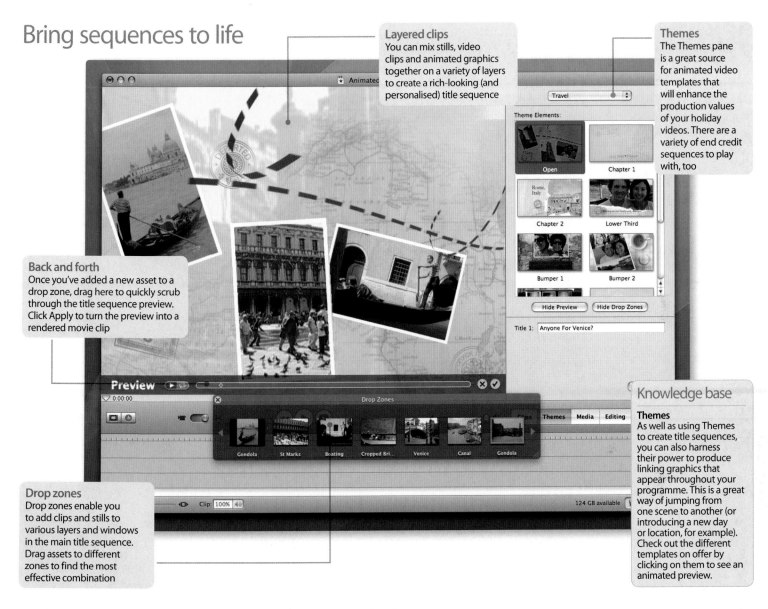

Layered clips
You can mix stills, video clips and animated graphics together on a variety of layers to create a rich-looking (and personalised) title sequence

Themes
The Themes pane is a great source for animated video templates that will enhance the production values of your holiday videos. There are a variety of end credit sequences to play with, too

Back and forth
Once you've added a new asset to a drop zone, drag here to quickly scrub through the title sequence preview. Click Apply to turn the preview into a rendered movie clip

Drop zones
Drop zones enable you to add clips and stills to various layers and windows in the main title sequence. Drag assets to different zones to find the most effective combination

Knowledge base

Themes
As well as using Themes to create title sequences, you can also harness their power to produce linking graphics that appear throughout your programme. This is a great way of jumping from one scene to another (or introducing a new day or location, for example). Check out the different templates on offer by clicking on them to see an animated preview.

7: Background video
Drag Venice into zone five. This pops the video clip onto a sepia-coloured background behind the floating photos in the title sequence.

8: Check duration
Add Canal to zone six and Gondola2 to seven. Zone seven needs to contain the longest clip, as it isn't visible until the end of the title sequence.

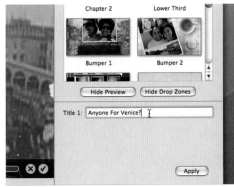

9: Add text
At the bottom of the Themes pane you'll find a Text field. Type in the name of your programme here to add it to the title sequence. Click Apply.

Tutorial: Cut footage creatively in iMovie

Jump creatively from one shot to another using clever cuts instead of traditional transitions. We show you how to create the effect of wipes and fades entirely through cuts!

Task: Create the effects of wipes and fades entirely through cuts

Difficulty: Intermediate

Time needed: 20 minutes

 In these digital days of non-linear editing, we take transitions for granted. iMovie makes it a drag-and-drop doddle to pop a transition between two shots, which can lead to mundane-looking movies. In pre-digital days it was a time consuming and expensive exercise to add transitions to movies. This challenged old-school editors to find ways to jump from one shot to another in more creative ways, using nothing but cuts. By careful composition and slick editing you can use the movement of on-screen subjects, and even camera movement, to mimic transitions like wipes and fades…

Step-by-step | iMovie Fake wipes and fades using nothing but cuts

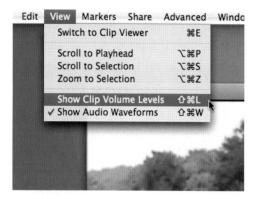

1: Wipe cut
Start by faking a wipe to take you from one shot to another. Create a new iMovie project and import 'Wipe Cut.dv' and 'Wipe 02.dv'.

2: Add clip
Drag Wipe Cut to the Timeline viewer. Turn Show Clip Volume Levels off in the View menu so you can trim the clip.

3: Trim the clip
Now drag the clip to the left to trim the shot by a few frames. It should end as the running soldier fills the frame.

4: Create the transition
Add Wipe 02 to the timeline. The running soldier acts as a wipe, creating a smooth transition from one shot to another (see 'EditedWipe.dv').

5: Whip pan
Create a new project and import 'Army 01.dv', 'Whip Pan.dv' and 'Army 02.dv'. Drag the clips to the timeline in that order.

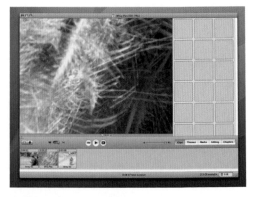

6: Test the transition
The Whip pan's fast pan to the right matches the panning in the adjacent shots. This movement links the shots together as a transition.

Use cuts to create wipes and fades

Alternative transitions
Many of iMovie '06's transitions can make your work look like every other iMovie users, especially 'showy' transitions like Ripple. Luckily you can create unique transitions from simple cuts

Whip pan
On location zoom your camera in tight and record some blurry whip pans of objects (like trees or buildings). You can use these abstract shots as cut-based transitions from one shot to another

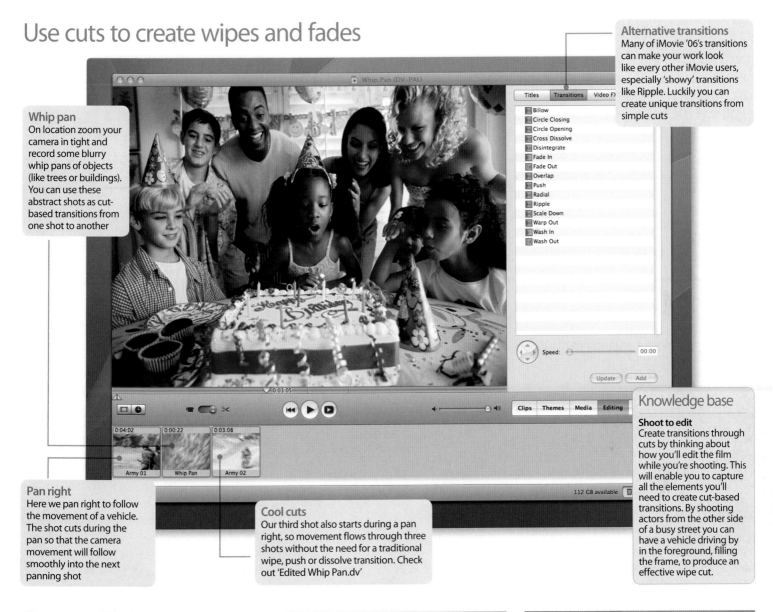

Pan right
Here we pan right to follow the movement of a vehicle. The shot cuts during the pan so that the camera movement will follow smoothly into the next panning shot

Cool cuts
Our third shot also starts during a pan right, so movement flows through three shots without the need for a traditional wipe, push or dissolve transition. Check out 'Edited Whip Pan.dv'

Knowledge base

Shoot to edit
Create transitions through cuts by thinking about how you'll edit the film while you're shooting. This will enable you to capture all the elements you'll need to create cut-based transitions. By shooting actors from the other side of a busy street you can have a vehicle driving by in the foreground, filling the frame, to produce an effective wipe cut.

7: Fake a fade
A common transition in any video is a fade to black. Use an actor as an alternative way to create this. Import 'Cut To Black.dv'.

8: Fade to black
Get the actor to walk straight up to the camera lens (without knocking it over!). This makes the image fade to black naturally.

9: Fade up
To introduce a shot (and mimic a fade-up transition), get the actor to walk away from the lens to reveal the scene.

Tutorial: Extreme shooting with iMovie '08

Combine creative camera moves, angles and shutter speed settings with iMovie's editing techniques to produce a wider range of exciting video sequences

Task: Shoot and edit extreme footage
Difficulty: Expert
Time needed: 10 minutes

In this tutorial we'll train you to 'shoot to kill' by demonstrating ways you can capture more exciting shots with your camcorder (or even your phone!). We'll look at ways to compose your shot to capture more dramatic camera angles, and tinker with shutter speeds so you don't miss a single frame of high-speed action. Learn how to whip-up some exciting transitions using camera moves. We'll also look at how to use iMovie's Crop tool to enhance your footage by creating jarring jump cuts from mid-shot to close-up, and even add dramatic camera zooms and pans to stills. We've referenced the files on the disc during this tutorial.

Step-by-step | iMovie Shoot and edit extreme footage

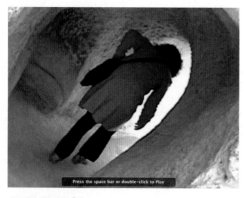

1: Go Dutch!
Tilt the camera to knock the viewer's expectations off balance and make them pay attention. This is called shooting at a Dutch angle (Dutch.mov).

2: Hit the deck!
Most people shoot from head height. By shooting from a lower angle, you can make the subject look more dominant (Low-angle.mov).

3: Down under
Let your camcorder shoot where you can't, like under the wheels of a passing car! This creates an extreme shot without putting you at risk (Car.mov).

4: Extreme shutter speed
When shooting fast-moving action, pop your camera on Sports mode to use a faster shutter speed. This captures blur-free details (Shutter.mov).

5: Jump cuts
Jump to a close-up even if you didn't shoot one! Split a clip and click the Crop tool icon. Crop to a tighter composition and click Done (JumpCut.mov).

6: Whip pan transition
On location, shoot some rapid panning shots. This will create abstract blurs that you can use to create an extreme whip pan from one subject to another.

Extreme footage in iMovie

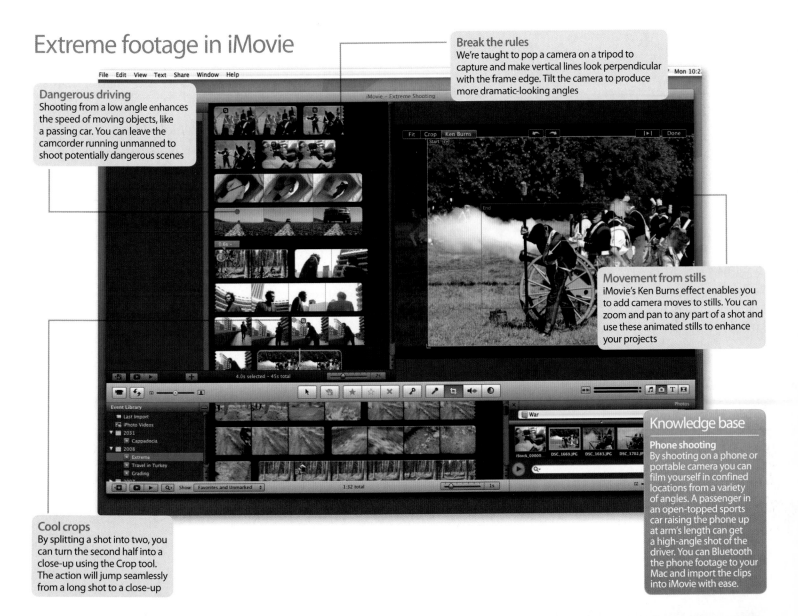

Dangerous driving
Shooting from a low angle enhances the speed of moving objects, like a passing car. You can leave the camcorder running unmanned to shoot potentially dangerous scenes

Break the rules
We're taught to pop a camera on a tripod to capture and make vertical lines look perpendicular with the frame edge. Tilt the camera to produce more dramatic-looking angles

Movement from stills
iMovie's Ken Burns effect enables you to add camera moves to stills. You can zoom and pan to any part of a shot and use these animated stills to enhance your projects

Knowledge base

Phone shooting
By shooting on a phone or portable camera you can film yourself in confined locations from a variety of angles. A passenger in an open-topped sports car raising the phone up at arm's length can get a high-angle shot of the driver. You can Bluetooth the phone footage to your Mac and import the clips into iMovie with ease.

Cool crops
By splitting a shot into two, you can turn the second half into a close-up using the Crop tool. The action will jump seamlessly from a long shot to a close-up

7: I'm the phone
Phones (and compact stills cameras) are light and small so they can shoot video where camcorders can't – and are cheaper to replace if you drop them!

8: On the move
Add extra motion to an action scene by moving from a crouching to a standing position. This is a called a crane shot (Crane.mov).

9: Zoom and pan digitally
Add dramatic camera moves to stills. Place the Ken Burns green Start box on a wide shot. Position and scale the red End box on a close-up (Zoom.mov).

Shake and bake
Fake the effect of an explosion's shockwave buffeting the camera by applying the ground-moving Earthquake filter. This post-production shake adds extra impact to the on-screen carnage!

Plug and play
Thanks to third-party plug-ins, like Gee Three's Matte-tastic, you can add stunning matte-painting elements from Photoshop to your clips (like an alien planet hanging in the sky, for example)

Video FX
The Video FX pane enables iMovie '06 to kick sand in the face of new kid iMovie '08. Here you'll find a host of post-production special effect filters to give your shots a Hollywood style makeover

Knowledge base

Perfect plug-ins
Unlike iLife 08's version of iMovie, there is a plethora of special effect plug-ins available for the older iMovie '06. Surf over to **www.geethree.com** and treat yourself to the Hollywood edition of their plug-in range: Slick 4. This dramatically extends the range of iMovie's filters and lets you add images to your clips (like the alien planet in our example).

Play misty for me
iMovie's Fog filter can be used to enhance a variety of Hollywood style scenarios. Use it to shroud a spooky scene in a moody mist, or make smoke drift across a battlefield

Tutorial: Create Hollywood effects in iMovie

Give your video footage a Hollywood blockbuster makeover (without blowing your budget) thanks to the special effect filters in iMovie '06

Task: Add Hollywood style digital effects to your footage in iMovie '06
Difficulty: Intermediate
Time needed: 15 minutes

iMovie '06 refuses to die! Although it no longer ships with new Macs, you can still download it from Apple's website due to popular demand. Many were irked when the feature-lite iMovie '08 took its place, and this is Apple's semi-apology. Unlike the latest incarnation of iMovie, the older version is packed full of cool filters that can enhance your footage in a variety of dramatic ways. We've popped a variety of video clips on the CD, and in the following walkthrough we'll show you how to create alien planets, enhance an explosion with some post-production camera shake and even turn back time to create a flashback style vintage film effect. Think about how you could utilise these tricks in your next project and you'll soon be wowing the crowds with your Hollywood-esque editing prowess. Prepare the popcorn and get ready to edit!

Step-by-step | iMovie Enhance footage with special effects

1: Brave new worlds
Import 'Alien Planet.mov' and drop the clip in the Timeline viewer. Click on the Editing button and the Video FX tab. Now select Adjust Colors.

2: Alien colours
Drag the Hue slider to the left to create an alien-style Colour palette. The sky will turn green and the rocks will be tinted magenta. Now click Apply.

3: Plug-in power
If you have the Gee Three Slick 4 plug-in (see Knowledge Base) then click on Matte-tastic. Now click Configure and choose 'Planet.tif' from the CD.

4: Move and scale
Use the Scale slider to shrink the planet. Drag it into position. Drag the Opacity slider towards Clear to blend the planet with the footage. Click Apply.

5: The fog
Import 'Fog.mov' and use the Fog filter from the Video FX pane to make an atmospheric shot look even more scary. Black fog creates clouds.

6: Big bang!
Import 'Big Bang source.mov', which shows a Hollywood cliché – the exploding car. To get more bang for your buck pop it in the Clip viewer.

7: Let's split
Scrub forward until just before the car explodes. Choose Edit>Split Video Clip At Playhead. Split the clip again a few frames into the explosion.

8: Shake it up
Click on the middle clip (Big Bang/1). Go to the Video FX pane and select Earthquake. The explosion will now make the camera shake!

9: Turn back time
To create a vintage film effect (for a flashback sequence, for example) import 'War source.mov'. Apply the Aged Film filter to it for a retro look.

 iMovie '06

Tutorial: Slow motion and freeze effects in iMovie

Enhance fast-moving scenes by re-timing your footage to create dramatic slow-motion and freeze-frame effects in our guide to tinkering with time…

Task: Insert slow motion sequences and freeze frames with iMovie '06

Difficulty: Intermediate

Time needed: 15 minutes

When something exciting or scary happens, time seems to slow down. This enables us to analyse the event from second to second. Thanks to iMovie '06's Video FX pane you can take control over time, and move seamlessly from real time to slow motion. You can even halt time in its tracks with a fabulous freeze frame. By changing video speed you draw attention to specific events, enabling the viewer to appreciate a particular action sequence. We've used footage of cyclists leaping off ramps, but any action-based footage will suit the slow-motion/freeze-frame treatment.

Step-by-step | iMovie Halt time in its tracks or slow it down

1: Too fast
In some shots the action happens so quickly that you can't see the identity of the subject (like a cyclist flying past the camera at high speed).

2: Let's split
Pop the clip on the timeline and scrub to where you can see the subject's face. Press Cmd+T to split the clip in two.

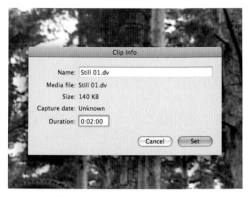

3: Be still
Go to Edit>Create Still Frame. A five-second frozen clip will appear in the clip bin. Double-click on it to change the Duration.

4: Insert freeze frame
Drag the still between the two clips and play the sequence. The footage will play, pause and resume, giving you a clear look at the cyclist.

5: Add graphics
Freezing time is a great way to introduce a character with a caption. Target the still and go to Editing. Select Titles and choose Centered Title.

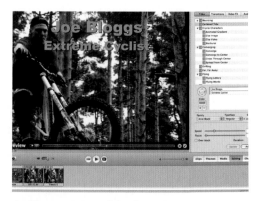

6: Change graphic duration
Drag the Speed slider to give the caption the same duration as the frozen frame. Reposition and colour the caption to suit the footage. Click Add.

Insert effects with iMovie '06

Video FX
The Video FX pane has tools that enable you to dramatically slow down a clip to enhance your footage with stunning slow-motion effects. Click Apply to re-render a re-timed version of the clip

Knowledge base

iMovie '06
When you buy a copy of the latest iLife suite of applications you'll find that iMovie '06 is relegated to a folder called iMovie (previous version). If you buy a new Mac then iMovie '06 won't be installed, which is annoying as iMovie '08 lacks the option to produce slow-motion effects. Luckily you can download iMovie '06 from Apple's site.

Real-time footage
After the action has been frozen or slowed down during the second clip, it will seamlessly return to the correct speed when the Playhead reaches the third clip

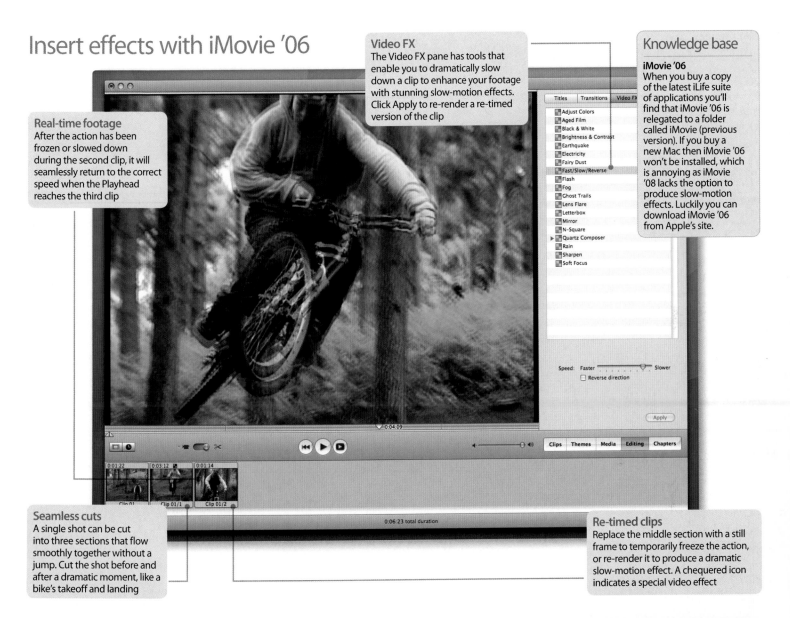

Seamless cuts
A single shot can be cut into three sections that flow smoothly together without a jump. Cut the shot before and after a dramatic moment, like a bike's takeoff and landing

Re-timed clips
Replace the middle section with a still frame to temporarily freeze the action, or re-render it to produce a dramatic slow-motion effect. A chequered icon indicates a special video effect

7: Playback
When we play the whole sequence our cyclist whizzes forwards, freezes for two seconds while a caption introduces him, and then whizzes away!

8: Slow motion
To jump seamlessly from real-time to slow motion, and back to real-time, split a clip in two places (when a bike lifts off and lands, for example).

9: Quick, quick, slow!
Target the middle clip. Go to the Video FX pane and click on Fast/Slow/Reverse. Drag the Speed slider to Slower and click Apply.

iCandy
MacBook Pro 17"

MacBook Pro 17" The new MacBook offers all the features of the 15" version, but with a bigger, non-removable battery

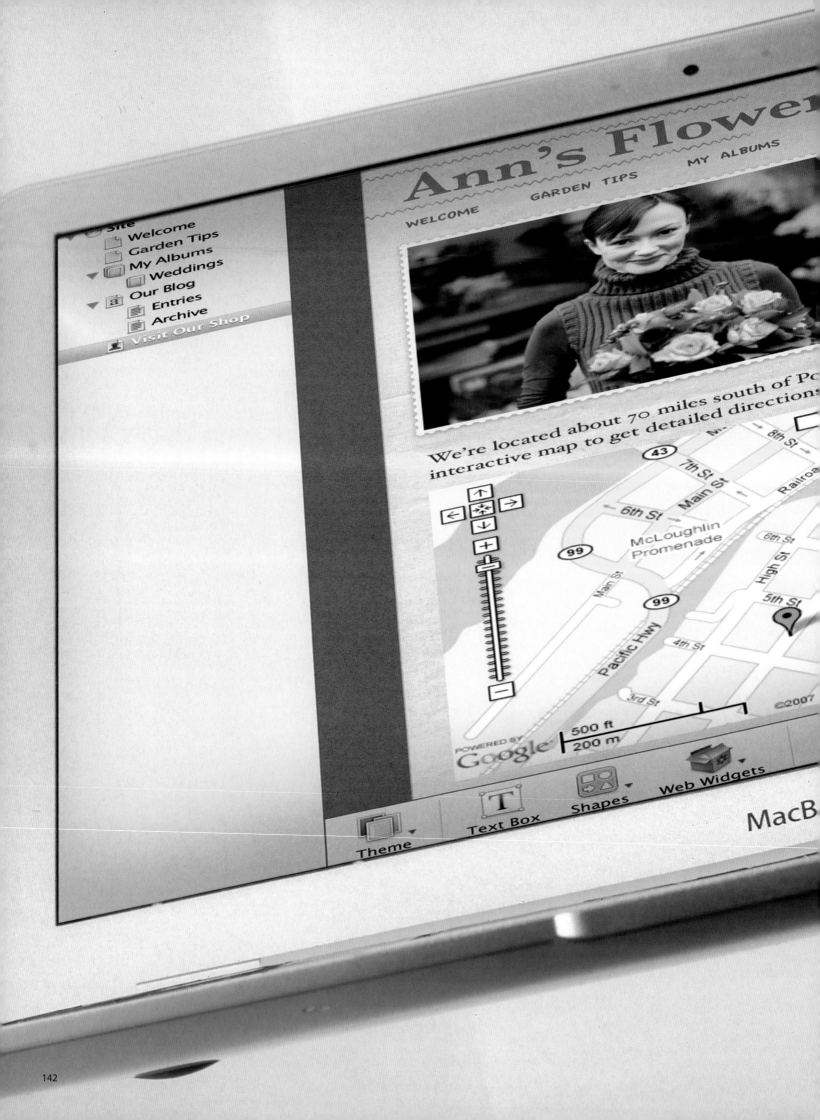

iWeb

Features

Tutorials

Publishing to the web has never been easier. iWeb enables complete novices to cut their teeth into web design, as well as allowing those people who are more advanced the flexibility to be more creative.

iCandy

iCandy
iMac 24"

iMac 24" The silver beauty of the Apple desktop line, the iMac is perfect for almost every creative task you throw at it

144

The iWeb Creative Cookbook

Design delicious websites

Get cooking with iWeb

What better way to get yourself acquainted with all the great new features of iWeb than to follow these fantastic recipes for delicious websites…

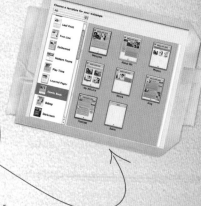

Recommended utensils
✓ iLife Suite
✓ Dedicated web space
✓ Stock photos
✓ YouTube and Twitter accounts

Have a browse through the available designs in the iWeb Template Chooser to pick your perfect style or select a blank page to start a site from scratch

Welcome to the iWeb creative cookbook

It may still have an unglamorous reputation, but from humble beginnings iWeb has turned into a powerful and versatile web-editing application.

For a long time iWeb's main selling point was ease of use, particularly for MobileMe users. Getting a website or a blog published online with iWeb really was just a matter of entering text content, pulling some images in from iPhoto and pressing the 'Publish' button. iWeb handled the background technical stuff for you.

The trouble was that many creative Mac users who tried it all too quickly came up against some of its notable limitations, in particular its lack of flexibility and its crude assumption that its user base was made up largely of MobileMe subscribers. If you didn't subscribe to MobileMe you had to go through hoops to upload content.

But two factors have vastly broadened the program's appeal. First, the introduction in iWeb '09 of direct FTP transfers. This makes it easier for you to upload your web content to the free space, often available as part of a monthly internet subscription or as part of a dedicated website hosting package. Rather than having to rely on the presence of a MobileMe account or having to fiddle around uploading iWeb-exported folders through a dedicated FTP client, everything takes place inside iWeb. Publishing, no matter where the destination, is now one click away.

The other factor that makes iWeb a much-improved all-round choice for web publishing is the growth in the number of add-on widgets it supports. Widgets are small pieces of self-contained functionality that can be embedded on an iWeb-authored page just by dragging them from the Media pane. If you've ever wrestled with pasting code to a particular place on a page, you'll appreciate the simplicity of this approach.

Some of the widgets offer specific functions. The countdown counter will count down to a specific point in time, and the YouTube widget embeds videos from YouTube – but others are almost infinitely flexible. For example, the HTML Snippet widget effectively lets you add any HTML element to your page just by cutting and pasting code into its window. That adds a whole new layer of power to the program, and your web designs.

In short, it means that you can put together any type of website with an app that comes free on your Mac. That's quite a lot of power in your hands and over the next few pages we hope to prove to you just how flexible it can be. We'll show you how you can put together some great-looking and functional websites using the simple ingredients at your disposal. We've chosen a smorgasbord of examples, from the personal sites to the professional, from travel sites to music portals – in fact, the sort of sites that you, the reader, are probably putting together every day. As we'll show, iWeb doesn't mean you're sacrificing functionality. You still have a voice. iWeb just makes it easier to be heard.

A tasty travel journal

Keep everyone up-to-date on your trip

One advantage of using a MobileMe gallery rather than your iPhoto library is that you can take pictures with your iPhone, upload them to MobileMe and they'll appear on your site in seconds

For this recipe you're going to need:

iMovie Map
Add interest with an interactive guide to your travels

Maps widget
Let your viewers know exactly where you're going

Weather widget
Just how hot is it? Let your friends and family know with this widget

Video greeting
The personal touch – record a quick message before you go

MobileMe image gallery
Add photos on the fly by linking to your MobileMe gallery

A video postcard is so much better than a tattered card through the post

Once upon a time, keeping friends and family up-to-date with the latest goings-on on a round-the-world trip or extended holiday meant regular scribbled postcards or expensive calls home. Not any more. Now iWeb is the only tool you need.

We've split this iWeb travel site into three sections. Its homepage is a blog page from iWeb's Travel template. To help readers follow along with the trip, there's also a 'Where we are' page that includes a map of our travels. iWeb's Google Maps widget is a good way to show a static location – just type in an address in the Google Maps widget and you'll get an instant map – but for more visual and interactive appeal you can create a map in iMovie and export it to the Media browser. You can then drag this straight into the iWeb window from iWeb's Media pane.

To keep people up to date with the weather on our trip we've added a live forecast from AccuWeather (**http://netwx.accuweather.com**). At the AccuWeather site you choose the size, theme and location of the forecast and then copy the code into iWeb's HTML Snippet window.

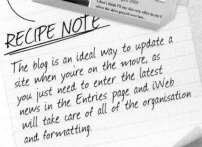

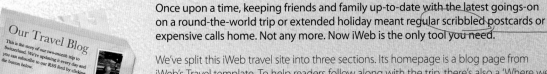

RECIPE NOTE
The blog is an ideal way to update a site when you're on the move, as you just need to enter the latest news in the Entries page and iWeb will take care of all of the organisation and formatting.

You're not limited to the widgets built-in to iWeb. Many other sites make their own that you can paste into your site

RECIPE NOTE

Take care with fonts: the straight lines and stature of a font like Helvetica make it ideal for a headline font, but avoid those like Comic Sans that scream amateurism. Stick with standard web fonts like Verdana or Georgia for body text.

A beefy business site

Use widgets to produce a polished site

For this recipe you're going to need:

Websites like iStockphoto.com provide fantastic photography bargain prices

Wufoo
The Wufoo service gives you easy access to online forms

Google Maps
Show everyone exactly where you're at with a map

PayPal
Want to sell your stuff over the web? PayPal is the easiest way

Stock photos
If your own images aren't up to scratch there are cheap alternatives

RSS feeds
RSS feeds get other sites' content into yours in the simplest way

Business websites can be dry affairs. Keep visitors coming back by offering links to up-to-the minute news and opinions about related subjects through the RSS widget

By plugging in fantastic services like Wufoo you can add impressive functionality to your site without having to fork out for expensive web developers

The design of a business website should reflect the professionalism of the person behind it and its message should clearly convey the product or service you are selling. As iWeb lacks a specific business template, you should start with a blank page from any of the templates.

The critical parts of a business website are an explanation of what you sell, an easy way to sell them and a way for customers to contact you. Often the best way to do this is through an online form that can be filled in on the website and delivered directly to you. iWeb lacks such online forms, but again it's widgets to the rescue with additional help from online forms manager Wufoo (www.wufoo.com), the free version of which lets you add up to three forms to your website. You design them on the Wufoo website and then, in the site's Forms Manager page, copy the code. In iWeb, drag the HTML Snippet widget over the page and paste the code. Click Apply and it will appear on the page.

While it's true that you'll find it next to impossible to create a database-driven, credit-card crunching behemoth like Amazon with iWeb, you can create something more modest with it. To get selling online you just need an account with PayPal (www.paypal.co.uk), which handles the drudgery of credit card management for a small take of the proceeds.

iWeb inspiration

There's no reason to reinvent the wheel! Take inspiration from some of the great business sites online…

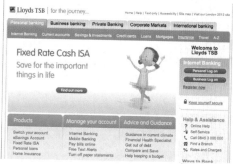

www.lloydstsb.com

This banking website offers a clean and easy-to-read homepage with all of the key services presented as buttons and images, plus tabs for navigation.

www.apple.com/store

Apple's online store can't be beaten for its style and simplicity. This style is possible in iWeb too, with all its content made up of links and images.

www.bloomberg.com

The Bloomberg financial site provides the latest financial info from one simplistic homepage with contrasting text and background colours.

A window is often the major focal point of a room so the design and treatment of your curtains or blinds is crucial to the design process. It deserves careful thought and attention.

I can help with the selection and supply of your fabric, trimmings, tie-backs, poles and tracks, plus all accessories. Curtains are made to measure with a combination of machine stitching and hand sewing for durability, strength and precision. In central and southern Scotland, the service includes measuring and hanging. Phone or email me for more information, advice or a quotation.

Keep your business message simple and don't try to say too much – it can put off visitors

Roman blind

Designed to your specification – and installed on site

Buy Now

£49

Curtains

Designed to your specification – and fitted on site, complete with pelmets

Buy Now

£79

Industry news

Rodnik Band's New Energie

T-shirt junkies, take note! To celebrate edgy English label (self proclaimed as "the first fashion rock brand") Rodnik Band's collaboration with Miss Sixty brother label Energie, the line has created five limited edition tees, to be sold at key retail stores including New York, Los Angeles, Miami, San Francisco, South Coast Plaza, and Georgetown starting April 15th. Chic Report is loving the art-inspired graphics (we spy Andy Warhol soup cans and a certain Marcel Duchamp readymade)…

Easy as One, Two, Three

For anyone who

Fashion Week Daily - Chic Report

Adding a PayPal button is a simple cut-and-paste job. Once you have created a PayPal account click the Merchant Services button on the PayPal site and follow the instruction in the Useful Links section to create a new button. When you've grabbed the necessary code, drag the HTML Snippets widget over the page and paste the code into the code field. Visitors will now be able to make payments directly to your account.

Google Docs:
http://docs.google.com
You can use the form builder in Google Docs to create forms with text, scale or multiple choice answers, which will then be added to an online spreadsheet. Perfect for contact forms, quotes and more.

Sprout Builder:
www.sproutbuilder.com
Sprout Builder lets you create your own widgets, which you can then embed on your iWeb site. Anything from a personal contact button to a promotional widget is possible with the Sprout Builder.

Feature: Get cooking with iWeb

We've adjusted the font to a more personal-looking handwritten font, which suits the subject matter better

Bun in the oven baby blog

Your baby's on its way, keep the world informed

For this recipe you're going to need:

Countdown widget
Count down the days to the birth with the Countdown widget

Stock photography
A great way to add some colourful images to your site

Kuler
Can't decide on a colour scheme? Kuler can help you choose

iPhoto images
New baby pictures can't be beaten, so make sure you add a couple

Amazon Wishlist widget
Make sure everyone knows what gift to get your new baby with this widget

If you start your site before the baby is born, the countdown timer widget is a great way to count down to the new baby's arrival. Drag the timer over the window and enter the babys due date in the field

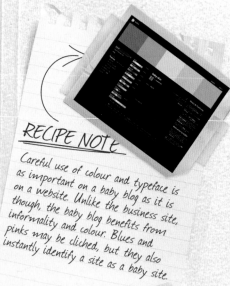

RECIPE NOTE

Careful use of colour and typeface is as important on a baby blog as it is on a website. Unlike the business site, though, the baby blog benefits from informality and colour. Blues and pinks may be cliched, but they also instantly identify a site as a baby site.

A blog-based site is the best way to keep people up to date with your pregnancy and the birth of your baby. iWeb comes with its own Baby theme, but if you don't know the baby's sex you may prefer to avoid cliched colours altogether. Kuler (**http://kuler.adobe.com**) offers great alternative colour schemes.

While the baby's arrival will inevitably produce a flood of photos, to add visual interest before the birth, investigate stock images, particularly for your homepage. iStockPhoto (**www.istockphoto.com**) offers inexpensive snaps, particularly for web use, and it's a good source for custom icons for web buttons too. Don't overlook cheaper sources. Flickr (**www.flickr.com**) is one of the world's biggest photography archives, and while its images are protected under the original photographer's copyright, many have been made available for non-commercial use. You can check restrictions, which appear on the same page as the main photo. But even better, just ask the photographer.

For all those doting relatives who would like to help with clothes, books and toys, but don't know your taste, how about putting an Amazon Wishlist on your site? Copy the code from **https://widgets.amazon.com/Amazon-Wishlist-Widget** and place in an HTML Snippet widget.

RECIPE NOTE

iSight Photo and iSight Movie files are stored, with other iWeb content, in a single file in your User's Library/ Application Support/iWeb folder. It's sensible to back this file up occasionally – and keep a close eye on its size too.

A spicier personal page
Make your homepage look as good as possible

For this recipe you're going to need:

Contact Me
Select Insert>Button>Email Me to add a button that links to your email address

iSight Photo
Add a photo of yourself the easy way by grabbing it with the iSight camera

Twitter account
Harness the power of Twitter on your own website

Flickr
Drag some interesting images from Flickr into your website

AdSense account
Sign up for an AdSense account and place ads in iWeb to make money

Penny for your thoughts? Google's AdSense (www.google.com/adsense) shows relevant adverts on your page and pays per click. It might not make you rich, but it could offset hosting fees

Add Flickr content by following the instructions at www.flickr.com/badge. gne and pasting the resulting code into an HTML Snippet widget window

Your personal site should not only help build your identity on the web, but also be a place where friends, family and even potential employers can see what you're up to.

The problem with personal sites is that they often feel like a daunting challenge. You probably already have a presence in different social media sites around the web, whether it's Twitter or Facebook. Won't adding a personal web page add to the digital clutter?

Not if you reuse that content. For example, you can add a display of your Flickr-hosted photos or add Twitter (**www.twitter.com**) feeds to your iWeb page. This will take the content of anything you add to the micro-blogging website and copy it to your own page. There are two ways to add it: either use the JavaScript code that Twitter offers on its website and pasting it into an HTML Snippets window, or more simply, from your Twitter homepage, copy the link to its RSS feed. Drag the RSS widget over your iWeb page and paste it into the Subscription URL field.

If you're using AdSense on your page, you can log in to your Google.com account in order to track the clicks and impressions recorded for your page, and find out if you've made any money. It's also a handy way to gauge traffic hitting your site.

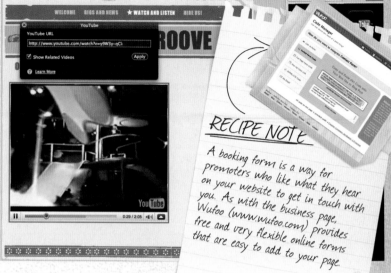

RECIPE NOTE

A booking form is a way for promoters who like what they hear on your website to get in touch with you. As with the business page, Wufoo (www.wufoo.com) provides free and very flexible online forms that are easy to add to your page.

Serve up a feast for the ears

Here's how to get your band's message across

For this recipe you're going to need:

 iMovie
Let others see your musical masterpieces with a clip from iMovie

 Yahoo! Media Player
A bit of a fiddle but, once embedded, this widget is well worth using for music

 YouTube widget
Transfer your MP3s to Flash format for better streaming

 GarageBand
Get recording those great tracks – and send them straight to iWeb!

 Contact form
Want to get booked? Promoters will need to contact you

 Audio2SWF
Transfer your MP3s to Flash format for better streaming

Here we've simply dragged a track from GarageBand over to the iWeb window, but there are other alternatives for streaming audio

The web offers a great way to promote your band and let friends and fans hear your latest tracks, watch you in action or catch up with the latest band news and gigs.

MySpace (**www.myspace.com**) is popular with musicians, partly because its mix of audio, blogs and comments gives a feeling of engagement, but you can replicate its features – and add a few of your own – with iWeb.

Over the page we've created a homepage for the band, which opens with a short biography and links to other pages that contain a band blog, an audio and video page, and a booking form.

Video on your website isn't the bandwidth-sucking exercise it used to be, thanks to YouTube (**www.youtube.com**). So there's no excuse not to include it. iMovie can export directly to YouTube, so as long as you have a YouTube account set up, it's easy to export your video to the service. Embedding the resulting video in your iWeb page is just as easy, and you don't even have to embed any code. Just drag the YouTube widget over the page and enter the video's URL in the URL field.

There are a couple of tweaks to note, though. It's best to turn off the 'Show related videos' option. Leaving this option on will show viewers other videos similar to your own, which is probably something you don't want

★ HOME   ABOUT US   MUSIC   TOUR

THE SHOWBOATS

TOUR DATES

LAZY JOE'S, CA
19/5/09

THE BERRY PATCH, CA
22/5/09

SOUL CAFÉ, NY
25/5/09

BIG PLANET, OH
10/6/09

THE ROCK SHOP, CA
15/6/09

HOPE FESTIVAL, FL
18/6/09

NEW ALBUM ON SALE IN:

32:23:53:24

Days   Hours   Mins   Secs

★ ★ ★ ★ ★ ★

UPDATES FROM THE BAND

THE TOUR STARTS HERE
20/5/2009
WE'VE KICKED THINGS OFF IN STYLE THIS YEAR WITH A SELL OUT SHOW IN THE MIDDLE OF GOOD 'OLE CALIFORNIA INFRONT OF A GREAT CROWD. WE'RE TRYING OUT A FEW TRACKS FROM OUR NEW EP SO CHECK THE TOUR DATES ABOVE AND GET TO OUR NEXT GIG!

MEDIA PLAYER

THE SHOWBOATS

LIVE IN COLORADO EP

iWeb inspiration
Stuck for some ideas to make your band's website rock? Check out these musical hotspots online

www.jasonmraz.com
Jason Mraz has a fun site along the lines of the iWeb Doodle theme with hand drawings and fun sounds. Navigation is simple too.

www.U2.com
U2's new album and tour brings about a brand new website complete with a handy navigation menu, large highlight images and an online store.

www.jackjohnsonmusic.com
Like his music, Jack Johnson's site is simple yet effective. You could easily copy this style with a gradient background and transparent shapes.

As you're in a band, audio is the most important aspect of your work. Adding audio to an iWeb page is a simple drag-and-drop affair, but if you want to stream your music, which helps discourage downloading, you could convert your MP3 files to Flash format with Audio2SWF (www.verticalmoon.com/products/audio2swf) and embed the resulting tracks as Flash files. You'll find instructions at www.iwebformusicians.com. For general audio playback, a simpler alternative is to use Yahoo!'s Media Player (http://mediaplayer.yahoo.com). Copy the HTML on that site into an HTML snippet window – replacing the URLs with your own – and you'll have a built-in media player.

MP3 Player
www.widgetbox.com
This very simple widget allows you to link to an MP3 you have uploaded and set it to autoplay when your site loads, or you can allow users to turn music on and off with the click of a button. It can be customised with colours to match your site too.

My iTunes
www.apple.com/itunes/myitunes
Share your iTunes favourites or, if you're lucky enough to be on the Store, your own music with this slick iTunes widget from Apple. Customise the widget from a set of default templates and include purchases, favourites and reviews for all to see.

Tutorial: Add a countdown widget to your website

Count down the days, hours, minutes and even seconds leading up to an event with the new countdown widget available in iWeb '09

Task: Add a countdown timer to your site
Difficulty: Beginner
Time needed: 10 minutes

iWeb didn't see too many changes in the last release of iLife, but the updates that were made were still great for fans of Apple's web design software. The most changes were seen in the widget category, which included simple ways to add iSight video and photos, RSS feeds and the countdown widget, which we're looking at here. The widget can be customised as you wish and counts down from the day you add it to a specified date in the future. A set of different designs are available to fit the timer to your website and you can even set the units shown such as days, hours, years, minutes etc for a precise indication of the time remaining.

In this tutorial we'll be using the example of a travel diary website with a countdown timer used to show the remaining time left on the trip. Of course, you can use the countdown for any purpose you require and with this guide you'll be able to make it your own. Time to start counting down with iWeb!

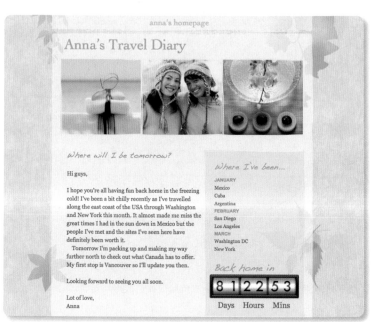

Step-by-step | iWeb Add a countdown widget

1: Drop in the widget

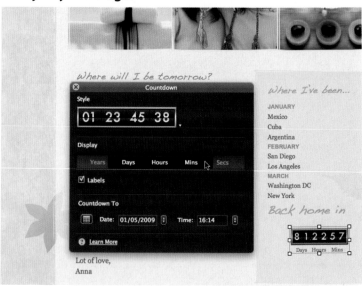

● Here is our travel diary page with space for our widget at the bottom-right of the screen. Click the Show Media button and, from the Widgets pane, drag the countdown widget onto your page.

2: Adjust your widget

● Once you have dropped the widget onto your page a new window will open with a variety of options to adjust your countdown clock. Here we're dragging the sliders to show only days, hours and minutes on the clock.

Add a widget to your iWeb site

Countdown style
Use this drop-down menu to select from one of four styles for your countdown widget that will help match it to your site design

Time display
You can use the handles on this slider to determine whether or not to show the countdown in years, days, hours, minutes or seconds

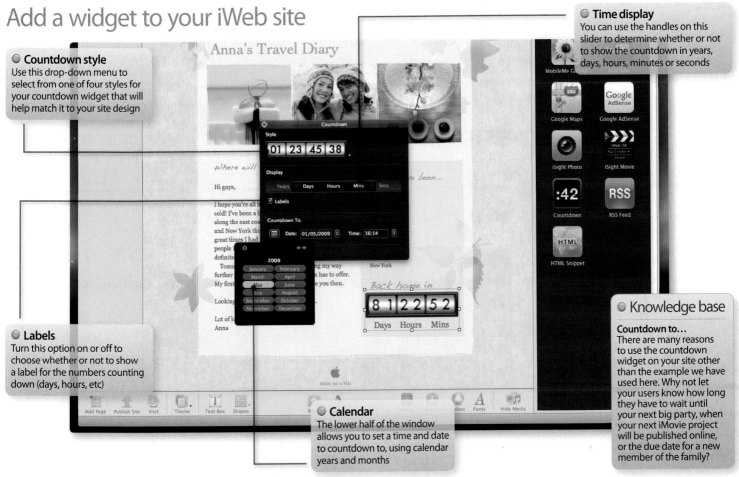

Labels
Turn this option on or off to choose whether or not to show a label for the numbers counting down (days, hours, etc)

Calendar
The lower half of the window allows you to set a time and date to countdown to, using calendar years and months

Knowledge base

Countdown to...
There are many reasons to use the countdown widget on your site other than the example we have used here. Why not let your users know how long they have to wait until your next big party, when your next iMovie project will be published online, or the due date for a new member of the family?

3: Counting down

Next set the month, day and time you want the clock to countdown to by entering the information at the bottom of the Widget screen. The clock will count down from the current date and time.

4: Final adjustments

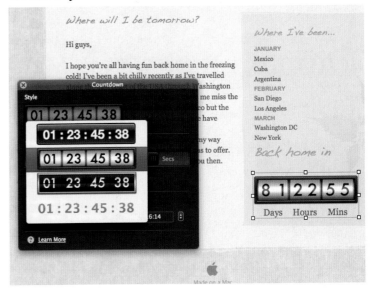

Now all that's left to do is to select the countdown timer style from the drop-down menu and resize the widget on your page so it sits comfortably within your site.

All your news in one place
By pulling news feeds from your favourite sites, you can see all your daily news on one page that you can visit from any computer, iPhone or web browser in the world

Fancy some photos?
Many other sites, such as Flickr, also use RSS feeds, so you can have automatically updating galleries live on your page

Knowledge base

What is an RSS feed?
RSS feeds are simply a standard form of stripped down summaries of the posts made to a website. Using the RSS widget in iWeb, you can embed the feed into your site so that all the updates posted to the original site also appear on your page. Clicking an entry takes you to the original post.

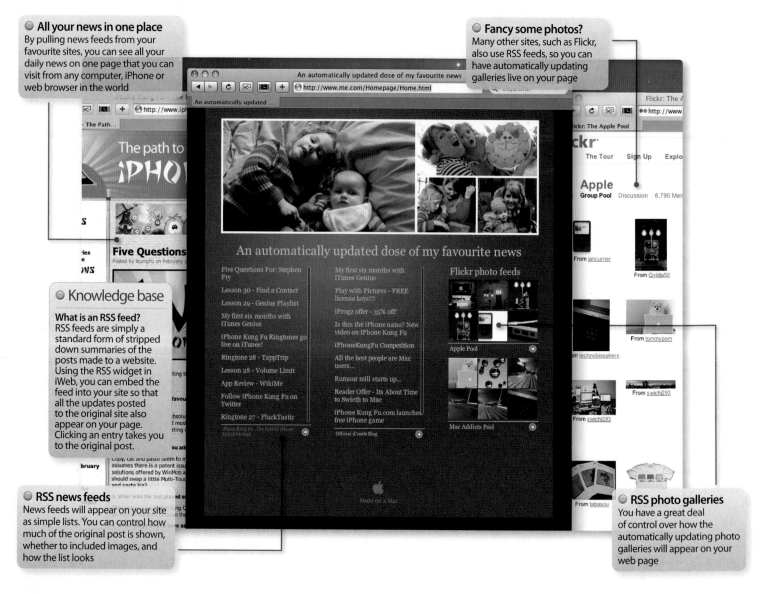

RSS news feeds
News feeds will appear on your site as simple lists. You can control how much of the original post is shown, whether to included images, and how the list looks

RSS photo galleries
You have a great deal of control over how the automatically updating photo galleries will appear on your web page

Tutorial: Create an iWeb page that updates itself

While iWeb makes it easy to design great looking web pages, it can't help you fill them with great content. That is until Apple introduced the RSS widget…

RSS Feed

Task: Add news feeds from your favourite sites to an iWeb page
Difficulty: Intermediate
Time needed: 30 minutes

iWeb received a fair amount of bad press following the slew of updates that made up iLife '09. There's a fear that with only a few, arguably minor, improvements Apple is quietly pushing the website creator back into the same dusty, spiderweb-filled cupboard that iDVD now calls home. A back corner of the iLife office that may never see a reasonable update again.

All is not lost though as – although iPhoto may have hogged the limelight with Faces and Places, and iMovie has set hearts a flutter again for the first time since HD – there's more to this edition of iWeb that many have considered. And chief among these over-shadowed playthings has to be, for us, the RSS widget.

Anyone who spends a decent amount of time online may well have noticed two clear trends. The first is the prevalence of news sites, otherwise known as blogs, while the second is

the way websites are sharing more and more content – it's now common to see headlines from one site appearing in the sidebar of another. These trends are connected; blog sites create RSS feeds which make it very easy for other sites to include automatically generated lists of their most recent posts and updates. In iLife '09 iWeb brings you this capability quickly and easily.

To see just how powerful RSS aggregation can be, take a moment to explore the categories on **www.alltop.com**, which is entirely powered by RSS feeds. While we're not going to go to quite that extreme over the next nine steps, what we will do is show you just how easy it is to create a simple, personalised home page that brings all the news and updates from your favourite web sites together on one page. Once you've mastered that, you'll quickly start thinking of the great ways the RSS widget can add great, fresh and regularly updated content to your pages.

Step-by-step | **iWeb** Create an auto-updating personal homepage – paged with news!

1: Open the Widget browser
If the Media sidebar isn't open, click the Show Media button at the bottom of the iWeb window. Now click the Widget button in the top-right corner.

2: Select the RSS Feed widget
Click on the RSS icon and, with the mouse button still held down, drag the icon left and onto your iWeb page.

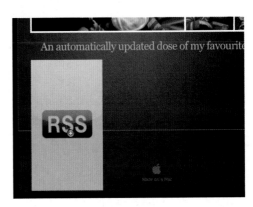

3: Drop it into position
As you move over the page the icon will turn into a grey placeholder rectangle. Position it and release the mouse button to drop it in place.

4: Find the feed in Safari
In Safari, open the page you wish to use as the source for your RSS feed. If it's compatible a blue RSS button will appear in the location bar. Click it.

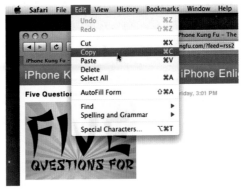

5: Get the feed address
The view will switch to Safari's RSS reader, with the Feed URL shown in the location bar. Select this address and copy it.

6: Paste it into the widget
Back in iWeb, paste the URL into the Subscription URL field and click Apply. After a few moments the feed should appear in the widget.

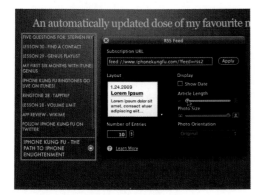

7: How much info to show
As we want as many stories as we can on our page, uncheck the Show Date checkbox and drag the Article Length slider all the way to the left.

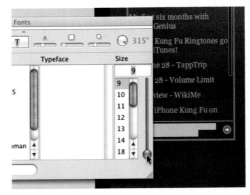

8: Style the text
To style the text in the feed, double-click the widget (until it gets a blue border) then click on the text. You can then use any of the type formatting tools.

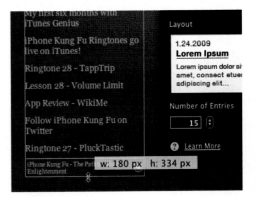

9: Size it to fit
Change the size of the widget to fit by clicking on it and dragging any of the square handles that appear. Repeat these steps for all the widgets you need.

Tutorial: Add an iSight photo to your iWeb site

Personalise your iWeb page with an iSight image that you can shoot and add from within the application

Task: Add an iSight photo to an iWeb website
Difficulty: Beginner
Time needed: 5 minutes

There are many reasons why you might want to add a photo to your iWeb site – be it for sharing holiday snaps or to illustrate a product or service. There's a feature in iWeb '09 that allows you to include photos of a more personal nature; those of yourself or friends taken in front of your computer. The new iSight Photo widget allows you to access your Mac's built-in iSight camera to snap a quick picture to add to a page describing you or welcoming visitors to your site. If you don't have an iSight camera on your Mac you can use a third-party webcam for the purpose too. In this tutorial we will show you how to add the widget to your page, take the photo you want and how to adjust it to fit the template of your choice. Of course, the picture doesn't have to be of you – you could use the camera to shoot your office or a particularly attractive view if you can manipulate your camera in the appropriate direction. However you wish to use it, this feature will save time snapping a quick pic.

Step-by-step | iWeb Add an iSight photo

1: Pick your page

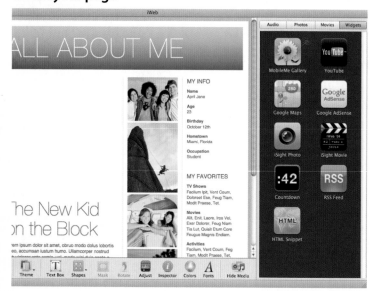

● Create a new iWeb project or load one you have already created and select the area you would like to add your photo to. Make sure the Widgets screen is showing by clicking the Media button and selecting the Widgets tab.

2: Drag in the widget

● From the Widgets tab, drag the iSight photo button to your page or, alternatively, double-click it to add a photo space to the site. A square will now appear on your page ready for the photo to be taken.

iSight photos in iWeb

Widget tab
Widgets can be found by clicking the Widget option from the Media menu, which can be shown and hidden with this button

Image adjustment
Your photo can be resized by dragging the handles and moved by clicking and dragging the image to a new location on the page

iSight Photo widget
This widget, just like the others, can be dragged on to your page to be added to your website

Change the shot
To take another photo simply click this button to start the camera and take another photo

Knowledge base

iSight secrets
If your Mac has a FireWire port you can use the original Apple iSight camera that was available when cameras weren't built-in. Still available on eBay and other sources, these cameras are more maneuverable and can help you shoot more varied images with a wider range and flexibility than the new internal versions.

3: Take your best shot

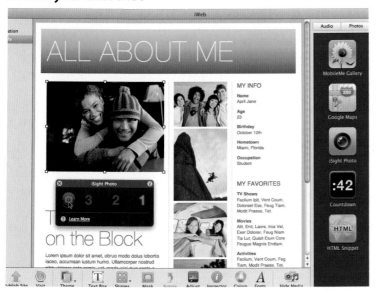

When you click on the photo square a preview will be displayed, allowing you to pose or position your subjects ready to take your shot. When you're ready, click the red Capture button to start the countdown.

4: Adjust your image

You can now use the handles to resize your image and drag it around to place it anywhere on the page. Of course, you can also re-take your photo by clicking the blue Start button and trying again.

Tutorial: Use Facebook notifications in iWeb '09

We show you how to use this innovative feature that lets your Facebook friends know when you've updated your iWeb site…

Task: Automatically alert your Facebook friends of your website updates
Difficulty: Beginner
Time needed: 30 minutes

iWeb has made blogging a breeze ever since Apple added the blog page templates, and the enhancements to the '09 version mean that you can now set up a permanent link between your iWeb site and your Facebook profile. With millions of people signed up to the social networking service, it's a great way to keep track of friends and family. Every time you update your blog with a new entry, not only does iWeb now upload only the changed material, making for a quicker update, but you can set it to notify all of your friends on Facebook that you've updated your site too, instantly increasing the draw of your site and the number of visitors to it. If that isn't enough, it also provides them with a link to your latest exploits so they can quickly find your page and check out your new post. In this tutorial we'll show you how to setup your iWeb site and let Facebook know about the incoming messages from the application when you hit the publish button.

Step-by-step | iWeb Facebook notifications

1: Select site

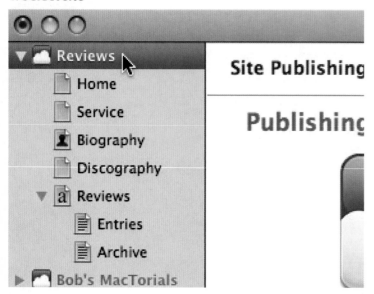

● In iWeb's sidebar, select the name of the site you want to republish. This will bring up the Site Publishing Settings pane.

2: Activate link to Facebook

● Scroll down and tick the 'Update my Facebook profile when I publish this site' checkbox to link the currently selected site to your Facebook profile.

Facebook notifications in iWeb

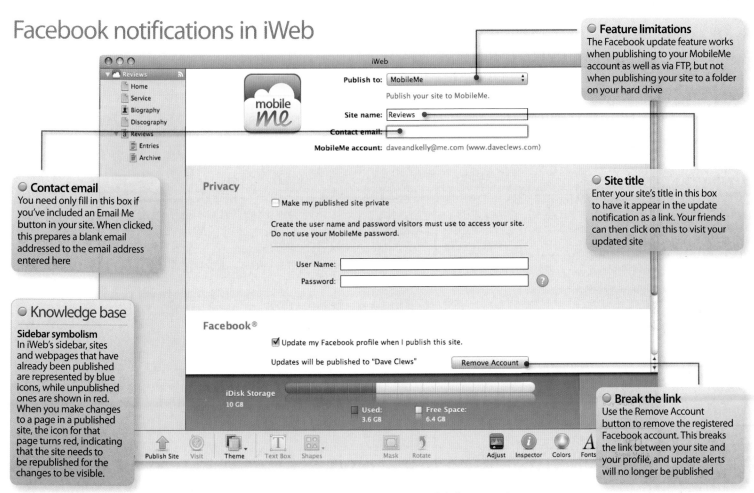

Feature limitations
The Facebook update feature works when publishing to your MobileMe account as well as via FTP, but not when publishing your site to a folder on your hard drive

Contact email
You need only fill in this box if you've included an Email Me button in your site. When clicked, this prepares a blank email addressed to the email address entered here

Site title
Enter your site's title in this box to have it appear in the update notification as a link. Your friends can then click on this to visit your updated site

Knowledge base

Sidebar symbolism
In iWeb's sidebar, sites and webpages that have already been published are represented by blue icons, while unpublished ones are shown in red. When you make changes to a page in a published site, the icon for that page turns red, indicating that the site needs to be republished for the changes to be visible.

Break the link
Use the Remove Account button to remove the registered Facebook account. This breaks the link between your site and your profile, and update alerts will no longer be published

3: Enter login

In the subsequent dialog box, enter the Facebook login details for the account you want to link your site to. Click Login, then Finish.

4: Republish your site

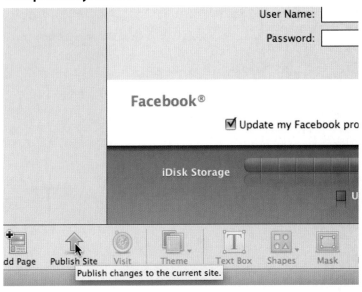

Click Publish Site and iWeb will update your site and post a notice on your Facebook profile containing a link to your updated site.

Tutorial: Publish your new site to MobileMe

Now you've created your dream homepage or business site, make sure the world can see it by publishing it to MobileMe from right within iWeb

Task: Publish your iWeb site to MobileMe

Difficulty: Beginner

Time needed: 10 minutes

So you've crafted an amazing iWeb site and now you're ready for it to hit the web. Once you have got your site up online, updates are only a click away with just the new information altered on the published pages to keep things snappy.

Before you can take advantage of this simplicity, however, you will need to follow a few steps in order to set up your MobileMe publishing preferences and let iWeb know a little more about your account. Of course, you will need a MobileMe subscription to follow this tutorial but, if you're still undecided on Apple's web service, a free trial is available at www.me.com for two months, within which time you can publish as many sites as you may wish. Give it a go while you follow this tutorial and there will be more than enough evidence to help make up your mind.

Step-by-step | iWeb Publish your site

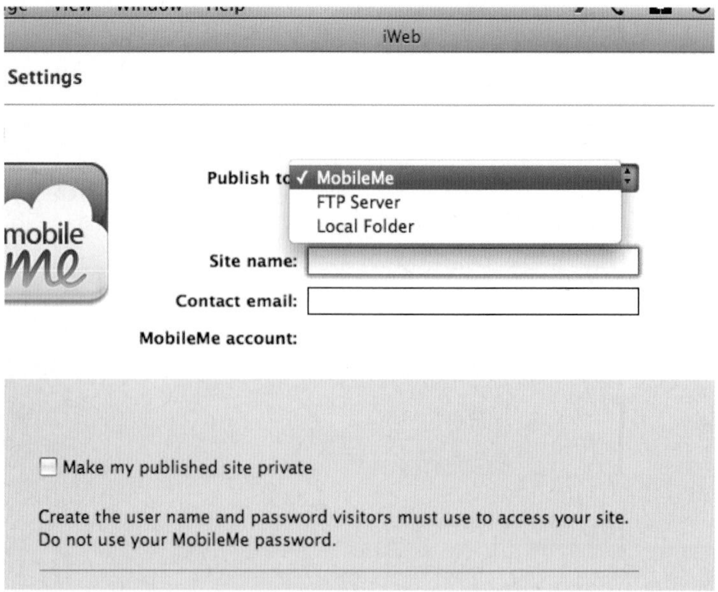

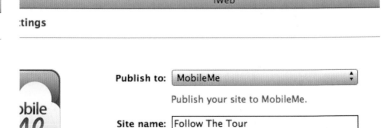

1: Publish Preferences
Start by selecting your site's name at the top of the Source pane on the left of the screen to bring up the Publishing Preferences. Now select MobileMe from the Publish To drop-down menu.

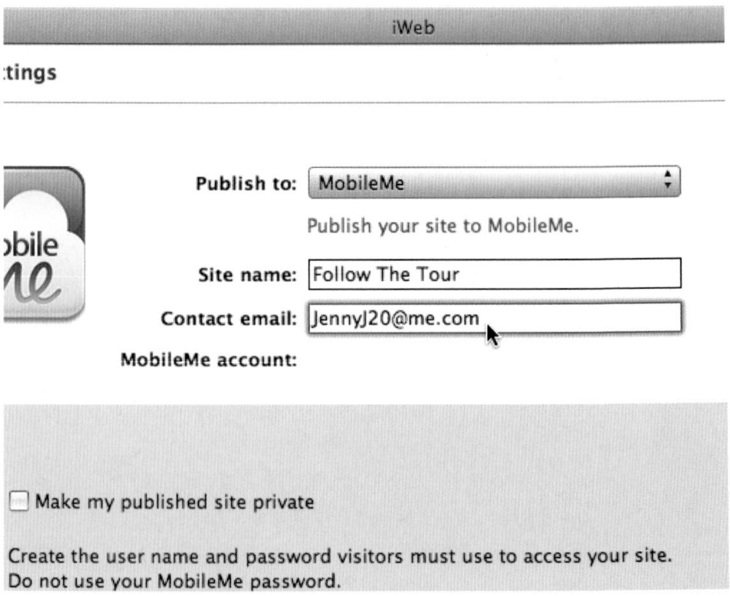

2: Finer details
Now enter a name for your site, as well as a contact email address in the boxes below the Publish To menu. Make sure you enter your email address correctly so that site visitors can contact you.

The publishing process explained
Make some sense of the publishing preferences in iWeb '09

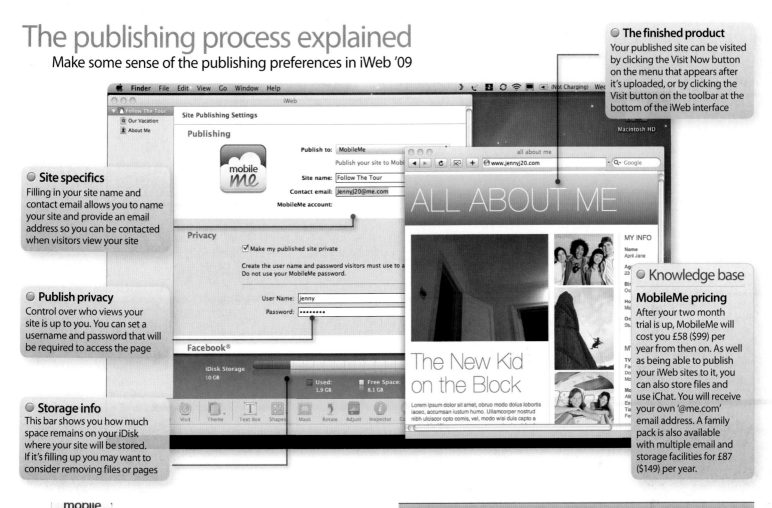

● The finished product
Your published site can be visited by clicking the Visit Now button on the menu that appears after it's uploaded, or by clicking the Visit button on the toolbar at the bottom of the iWeb interface

● Site specifics
Filling in your site name and contact email allows you to name your site and provide an email address so you can be contacted when visitors view your site

● Publish privacy
Control over who views your site is up to you. You can set a username and password that will be required to access the page

● Storage info
This bar shows you how much space remains on your iDisk where your site will be stored. If it's filling up you may want to consider removing files or pages

● Knowledge base

MobileMe pricing
After your two month trial is up, MobileMe will cost you £58 ($99) per year from then on. As well as being able to publish your iWeb sites to it, you can also store files and use iChat. You will receive your own '@me.com' email address. A family pack is also available with multiple email and storage facilities for £87 ($149) per year.

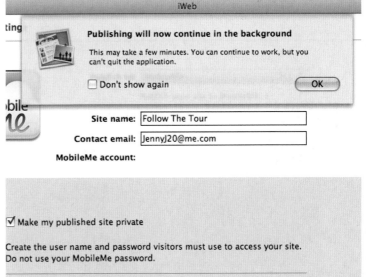

3: Limited access
You can also choose to make your site private if you wish in order to preview it in its published form or deny public access. Check the box and enter a username and password if you would like to use this option.

4: Publishing power
When you're done, click the Publish button in the bottom-right of the screen. A message will tell you that publishing will continue in the background and another will let you visit or announce the site.

Tutorial: An iWeb blog you can update from your iPhone

Fed up of thinking up a great blog post while you're out and about, only to forget it by the time you get back to your Mac?

RSS Feed

Task: Use the RSS widget with a Tumblr blog

Difficulty: Intermediate

Time needed: 60 minutes

We couldn't help but have mixed feelings about the updates made in iLife '09. On the one hand, we were hoping for great improvements to the blogging abilities of Apple's online app – we're tired of being tied to our Mac to make a post when it would be so much more convenient to post from a web browser or, even better, an iPhone app. On the other hand, Apple added the RSS widget. Admittedly not the most exciting addition at first glance, but combine it with some of the coolest web services and you suddenly have an incredibly powerful tool. Tumblr is one of those services – a free blog service that is very easy to set-up and use, allows you to post online or from your iPhone, and is easy to import into iWeb. Over the next four pages we're going to show you how to sign-up for a Tumblr blog, how to post from a browser or iPhone, and how to automatically import those posts into your iWeb site.

What you're going to create…

Mash up Safari, Tumblr, iWeb and your iPhone for on-the-go goodness

● The blog in iWeb
By importing the Tumblr blog into your iWeb site you'll have a mini-blog that's automatically updated every time you upload a post or photo

● The blog in Tumblr
You can post to your Tumblr blog using any web browser in the world, or by using the excellent, free Tumblr app for the iPhone when you're out and about

● The blog in your site
Readers of your site will have no idea that they're viewing an embedded blog, unless of course they click a post, in which case they'll be taken to the full Tumblr blog. There is a cheat for this though, if you'd rather keep that a secret; check out the Knowledge Base to the right

● Knowledge base

Blocking clicks
Because of the way the RSS widget works, if your readers click a post in the embedded blog they'll be taken directly to the original Tumblr page. If you'd rather this didn't happen, just place an empty shape box over the top of the RSS widget in iWeb. That should block the clicks!

Step-by-step | iWeb Sign up for a Tumblr blog

1: Take a tumble
First you need to set up your Tumblr mini-blog, which we'll later import into an iWeb page. Open up Safari and head to www.tumblr.com.

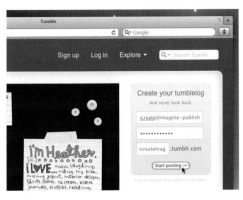

2: Sign me up
Creating a blog takes seconds. Enter your email address, a password and the blog name into the box on the right-hand side and click Start Posting.

3: That was quick
With sign-up completed you'll be automatically taken to your blog. Click the Customize link that appears on the Info panes that appear.

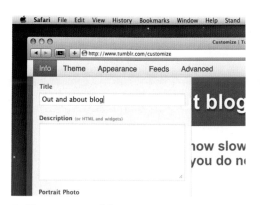

4: Name your blog
Click on the Info tab and enter a title for your blog. You can also apply a theme if you wish. Click on the Save Changes button to return to the Dashboard.

5: Your first post
Posting via the web is easy. Hit one of the Post buttons at the top of the Dashboard, enter your update and click the Create Post button.

6: Take a look
To see how your mini-blog will look to readers, click the link under the blog title on the right – this takes you straight to the web address of your blog.

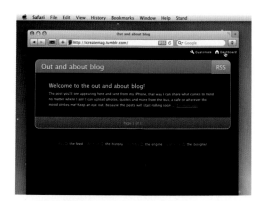

7: Back to the Dashboard
Check out your first post, and then click on the Dashboard icon in the top-right corner to return back to the Tumblr Dashboard.

8: Goodies, goody goody gumdrops
Now to the iPhone bit. Click the Goodies link at the top of Tumblr and then click 'Download Tumblr for the iPhone' to launch the App Store in iTunes.

9: Get the iPhone app
You'll head straight to the App Store page for the Tumblr app, and the good news is that it's free. Click the Get App button then sync your iPhone.

Step-by-step · iPhone · Set up and use the free Tumblr iPhone app

10: One app among many
Now that the Tumblr app is installed on your iPhone, find the icon on one of your home screens and touch it to get started.

11: Sign in
In the Settings screen that appears, enter your account information from step 2. The app will validate your account and you're ready to go!

12: Post from your iPhone
To post an update directly from your iPhone, wherever you are, touch the Post button in the bottom-left corner of the app.

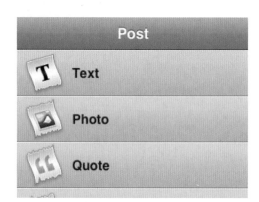

13: Pick a post
The list of posting options will appear, so touch whichever one suits your purpose. We're going to start by posting a quote.

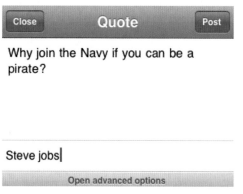

14: Touch typing
The screens that appear when posting should feel familiar. Use the keyboard to enter your text then touch the Post button in the top-right corner.

15: And just like magic…
Head back to Safari on your Mac and open up your Tumblr blog. You should see that your new post is already up and online.

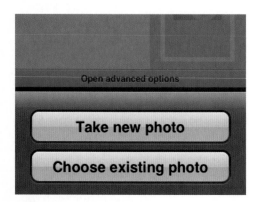

16: Post a photo
Uploading photos is just as easy. From the Post screen choose Photo and then click 'Choose existing photo' to pick one from your library.

17: Pick an album
The standard Photo Album screen will open up, so scroll through it, choose an album and then pick the photo you want to upload.

18: Caption contest
In the resulting screen you'll be given the option to add a caption to the photo before clicking the Post button to upload it to your blog.

Step-by-step   iWeb Add your Tumblr mini-blog to your site

19: Finally, into iWeb
Now to get your Tumblr blog into iWeb. Open up your iWeb site and click the Widgets button in the top-right corner.

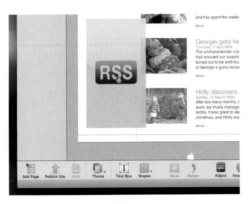

20: Drop in the widget
Click on the RSS widget and drag it across into an empty section of your site. Where you place it depends on how prominent you want it to be.

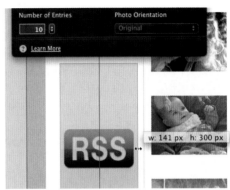

21: One size fits all
You can easily resize the RSS widget to fit the space by dragging any one of the handles that appear on the edges or corners.

22: Find the feed
Now head back into Safari and open up your Tumblr blog. Click on the RSS logo in the location field at the top.

23: Click and copy
This will load the RSS address into the location field (or into Mail if you have that set as the reader). Select the address and choose Copy from the Edit menu.

24: Paste in the feed address
Back in iWeb, click in the Subscription URL field of the black window that pops up over the RSS widget. Choose Paste from the Edit menu.

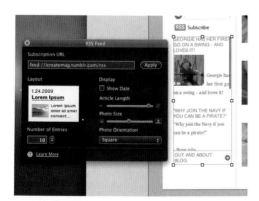

25: Play with the settings
You can now customise the appearance of your Tumblr blog feed by experimenting with the settings in the black window.

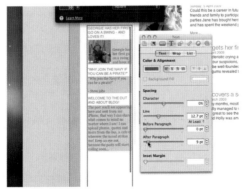

26: Change the text formatting
To edit the appearance of the text, click once on the RSS widget and then double-click on the text. You can then use iWeb's normal tools to change it.

27: Give it a title
Finally, add a text box above the feed and give it a title and description so that your visitors know what they're looking at.

Spotlight You can also add a visual hit counter to your site in the same way you do the Email Me button. Simply choose Hit Counter from the Insert menu instead of Email Me.

Tutorial: Add an Email Me button to your iWeb site

It's no good having a great website online if nobody can tell you how great they think it is. Here's a way to put that right…

Email Me

Task: Add an Email Me button to your iWeb site
Difficulty: Beginner
Time needed: 5 minutes

No matter what you've built your iWeb site for, you need a way for visitors to contact you. Whether they're friends checking in to see how you are, customers making orders or others providing feedback, a quick link to an email address is the easiest way to do things. Fortunately, iWeb offers just such a method and it's a breeze to implement. iWeb's Email Me button is a simple logo that immediately suggests its purpose without getting in the way of the design of your site. Its rectangular shape makes it perfect for dropping into the corner of a site or onto a list of links. Once you've added it your work is done, and iWeb will handle the rest. Make sure your default email is set up for the page. Now, every time anyone clicks the link, they'll be taken to their mail application with your address added to a new message.

Step-by-step | iWeb Add an Email Me button to your website

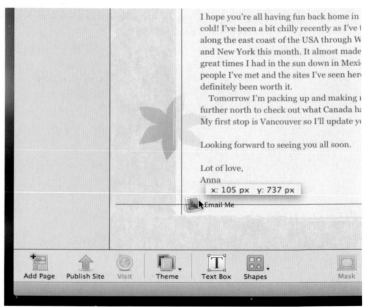

1: Insert the button
Load up the page you want to add the button to and head to the Insert menu. From here select Button, and then click on the Email Me option to drop the button on your page.

2: Position to perfection
You are now free to move the Email Me button to any position on your page. Use the guides to line it up with other elements and make sure that it's in a visible position so visitors can spot it.

iCandy

iCandy
MacBook Pro 17"

MacBook Pro 17" Even when in dim light, the new MacBook Pro
looks remarkable with its backlit keyboard

iWeb Inspirations

How do you design an iWeb site that doesn't look like an iWeb site? Learn the techniques to create your unique webpage today…

Add an online store

Link to Facebook

Add Google maps

"A unique site is only limited by your imagination"

Why not create a family tree?

Share photo and movie galleries

Online forms

Customise themes

The disc is dead. Forget the rise of the Blu-ray, fresh from its victory over HD-DVD, discs in general are on their way out. Nowhere is this more true than within the walls of Apple's HQ. Not only has the company recently released a laptop without an optical disc drive in the form of the MacBook Air, but it also practically ignored its DVD burning application iDVD in the last iLife update, while heavily enhancing iWeb and .Mac. iTunes is slowly erasing the compact disc from our memories, and the iPod is the DVD player and Walkman that you can take anywhere.

Is everything Apple heading online? Even iMovie now snubs its brother iDVD, by offering Export options to .Mac Web Gallery, YouTube and, of course, iWeb. With this in mind we've decided to delve into the unsung hero of the iLife suite: the incredible iWeb.

For too long people have had to put up with pretty awful web-based site-making tools or, at the other end of the spectrum, shell out time and money on the steep learning curve (and even steeper price tag) that comes with professional apps, like Adobe's Dreamweaver. iWeb does away with the preconceived notion that web design is difficult and that you have no freedom to be unique when creating your own homepage, blog or site for a small business. WYSIWYG (What You See Is What You Get) is a much hyped idea that is rarely as simple as it claims in the world of software. iWeb redefines the abbreviation. Add an image, make shapes, paste text, drop in movies, music and more, and what appears in the iWeb Interface is what visitors to your site will see once it's published. The available themes in iWeb should provide you with a good starting point, but how unique a site looks is only limited by your own imagination.

The process of building a professional-looking site in iWeb is so simple that we're not going to waste pages showing you the basics. Most Mac users are used to the simplicity of dragging and dropping and that's really all there is to it. Here we're going to look at the exciting extras, inspirational ideas, and little-known features and functions that will make your iWeb site stand out from the myriad of heavily templated offerings which are already available online. We aim to show you the many additions that you can use for your site that will not only make it a great deal more impressive, but even easier for visitors to use. Whether you're planning to sell products online, share your family news, videos and photos, promote a body of work or simply give yourself an online home where you can write and post what you want, this feature will provide you with the information you need and more.

If you can burn a DVD and share your work with only a couple of people, just imagine the possibilities of sharing the same content online – accessible to anyone who has access to the internet. That's millions of people! So no more excuses – read the following iWeb Inspirations feature and realise what you've been missing by creating your very own iWeb site today.

"Whatever you want from a site, iWeb can offer it"

So you've got this far, and you want to make an iWeb website. Not only do you have one of the best consumer web design applications installed on your computer (assuming you bought your Mac or a copy of iLife in the last few years), but you have everything you need to get going, right on your Mac. Whether it's photos, videos, music or business plans, you have the raw materials (as well as access to the treasure trove that is the net) at your fingertips.

So what's your site for? Who's going to look at it? What do you want it to achieve? These are the questions you need to ask yourself as you begin to plot your online home. More often than not, it may just be a fun project for you to find your own corner of the web to reside in. Some of you might want to keep family and friends abreast of your movements, and some may want to take advantage of the second coming of the dotcom boom, and make a little extra

money without the danger of founding a multi-national corporation. Whatever you want from a site, iWeb can offer it. While it's a consumer application, a few tweaks and a little imagination will see you succeed in most tasks – even those not mentioned in the iWeb manual.

Let's consider some of the basics to begin with. There's no point in building your dream site, only to find a meagre percentage of users can view it. This could be down to a number of reasons, with the most prominent being the browser viewing your published site. Unfortunately, with browsers being constantly updated and refined, and web technologies ever developing, there's no true science to complete compatibility. Your best bet is to make sure you have a recent copy of the big three web browsers: Safari, Firefox and Internet Explorer. The more savvy among you will be noticing a problem here however, as there is no longer a Mac version of IE for Mac OS X. There are, then, two options open to you. If you're running an Intel Mac you can run Boot Camp or other virtualisation software to run Windows and then Internet Explorer on your Mac. A laborious and certainly over-the-top effort for such a simple task. The second option is more efficient; borrow a friend's PC or get a PC-using friend to check your site. Fortunately, in these times of ever growing Mac popularity, Safari is the best and fastest browser on both Windows and Macs, so a simple note and link to the Safari downloads page on your site should

The Colour pane explained
Make the most of colour on your iWeb site

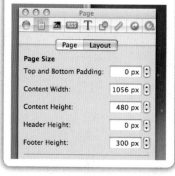

The buttons along the top select different colour selection styles, including sliders, crayons and the Colour wheel

To adjust the saturation of the Colour wheel, drag this slider up or down

The colour displayed in this window is your current colour, and will be applied to the selected object or text on your page

By dragging the cursor over the Colour wheel you can select different colour shades, and fine tune them with the other controls

To determine the opacity of your colour (the amount of colour allowed to pass through it), use this slider

If you wish to use a colour again, drag it from the colour area (next to the magnifying glass) and drop it into one of these squares

NEW DIMENSIONS

Size matters
The size your site displays at is very important. As computers come with increasingly larger displays it's best to make the most of the screen's real estate, without forgetting those with traditional-sized viewing areas. You can easily adjust the size of your page from the Inspector's Page Layout screen. By default, a page is 700 px by 480 px – but you can push this up to 1024 px by 768 px for a larger canvas. Don't forget to take mobile devices, like the iPhone, into account.

Page Size	
Top and Bottom Padding:	0 px
Content Width:	1056 px
Content Height:	480 px
Header Height:	0 px
Footer Height:	300 px

Colour me blind
Website colour is important. Learn some tips from the top!

All of the colours that you can specify for your website's design are based on the RGB (red, green and blue) colour space. This system is called the additive colour space, as you add colours together to get individual hues. Based on the ability of the cathode-ray tube to combine these three wavelengths of light, the RGB system is the basis for the creation of all screen-based colour.

The colours that the RGB colour space can produce are often grouped into two categories: warm and cool. Warm colours, such as red and orange, are described as warm colours due to their association with sunlight. Conversely, blue and green are cool colours as they are associated with the earth. Colour can certainly evoke emotions. Colour psychology has developed, attempting to assign emotions to colours. For instance, red is associated with passion, green with nature, black with power and pink with marriage and femininity.

The age, sex, and the culture of a person viewing a colour will influence any empathy they feel. When designing Colour palettes for your own websites,

it's imperative to know as much about your audience as possible. If your site is global, then checking out how a colour is interpreted in different countries might well mean a redesign of some of your proposed site. The subject matter and the target audience will give you a guide to the Colour palette, "Colour is one of the great tools we as designers wield in creating the emotional aspect of our designs," says Greg Huntoon, senior art director at Real Pie Media [www.realpie.com].

"On a fairly universal level, there are colour combinations that evoke a mood, or call in specific ideas or feelings. Warm colours remind us of sunshine and heat. Cooler colours suggest cloudy skies or rain. A collection of drab shades of olive greens will nearly always invoke a military or militant feeling. Pastels will add a soft and light air to nearly any composition."

These colour tips were provided by iCreate's sister title – Web Designer magazine. Learn more at www.webdesignermag.co.uk.

help things. At worst, a few glitches will appear in a non-conforming browser. But with any luck, you won't see anything too drastic. Testing is the key though, so make sure all is well before announcing your site to the world.

The next compatibility consideration is fonts. If you're using a font that isn't available to your website viewer then you're likely to run into trouble with their browser defaulting to another font to replace yours and, in doing so, losing the style you intended. It's best to play things safe here by opting for the fonts found in the Web category of the iWeb Font window. This section includes popular fonts like Arial, Impact and Georgia, all clean and legible scripts. While you might not be able to go to town with your font choices, it's better to be safe than sorry. Should a browser not recognise your font you'll run into a number of problems, from ugly default through to dreadful alignment, overflowing text boxes and worse.

If you have to use a font that doesn't fall under the 'web safe' category, there is another way. Any alterations you make to a font beyond the normal formatting, like adding shadows, will force iWeb to turn the text into a PNG image – which shows up in any browser. While this will be annoying to apply to all the text on your website, it will work for buttons and titles and allow you to use any font. ►

Create a photography portfolio
Use iWeb's sleek, sophisticated themes to display your work online

Recommended themes:
Most of iWeb's photo pages will do a decent job of displaying your photos, but for portfolio pages you'll need clean, striking styles like Darkroom, Formal, Elegant & Modern…

"For some style and interactivity on your site, you can't beat a .Mac Web Gallery"

Work with photo pages:
It's easy enough to add a photo page to your site and drop images into it. But you can be a little more creative, by creating a photo page to link to your individual photo pages – similar to the My Albums pages.

Use My Albums:
A My Album page is a useful way to provide navigation to all of the media on your site. Rather than having links to each photo and movie page, a My Album page provides an elegant way to link to them all from one location.

.Mac Web Gallery:
For some style and interactivity on your site, you can't beat a .Mac Web Gallery. Capable of hosting video and photos, it can be customised to allow for visitors to download images and movies, as well as upload some of their own – creating many options for community-based photo sharing.

Linking to a .Mac Web Gallery in iWeb is really simple; just select the gallery you want to add to your page from the Insert menu. Once you're on the page you can skim through photos as you would in an iPhoto Event, and click on the preview to be taken straight to the Web Gallery page.

Feature: iWeb inspirations

iWeb font gallery
Some of the best fonts for your site, seen in many templates

Arial
Arial: A clean, legible and web standard font that offers solid bold and italic options. A safe choice for compatibility in most browsers.

GEORGIA
Georgia: Another web-safe font, Georgia is not only a very clear font but the italic variant adds some real class to a site's design.

Chalkboard
Chalkboard: Like the much maligned Comic Sans, this font should only be used for titles and buttons on your iWeb site.

Helvetica Neue
Helvetica Neue: A simple font, Helvetica Neue offers a wide range of variants, including UltraLight and Condensed for keeping consistency across a site.

Hoefler Text
Hoefler Text: This elegant font will provide a touch of class to your portfolio or business site, and also provides a variant of page ornaments.

MARKER FELT
Marker Felt: Making up the titles of the Comic Book theme, this is a vibrant font for colourful websites.

CRACKED
Cracked: This urban-style font works well with a number of iWeb themes, including Nightlife and Freestyle.

PORTAGOL
Portagol:
Portagol is a stencil font that can be used on a variety of backgrounds, while still standing out on the page.

Zapfino
Zapfino: While a little more script-like, and therefore a bit more difficult to read, if used sparingly Zapfino is a very classy font for portfolio sites.

"The illusion of a perfectly good website can be shattered by the tiniest imperfections"

It's the little things that will make a big difference to your iWeb site. The polish and the attention to detail not only makes a site stand out, but gives it a depth of quality that enriches the visitor's experience. The illusion of a perfectly good website can be shattered by the tiniest imperfections, like broken links, out of place page elements and inactive buttons. Poor alignment can also distort the perception of your page. Make sure you use the guides to help you keep things lined up – be it images, Widgets or text. The iWeb Preferences pane provides options for the guides, including the option to show guides at object edges. This feature is turned off by default, but will help you to make sure everything sits perfectly on your page.

When adding an object to your page such as an image or video, question how it should sit on the page. Does it look too square by comparison to the rounded edges found elsewhere on your site, or vice versa? The easiest way to fit an object into the design of your web page is to use the Masking feature. Simply select an object and choose the Mask With Shape option from the Format menu. From here you can choose a shape to fit your object within. For example, you could mask a square shape with a rounded rectangle shape, and apply a soft shadow behind it to reduce the harsh edges. The Inspector's Object pane offers a number of effects to help enhance your site, including drop shadows, reflection and opacity.

While shadows will help add depth to your page, reflections will add a more Web 2.0, Apple-esque style, and opacity can be used in a variety of ways to blend objects and media on your page. Creating large shapes as backgrounds on your site can help you organise the layout of your page and, by using the Opacity slider, you can even add shapes on top of others to define regions.

The overall background of your page is also an important consideration and should be used carefully to make the most of your page, and show off its contents in the most effective way. Check out the Page Layout pane of the Inspector and you'll see that the background of your site is divided into two distinct regions; the page background (which is the colour behind your site and its content), and the browser background (the area surrounding your site when inside a Browser window). Clever use of colours and/or gradients on these backgrounds can create effective contrasts and serve to enliven your site but, on the other hand, they can also be its downfall. The last thing you want is for the background

CUSTOMISE YOUR URL

Make use of a Favicon
Download the excellent iTweak from **www.itweak.guimkie.com** to add your own custom favicon (the icon next to your site's URL) to an iWeb site. You can use any image you want as a favicon, but you will first need to convert it by using the excellent Favicon From Pics tool at **www.chami.com**. Once you have created and downloaded your icon, open up iTweak and head to the Favicon tab. Start by dragging your icon into the Favicon File box, and then enter your default website location for the file. In most cases this will be 'http://web.mac.com/your_username/your_site_name/favicon.ico', replacing the username and site names with your .Mac and website names. Click the Options button, check the Add Favicon box and click Close. Now click the Choose Published Site button, locate your site folder on your iDisk in the Web-/Sites/ location and click Choose Published Site. When you're done, click Process Site to upload your changes. Check your iWeb site to see your new favicon. Unfortunately, however, you will have to carry out this technique each time you publish your site.

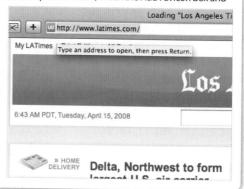

C-Name Game: Personal domains in iWeb

To truly personalise your site, you'll want its URL to be something more interesting than the default homepage.mac.com address. First, in order to do this, you need to purchase your chosen URL from a website like **123-reg.co.uk** or **namesco.com**. These sites will help you determine if the address you require is available and can be anything from yourname.com, to the '.org', '.co.uk' and '.biz' extensions. Some sites will even allow you to purchase more than one of the extensions for a fixed price, '.com' and '.co.uk', for example.

Once you have registered your domain, you need to set up your .Mac account to recognise it by logging in to **www.mac.com**, heading to the Account screen and clicking the Personal Domain button. You will then be prompted to define web.mac.com as the 'www' CNAME for your domain with your registrar. Most registrars will have an online control panel for you to make these changes from, but if you have difficulty you can always contact the provider of your domain for help. Once you have updated the CNAME details, head back to your .Mac Account and its Domain Settings screen and click Continue when you receive a confirmation message. Do note, however, that it may take the registrar up to 48 hours to complete your CNAME request.

of your page to catch the eye more than the actual information on your site. Another background option is to add an image in place of colours. In many situations this can work well, and even become incorporated with elements on your site (for example, vines and plants could form a border to text boxes, pictures and titles). Make sure you avoid tiling any images other than particular textures, and even then be careful. You don't want your site to look like the awful design-by-numbers pages, so popular in the early Nineties, featuring a repeated image behind the content.

When you look at the sites you visit on a day-to-day basis, you'll notice many of them provide banner advertising or animated buttons at the top, bottom and down the flanks of a site. While these areas are primarily reserved for advertising, and you can certainly fill them with AdSense ads, you can get a bit creative and include your own banners and buttons to link to highlights on your site. Anything from 'Check out my new blog' through to 'buy online today' messages can be included and will provide points of interest to lure your visitors. If you're serious about banners you can even add animated versions using the BannerZest from Aquafadas (www.aquafadas.com), which provides a number of themes for you to add your images and text to. You can then simply add the banner as an HTML snippet in iWeb for a pro touch. ▶

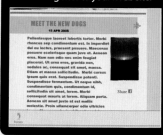

Create a family blog
Make the most of iWeb's built-in Blog tools to create your own online community

Recommended themes:
The safest blog template is found with the White or Black themes. But you can be more creative with those found in the Goldenrod, Modern Frame and Doodle templates.

"Once online you can even add photos from an iPhone to a .Mac Web Gallery"

Basic blogs
Add a blog page to your site, or customise a blog page as your Welcome page so you can use it as the 'latest news' section.

Comments
Use the Inspector's RSS pane to allow comments on your blog, so others can add their opinions on your posts via your site.

.Mac community
If you link to a .Mac Web Gallery from your blog, not only can you allow comments on the blog itself, but you can also encourage users to upload their photos and movies to your Web Gallery. This will create a communal pool of media from specific events that you can share with family, friends, colleagues and… well, the rest of the world!

Uploading and downloading photos, as well as adding photos via email, are available when you publish to .Mac from iPhoto or iMovie. Once online you can even add photos from an iPhone to a .Mac Web Gallery.

Feature: iWeb inspirations

iWeb isn't the most advanced web design package, and certainly doesn't provide the high-end tools you would expect in professional applications. But we wouldn't want it any other way. Why struggle to master an application when, with a little ingenuity and imagination, you can make such a simple consumer application do nearly everything you want it to? Many have bemoaned iWeb's lacking features but, if you're dedicated, just about anything is possible with a little effort. The Web Widget feature in iWeb 2.0 has improved the application no end. With the HTML Snippet option for web Widgets, almost anything made up of HTML code can be added to your site and, if you really want to get into detail, can be refined to work in perfect harmony with your page.

If you're familiar with social networking sites like Facebook and MySpace you'll already know about web Widgets and web Apps, even if you didn't know that's what they were called. These nifty little devices can take the shape of something

as simple as a clock, all the way to a complex photo manipulation tool or a game. In reality, all they are is strings of code that a web browser reads and runs. Every time someone on Facebook 'hugs' you, or you see a swirling set of animated photos on someone's MySpace page, what you're seeing is just a string of code in action. In most situations you can easily grab this code yourself, just as you would copy the embed code of a YouTube video and paste it into an HTML snippet in iWeb. With access to anything from news feeds to music and video players, you don't have to gaze longingly at the content on other sites when you can drop the same elements into your own page.

A good place to start looking for these exciting add-ons is www.widgetbox.com, which provides a comprehensive list of web Widgets with most providing the code you need to apply them to your own site. Be warned: as cool as a Widget may be, the chances are that it will require quite a bit of bandwidth to

receive its information and appear on your page, so use them sparingly (unless you want your site visitors to wait a while before your page loads).

As well as custom HTML snippets, iWeb provides web Widgets for more common elements too, such as Google Maps, AdSense ads and .Mac Web Galleries. We'll come on to AdSense a bit later, but if you're after exciting, interactive elements on your page then you can't go wrong with a map

⊗ Top tip

Animated buttons
Animated page elements aren't solely available in professional web design applications. Drop a sequence of images or titles into iMovie, export them as a video file at mobile size and add them to your iWeb site. Set the video to loop and autoplay. Opt not to show the video controls from the Inspector pane, and frame it with a shape if you wish. Now add a shape over the top of your video, and create a hyperlink to the page you want the button to link to. Once done, set the opacity of the shape you added to 0%. Now you have a working, animated button.

> "Just about anything is possible with a little effort"

THE iWEB WEBCAM TRICK

While it's a little tricky to show an actual webcam feed on your iWeb site, you can share frequently updated images from your iSight camera live on your site. The technique is very simple and requires a great app called Periscope from **www.freeverse.com**. The application uploads stills from your iSight camera at predetermined intervals, which are then displayed on your site. For more information just head to its website where you can download the app.

Welcome to Widgets

The true power of Apple's inclusion of web Widgets in iWeb 2 has not received the coverage it deserves. With the ability to drop in HTML snippets from almost any source, you can take an iWeb site well beyond the expected capabilities with Flash Widgets that add anything from live clocks, news feeds or media players to your site. The best source for Widgets to use in iWeb is **www.widgetbox.com,** which enables you to directly copy the source code of a Widget from its gallery onto your clipboard, so you can quickly paste and HTML snippet it in iWeb. **Picturetrail.com** offers a unique way to show off your photos in a customised web Widget with a variety of styles available. All you need to do is sign up to the site, upload your photos and request the code for your website. **Finetune.com** is another top site that, after registration, allows you to build a custom playlist and turn it into a Media Player Widget on your site for visitors to sample your taste in tunes. Of course, you don't need to go beyond iWeb for Widgets with the ability to include Widgets on your page, such as: Google AdSense ads, Google Maps and YouTube videos via HTML snippets. You could even go as far as to devote an entire site to showing the world your favourite places to browse. Not only would this be a collage of colour and web personality but it would also offer people a great insight into the places online that you love to visit. Again, this is a wonderful example of iWebs versatility and one of its many strengths.

or skimable gallery preview. There are a number of reasons to make use of Google's maps on your page. The most obvious is to show others how to find you (although in this day and age, that might not be the best idea unless your site is password protected). Other options are to show off where you're planning on travelling to, point out areas of interest, or back up a set of photos and videos with the exact geographical location they were taken in.

We all know how great .Mac Web Galleries look, and you can add some of this style to your site by linking to one with a web Widget. Whether you're linking to a movie or a photo album, running the mouse over the Widget on your page will skim just like in Events in iPhoto and iMovie '08. With a collection of web Widgets for .Mac Web Galleries on one page, visitors will be able to scroll across the images to determine which of your collections they want to visit rather than having to wade through all your shots.

One oversight by Apple is the lack of framing for Web Gallery links. The Widgets tend to look a little blocky on the page with their square edges, and there's little option to manipulate their shape. A simple workaround is to add a shape as a frame for the Web Gallery link, such as a rounded rectangle, to help blend the Widget into your page a little more. One of the more common Widgets you'll find on a website is the standard RSS Feed viewer. These normally take the shape of a small banner running across the page, which scrolls headlines from the RSS feed of a newswire. Of course, once you have the RSS Widget in place, such as RSS Scroller from Widgetnest (**www.widgetnest. net**), it's completely up to you what you choose to run through it. Whether it's sports scores, news headlines or music releases, any valid RSS feed can be added and displayed on your site. If you want to be really clever, you can even add the RSS feed from your own blog and add the scrolling Widget to your homepage. This way, visitors to your site are instantly informed as to what's going on in your world, with the headline of your blog posts running across the Widget. Make sure you flag up where your blog is on the site, so people can get to the page quickly once the Widget entices them to check out your writing. ▶

Media sharing
Choose the best way to share and show off your media

Recommended themes
Make sure you pick a solid and colourful theme to show off the media on your iWeb site; choices include Bepop, Highlighter, Main Event and Modern.

"iWeb handles videos just as easily as photographs and audio files"

Autoplay music on your site
For a simple way to play background music on your iWeb site, drag a file from your iTunes library onto the page and set it to loop and autoplay. Also, hide the controls from the Inspector's QuickTime menu. If you don't want the file to be seen, reduce it to its smallest size and place it behind an object on your page.

Family tree blog
You can use the iWeb Blog pages for more than just informing friends and family of your news. By using the blog's structure, you can create databases of information – like an interactive family tree, for example. Family trees are a great way to share news between relatives as well as charting who's who.

All kinds of video
iWeb handles videos just as easily as photographs and audio files. Simply drag your clips into iWeb to add them. It's worth using iMovie's Export options if you want them to display quickly, or just link to an already published movie on your .Mac Web Gallery. Alternatively, you can use iMovie to publish your movie direct to YouTube where you can then embed a web-ready version directly into your iWeb site using the HTML snippet web Widget and the embed code provided by YouTube that appears next to your video.

Since its conception, the internet has been this generation's gold rush. With the dot com boom and subsequent bust, and now another boom on the cards (if we're not already in the middle of it), there has always been money to be made from the internet – be it through advertising, sales or subscriptions. Like most media formats, pornography has found a very lucrative home online in the darker areas of the web. Record labels and movie studios have followed suit, and even TV shows are now available for download. Even the most ludite-minded companies have had to concede that net business is the future, and have established an online presence. It's rare that a high-street chain doesn't have an online store these days, and even

the smaller retailers make sure they can receive orders via the web. With all this big business out there you'd be forgiven for assuming that every last opportunity to make money from the internet has been bled dry but, with the right marketing and an efficient iWeb site, it's still very possible to successfully trade online. Just as eBay made the community auction a global market, you can turn your iWeb site into a profitable platform with just a few simple techniques.

Even if you've never thought of using your iWeb site for sales, think what you've got to offer and give it a go. What's the worst that could happen? It's not just the business gurus who stand to benefit from the flexibility and low overheads of web marketing, either. More and more creatives are finding audiences for their art, and even racking up sales from their own sites. Whether you're a musician, painter, animator or photographer, your site can not only provide an impressive stage for your talents, but also a shop front for your product. Self-publish a book, put your GarageBand EP up for digital download or provide stylish wedding photography services. The possibilities are, quite simply, endless. Of course, iWeb doesn't

offer any e-commerce abilities as standard, so you'll have to look outside its windows at services like Woofu (see boxout) to add shopping carts and order forms to your pages. But once you're up and running, things couldn't be simpler. And the person asking for rent for your store each month is an ISP, and not a letting agent.

Unlike iDVD, it seems iWeb is Apple's current darling in the iLife line-up and should see plenty of revisions in the years to come. As a first effort, most were very impressed with Apple's debut in the consumer web design market and, if the 2.0 update is anything to go by, we'll be seeing more impressive additions soon. The web is increasingly becoming the platform of choice for developers, and it's where most of our iLife creations will be heading, rather than cramming everything on to a DVD. Blu-ray may make the difference to the current shift in the iLife app power struggle with iDVD making a triumphant return (although iBlu-ray would be an awful name), but until that time it's safe to say we'll be seeing a primary focus on iWeb.

Take a look at the websites that impress you. What is it that appeals to you, and what elements would you like to see on your own site? Pick your

PAYPAL DONATIONS

Get donations with PayPal's help
If you are registered with PayPal and want an easy way for people to make donations to your site, you can easily obtain the HTML code from the Merchant Tools section of the PayPal site. This can then be pasted into an HTML Snippet Web Widget in iWeb, which will add a Donate button to your page once published.

"With the right marketing and an efficient iWeb site, it's still very possible to successfully trade online"

The easy way to add forms and shopping carts

Sign up for a free trial at **www.wufoo.com** and have an online form for your website in minutes. With a wide range of form styles, from surveys to order forms in a variety of different themes, it has never been easier to allow users to enter details into your iWeb site. You can even integrate your forms with payment transactions through Google Checkout, Authorize.net and PayPal, so people can pay for items on your website. This could be anything from access to password protected areas of your site, physical items for sale, or digital downloads of music, movies or artwork you have made. The possibilities are limitless, from self-publishing books through to selling software and plug-ins from your own homepage.

Information entered into forms on your site can be accessed via **wufoo.com**, and you can opt for email notifications every time someone fills out a form on your site. Forms are added to iWeb through an HTML snippet, and Wufoo allows you to customise each form in a number of ways to fit it into your iWeb site's design. Once in place, a form can be used to provide survey information, site feedback or online sales.

colours, determine your content and sketch out a site map on a piece of paper. This, your Mac, and a copy of iWeb is all you need to create the iWeb site you always wanted to. Of course, don't ignore good old Google either. Something you can't do to your site you would like to? Chances are someone else has wanted to do the same, and has quite likely posted how to do it. Hunt around and you'll find all sorts of secrets you never thought possible. So forget the excuses, stop procrastinating and build your own iWeb site today.

Over the page we have provided you with another little inspirational kick: all 26 of the available iWeb themes displayed across a spread. Take a look at them, decide on the tone and mood of your site and realise just how brilliant your pages can look with very little effort. Obviously, it's best to move as far from these themes as you can in order not to produce a 'copycat' website, but by all means start with one of the themes and create your own hybrid from there. You can even copy and paste page elements between themes. The rest is up to you. Good luck.

Promote your business online
Add that professional touch when sharing info in iWeb

Recommended themes:
Add a professional touch to your iWeb site with a clean, elegant theme, such as Layered Paper, Elegant, Watercolour or Modern Frame. Perfect for providing details about a business, or offering a home for an online store

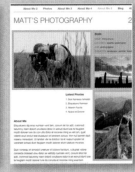

"It's handy to see how many hits your site is getting, as well as more advanced information"

Make money with AdSense
Built into iWeb is the ability to add Google AdSense adverts to your page. Set up an account within iWeb and add a variety of advert shapes to your page. These will update when published, with advertising tailored to your site's content. Every click on an advertisement on your page earns you money. Bonus!

Adding web forms
www.freedback.com provides a very convenient form-building service that enables you to create a custom form and embed it on your site. When a user submits a form on your page they will be sent to a page of your choice, and an email will be sent to inform you of the form submission details.

Is anyone visiting your site?
While you'll be informed with contact emails, blog comments and .Mac Web Gallery uploads, it's handy to see how many hits your site is getting, as well as more advanced information about your visitors – especially if you are creating a business site. The easiest method to gauge visitors to your site is to add a simple hitcounter from the iWeb Insert/Button menu. This will drop a small box onto your page that updates the hit count each time someone visits your site. For more detailed information you can use services like **Statcounter.com** and Google Analytics, and paste the HTML code into your site. The only problem with this method is that you'll have to use iTweak in order to embed the tracking code into each of your pages before stats can be generated. For more info, see **www.itweak.guimkie.com**.

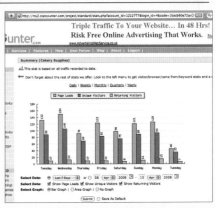

iWeb themes

All 26 of the amazing iWeb themes available are shown here, in all their glory, for your viewing pleasure. Make sure you update your software regularly, as new themes pop up from time to time…

White

Black

Golden Rod

Modern Frame

Playtime

Layered Paper

Comic Book

Bebop

Darkroom

Main Event

Gazette

Highlighter

Elegant

Notebook

Doodle

Cloud 9

Watercolour

Travel

Baby

Kids Blue

Kids Pink

Modern

Nightlife

Freestyle

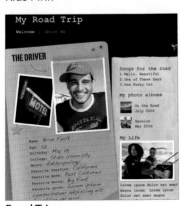
Road Trip

Formal

THEME SWITCHING

The Apple themes in iWeb make it easy to create simple yet stunning websites. Part of their appeal is that its easy to refresh your website at any time by switching themes. All it takes is a click and you're site updates.

You're never locked into a theme. Just select a different one from the theme panel and your page design updates automatically, giving your site a fresh new look.

 iWeb '08

Tutorial: Optimise iWeb videos for iPhone users

The iPhone is a booming web-browsing platform – but there are a number of limitations when it comes to movies. How do you ensure video on your iWeb site looks great on an iPhone or iPod touch?

Task: Optimise videos for your iPhone

Difficulty: Beginner

Time needed: 30 minutes

The iPhone and the iPod touch were built for playing videos, but if you've surfed some video sites on your iPhone you'll probably have encountered some big problems. First, it can be tortuous to play videos on a standard Edge mobile phone connection. Second, video previews sometimes don't appear properly. Instead of a video preview, visitors get a daunting QuickTime icon on a grey screen. And videos often aren't optimised for the iPhone's superb screen.

You can't ignore the growing importance of the iPhone, so it's crucial that any video you host on your website, whether built in iWeb or not, is optimised for iPhone use.

Adjusting video for the iPhone isn't difficult, and it's worth the effort to tailor it. After all, embedded QuickTime video played on the iPhone appears in full screen, so iPhone visitors to your site get an impressive multimedia experience.

Step-by-step | iWeb Watch videos on your iPhone

1: Export the video

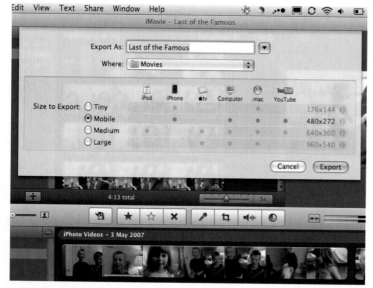

● Use iMovie to export your video in a suitable format. Select Share>Export Movie. In the resulting dialog box choose Mobile under the Size To Export options to export the iPhone-compatible video. Now click the Export button.

2: Adding to iWeb

● Open the Media browser in iWeb. Click the Movies tab and select the name of the video you just exported. Drag the video from the list over your iWeb page. Drag the handles of the video to resize it.

Optimise videos

Knowledge base

Using Web Gallery
The easiest iPhone-compatible way to share video online is to publish it as a Web Gallery directly from iMovie. The advantage is that you can export multiple versions of the same video, including those at Tiny and Mobile formats. When you connect to the Web Gallery on your iPhone, it automatically offers the appropriate video depending on your connection speed.

Optimum sizes
The optimum iPhone video dimensions, for sharp video in full-screen mode, is 480x360 for non-widescreen content. Try to get as close to that as you possibly can

Avoid the QuickTime logo
iPhone doesn't decode video until the user presses the play button on the page, so without a poster frame set users will see a grey rectangle with a QuickTime logo

Don't overload the page
You can't play a video on your iPhone until all page elements have loaded, so keep your page free of big image files and other bandwidth-hogging media

Poster frames
As the iPhone doesn't decode video until the user clicks the play button, a poster frame is a useful way to preview a still from the video while it's being loaded

Layout flexibility
The dimensions of the video on your iWeb page do not matter much for iPhone users; on playback the video will be resized automatically to fit the iPhone's screen

Playback options
These Loop and Autoplay settings govern playback on a Mac or PC browser. iPhones play videos in their own windows and seem to ignore any settings here

3: Create a poster image

4: Publish

○ To avoid presenting the visitor with a blank grey preview before they play the video on an iPhone, create a poster image for it. Open the Inspector (View>Show Inspector) and click the QuickTime icon.

○ Drag the Poster Frame slider to a suitable point in the video. This frame will be the preview icon for the video on your site. Click the Publish button to upload the site to .Mac.

 iWeb '08

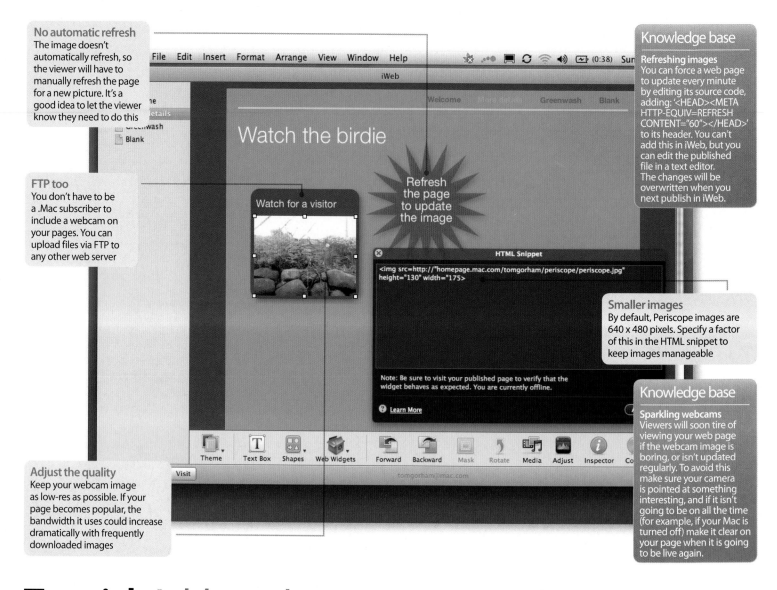

No automatic refresh
The image doesn't automatically refresh, so the viewer will have to manually refresh the page for a new picture. It's a good idea to let the viewer know they need to do this

FTP too
You don't have to be a .Mac subscriber to include a webcam on your pages. You can upload files via FTP to any other web server

Adjust the quality
Keep your webcam image as low-res as possible. If your page becomes popular, the bandwidth it uses could increase dramatically with frequently downloaded images

Knowledge base
Refreshing images
You can force a web page to update every minute by editing its source code, adding: '<HEAD><META HTTP-EQUIV=REFRESH CONTENT="60"></HEAD>' to its header. You can't add this in iWeb, but you can edit the published file in a text editor. The changes will be overwritten when you next publish in iWeb.

Smaller images
By default, Periscope images are 640 x 480 pixels. Specify a factor of this in the HTML snippet to keep images manageable

Knowledge base
Sparkling webcams
Viewers will soon tire of viewing your web page if the webcam image is boring, or isn't updated regularly. To avoid this make sure your camera is pointed at something interesting, and if it isn't going to be on all the time (for example, if your Mac is turned off) make it clear on your page when it is going to be live again.

Tutorial: Add a webcam to your iWeb page

Webcams are a great way to draw in web traffic, or even let you see what's going on at home. Adding one to iWeb couldn't be easier

Task: Add a webcam to an iWeb website
Difficulty: Beginner
Time needed: 20 minutes

You can't beat webcam sites. Adding one to your .Mac-hosted website is not only a great way to keep an eye on your home or office, but it can also be a sure-fire way of boosting visitor traffic, appealing to the voyeur in all of us. However, it's still regarded as a novelty extra rather than a fundamental feature of a website.

If you're worried that a webcam will be too much of a palaver to add, don't be – it's really not difficult to set up. The only extras .Mac users need is an iSight-compatible webcam, a copy of iWeb and the excellent £20 webcam utility, Periscope (www.freeverse.com). As the name suggests, Periscope is an easy-to-use tool that can take pictures at user-defined intervals, or snap an image when it detects noise or movement.

Follow our nine-step tutorial to make your iWeb website more professional, and hopefully increase the traffic passing through.

Step-by-step | iWeb Embed a webcam on an iWeb page using Periscope

1: Install Periscope
Download Periscope and launch it. In the opening screen, under the Capture tab, you can set your Mac up to take a picture.

2: Choose picture settings
Now, in Periscope, choose how the program takes a picture under the Capture tab. Here we've set it to take pictures at automatic intervals.

3: Send to .Mac
Under the Share tab, check the box next to .Mac. You may need to set up your .Mac settings if you haven't done so already.

4: Add the time
Check the Timestamp box to superimpose the current time on the webcam picture. This way, visitors will know when the image was taken.

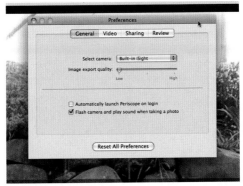

5: Reduce file size
Webcam snapshots can be hefty. Limit their size in Periscope's Preferences. Under the General tab, drag the Image export quality slider to the left.

6: Set up iWeb
In iWeb, create a new page by clicking the '+' button in the source list. Click the Web Widget button and select HTML Snippet.

7: Add the necessary code
Add this code to the Snippet window: <img src="http://homepage.mac.com/icreate/periscope/periscope.jpg". Enter your username. Click Apply.

8: Shrink the image
The width and height of the Periscope image is too big for a web page. Limit its dimensions by adding height=130, width=175 before the closing tag.

9: All is not lost
Smarten up the webcam image by dragging a shape from the window into the iWeb canvas and adding text around it.

Tutorial: Add custom links between pages in iWeb

Break free from iWeb's default navigation bar by using the hyperlink function to create your own custom links between pages, links to external sites and more

Task: Add custom links to an iWeb page
Difficulty: Beginner
Time needed: 30 minutes

The default method of navigating between your iWeb site pages is a pretty neat solution – as you add pages, iWeb automatically adds navigation links to the menu at the top of each page. However, iWeb also provides a simple method of transforming any text or image into a hyperlink that can be set to summon up another one of your pages, and these links can be formatted and arranged like any other object. Once your site is published, visitors can click on the text or image and their browser will navigate to the required page.

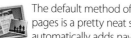

Step-by-step | iWeb Create your own custom links between pages

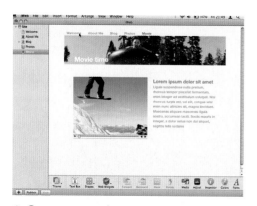

1: Create your site
It's best to set up a site with a few pages first, using the conventional default navigation bar to link between the pages.

2: Reveal inspector
To remove the first link, select a page in the sidebar. Click the 'i' button to reveal the inspector and select the Page pane.

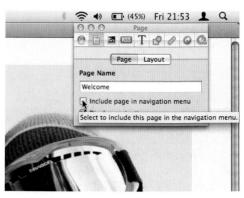

3: Remove links from header
Uncheck the Include Page In Navigation menu checkbox; the link to the current page should disappear. You can also hide the menu altogether.

4: Create new link
To create a text link, click the Text box button. Enter the required text and drag it to the right spot on the page.

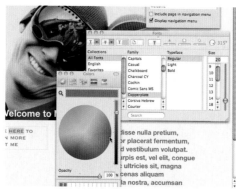

5: Format text
Use the Font menu and Colors palette to alter the appearance, then select the portion of text you want to convert to a link.

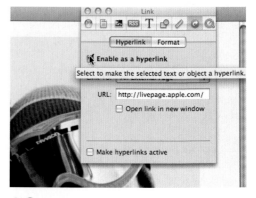

6: Convert
To convert the text, open the Link inspector pane and tick the Enable As A Hyperlink box. Click the Format tab to alter its behaviour.

Liberate your site's layout

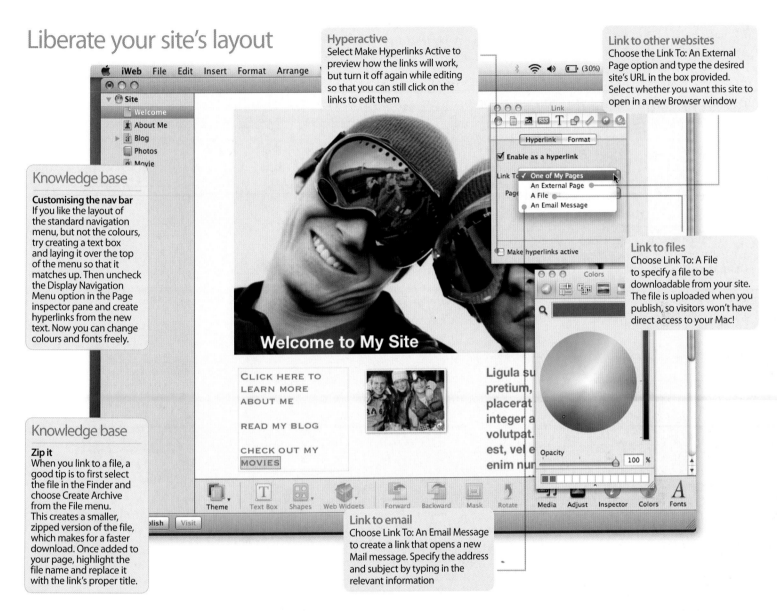

Hyperactive
Select Make Hyperlinks Active to preview how the links will work, but turn it off again while editing so that you can still click on the links to edit them

Link to other websites
Choose the Link To: An External Page option and type the desired site's URL in the box provided. Select whether you want this site to open in a new Browser window

Knowledge base

Customising the nav bar
If you like the layout of the standard navigation menu, but not the colours, try creating a text box and laying it over the top of the menu so that it matches up. Then uncheck the Display Navigation Menu option in the Page inspector pane and create hyperlinks from the new text. Now you can change colours and fonts freely.

Link to files
Choose Link To: A File to specify a file to be downloadable from your site. The file is uploaded when you publish, so visitors won't have direct access to your Mac!

Knowledge base

Zip it
When you link to a file, a good tip is to first select the file in the Finder and choose Create Archive from the File menu. This creates a smaller, zipped version of the file, which makes for a faster download. Once added to your page, highlight the file name and replace it with the link's proper title.

Link to email
Choose Link To: An Email Message to create a link that opens a new Mail message. Specify the address and subject by typing in the relevant information

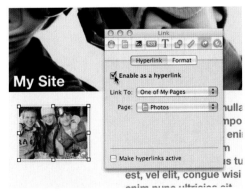

7: Select destination
Four options appear in the Link To menu. Select One of My Pages and choose the relevant page from the pop-up menu.

8: Picture this
You can also make images into links – simply select the required image and click Enable As A Hyperlink in the Link inspector.

9: I link, therefore I am
Continue in a similar vein for all the pages in your site, until all required links between pages are established.

Tutorial: Create a YouTube movie gallery in iWeb

You don't need a .Mac account to host a movie portfolio on your website – not when you can embed YouTube videos in your own iWeb-created gallery

Fans of iMovie '08 need no telling just how easy it is to upload movies to their .Mac web space and import those movies into iWeb. But if you don't have a .Mac account – or enough free space on your iDisk – what other options are there?

One of the best ways to showcase your video's content is to use YouTube, the online video-sharing service. And thanks to iWeb '08's web snippets, you can embed YouTube videos on your iWeb-created site. With iWeb's excellent templates and layout tools, you can create an impressive video gallery with ease.

Task: Create a YouTube movie gallery in iWeb
Difficulty: Beginner
Time needed: 20 minutes

Step-by-step | iWeb Create an iWeb video gallery with YouTube

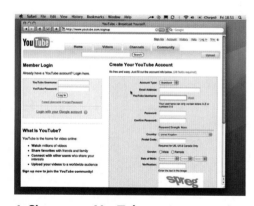

1: Sign up to YouTube
If you haven't already signed up for a YouTube account, visit its website at **www.youtube.com** and click the Sign Up link to register.

2: Enter video details
Click the yellow Upload link. On the next page, enter information about the video in the fields and click the Upload A Video button.

3: Copy the HTML snippet
Click the Choose File button and select the video to upload. Once it has completed uploading, copy the text contained in the Embed field.

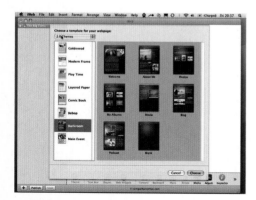

4: Create a new page
Open iWeb and use the Template gallery to create a new page or a site to host your gallery. Here we've chosen one of the Movie themes.

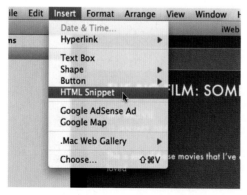

5: Paste the HTML snippet
To embed the YouTube content in your web page, you need to paste the embedded link into your iWeb page. Choose Insert>HTML Snippet.

6: Paste the snippet
In the HTML Snippet window, paste the text copied in step four. Click the Apply button and a dragable movie preview appears on your page.

YouTube and iWeb combined

Easy alignment
Use the built-in automatic alignment tools to make sure your videos are all neatly aligned with each other

Built-in controls
When you upload your site the videos are hosted on YouTube, but each video can be controlled from your own website

Knowledge base

The limitations of YouTube
YouTube is a fantastic resource for uploading videos, but it isn't without limitations compared to .Mac's web gallery. You can't upload a video to YouTube longer than ten minutes, or greater than 100Mb in size. Longer scenes have to be split up. Resolution is limited to 320 by 240 pixels, a restriction that doesn't apply to .Mac content.

THE BIG FILM: SOME OF MY FAVOURITE FILMS

A GALLERY OF THE BEST SHORT FILMS I'VE MADE - OR OTHERS HAVE

11 JANUARY 2008

These are some of the movies that I've always loved – just click on them to play.

x: 15 px   y: 241 px

HTML Snippet

```
<object width="425" height="355"><param name="movie" value="http://
www.youtube.com/v/VV3Xuv_jQtY&rel=1"></param> <param name="wmode"
value="transparent"></param> <embed src="http://www.youtube.com/v/
VV3Xuv_jQtY&rel=1" type="application/x-shockwave-flash" wmode="transparent"
width="425" height="355"></embed></object>
```

Note: Be sure to visit your published page to verify that the widget behaves as expected.

Learn More

Pasting code
If your scripting skills are up to it, you can amend the code that appears in the Snippets box when you double-click the YouTube preview

YouTube preview
A preview of the YouTube video appears as a single frame from the movie. You can't edit this preview in iWeb

---

7: Add more videos
Repeat to add more content from YouTube. You can link to other YouTube videos by copying the text from the Embed link on their pages.

8: Adjust page size
As you add videos, adjust page dimensions. Choose View>Show Inspector and click Page Inspector. Click Layout and enter larger values in the Content fields.

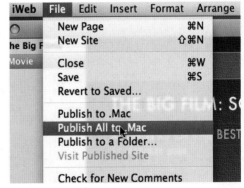

9: Upload the site
Select File>Publish to .Mac to upload your site to the web. Visitors can now browse and view YouTube videos within your web page.

GarageBand

Features

Tutorials

There's no doubt that GarageBand is a
total powerhouse. It has an interface that is
extremely easy to use and yet has features
that appear in professional software costing
hundreds of pounds.

BECOME A GARAGE MASTER!

Create music and effects for your iLife projects, learn an instrument and much more...

Apple created the iLife suite of applications back in 2003, but it wasn't until the following year that GarageBand joined the family. Having recently acquired German pro audio specialists Emagic, Apple based GarageBand on technology found in its industry leading sequencer software Logic, and so made the first music creation and recording software it had ever created. Best of all, it was included for free with all new Macs, meaning that as well as movies, DVDs and photo albums you could now make music on any Mac for little or no extra cost.

As GarageBand has evolved it has taken on more and more features, such as time stretching, notation, podcasting, automation, movie scoring, ringtones and, most recently, Artist Lessons. As a music application it's suitable for everything from quick recordings or sketches to creating music beds for podcasts, audio and MIDI editing, and even full-blown productions. One curious thing about GarageBand is that many of its features are located just out of sight, in a menu or perhaps an expandable window. And as such, it might not at first look particularly exciting. But this is far from the truth – in fact it's a powerhouse of music production, with a surprisingly gentle learning curve. It's able to record from your Mac's built-in soundcard and output through its speakers, so at a very basic level you don't need any extra tools to make music. And thanks to the loops you get included you can be up and running in no

time. With this guide we'll show you how to get creative with GarageBand, how to add soundtracks to your movies, create your own podcasts, add effects and virtual instruments and mix your tracks. You don't have to be an expert to make music, so read on to find out how it's done.

Like other music recording and production packages, GarageBand has a project area that contains audio and MIDI tracks and it works on a left-to-right timeline system. The playhead represents the playback of the project and the tracks, ordered from top to bottom, represent the layers of the music or podcast. Any loops or parts that exist at the same point on the timeline will be heard at the same time – for example, drums, bass and piano might typically be layered up to form the backing of a track, then guitars or vocals recorded over the top.

For the most part, GarageBand keeps all its different sections and browsers within the confines of a single main window, and the sections can be shown and hidden using the Track and Control menus, resized by dragging the boundaries and, in many cases, scrolled to access more of a section without having to resize. Keeping pop-up windows to a minimum makes the software easier to navigate, and means that it's possible to work efficiently on a laptop where screen space tends to be at a premium.

The Track view is where you build the structure of a project, adding tracks and either recording or dragging and dropping parts into them. Each track can be renamed

BAND

No skills? No problem!

GarageBand '09 has a great feature called Artist Lessons. From the Start screen choose Lesson Store. You can now choose from either free basic piano or guitar lessons, or advanced lessons from well-known musicians that you can preview. These videos cost £3.95 and can be downloaded on any Intel-based Mac. They appear in a special screen with easy-to-follow tools to help you.

What you'll need for...
• Podcasting

Podcasting is one of the simpler things you can do in GarageBand. To record your voice onto an audio track you just need a microphone, or even the Mac's own built-in one, plus maybe some loops or preset podcast music beds to use as backing music.

To send the finished podcast to either the iTunes Store or another website you will need an internet connection.

When composing a song you will probably start with a beat then layer up more elements like guitars, vocals, bass and keyboards to build up the production. Keep an eye on the structure to see how the song is working in terms of verses, choruses and instrumentation.

"With any track, if you select the Edit control, you can change the source instrument, the effect types and the settings"

to help you keep up with what's going on, and they also have a Level Meter, Volume slider, left/right pan control and several buttons including Record Enable, Mute and Solo, Lock and View Automation. Automation is the process of having the software re-create movements for you – say, for example, bringing the volume of a track up or down at different points in a project. Doing this by hand is very difficult, but use Automation and it's easy. It has many applications, such as panning a signal from left to right over time or changing effect settings. So you might want to gradually increase the amount of reverb on a vocal part and then have it brought back to a low setting. To do this you would expand the Automation Track, which would then appear underneath the desired music track, and use the mouse to draw in points.

Each point has a different value and GarageBand will transition between them. The Transport controls running along the bottom of the window are crucial for controlling playback and there's a loop control for repeating a section, as well as a master volume control. By clicking in the LCD style display you can change the visual feedback to display information about the current project time, the chord you have played or the project's tempo and time signature. In the bottom-right you can also switch between the Loop and Media browsers. From either of these you can drag-and-drop loops and sounds from your hard drive, iTunes library or the bundled loop collection straight into your project. You can also drop images into podcasts from your iPhoto library and movies from your Movies folder if you're creating

a score. It's easy to instantly preview MIDI or audio loops by clicking on the blue or green square that appears next to them, so you can audition them without committing to use them in a project.

By double-clicking on any audio or MIDI track in a project you can show its track controls section in the panel on the right of the screen. If it's a software instrument track, you can choose from a selection of preset track types – combining a software instrument and effects – all ready to go. If it's an audio track you can select a track preset containing a ready-made effects chain, for a blues guitar sound for example. With any track, if you select the Edit control, you can change the source instrument, the effect types and the settings, and then of course save the track preset under a new name for future use. For audio tracks you can set the input channels on which you want to record, and there's a handy Automatic Level control to make sure your input isn't too loud or quiet.

The Share menu at the top is how you get your finished projects out of GarageBand, and there are shortcuts to send mixed tracks straight to

MAKE MUSIC ON YOUR MAC
GARAGEBAND
NO EXPERIENCE NEEDED

Find your way around GarageBand

The track list
All the tracks in your project will live here, including audio and MIDI, podcast and movie tracks

The playhead
The playhead controls the playback of a project. Drag it left and right to zoom forwards or backwards

The Loop browser
All GarageBand loops that are supplied or that you add later yourself appear here, and are easy to search by category

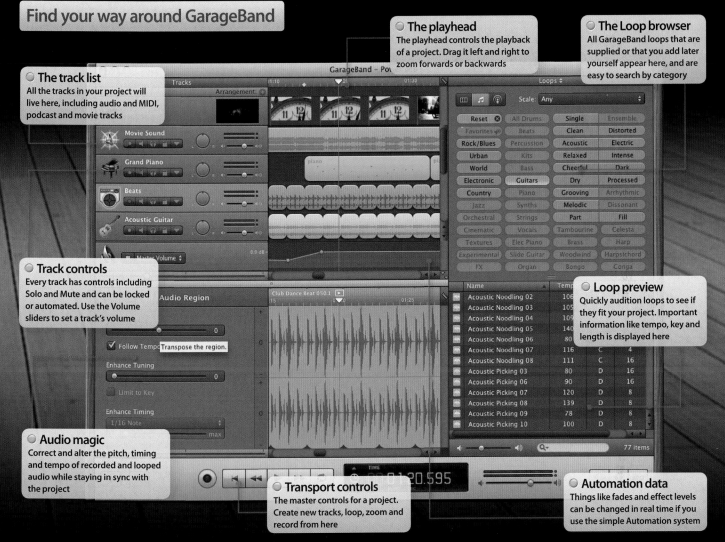

Track controls
Every track has controls including Solo and Mute and can be locked or automated. Use the Volume sliders to set a track's volume

Loop preview
Quickly audition loops to see if they fit your project. Important information like tempo, key and length is displayed here

Audio magic
Correct and alter the pitch, timing and tempo of recorded and looped audio while staying in sync with the project

Transport controls
The master controls for a project. Create new tracks, loop, zoom and record from here

Automation data
Things like fades and effect levels can be changed in real time if you use the simple Automation system

1: Track presets
Click on an effect's Preset tab to choose from a list of ready-made effects set ups.

2: Equalization
You can use the EQ plug-in to either raise or lower certain frequencies on a track.

3: Compressor
Double-click on an effect to open its window, where you can make detailed settings.

4: Virtual instruments
Use the built-in instruments to generate sounds like pianos, organs or brass.

iTunes as music or ringtones, a movie with a new soundtrack to iWeb or iDVD, or to export the song to a file or burn it to CD.

There are many different kinds of projects that you might want to undertake with GarageBand, and the software itself has been gradually growing since its creation to incorporate all sorts of new features. It's a curious application because although it looks friendly and inviting, it is actually capable of some fairly advanced techniques like musical notation and time and pitch stretching – things that are usually only found in more 'professional' software. You might be surprised to know that, although it comes free with new Macs or as part of iLife, GarageBand is quite widely used by music pros for working on the move with a laptop, either jotting down musical sketches, audio editing or just brainstorming through ideas. Unlike most music software GarageBand doesn't use any kind of security device like a dongle, so there's no chance of losing it. Plus, since it's designed for the Mac, you know that you're not going to have any issues or problems with driver or

►

Feature: GarageBand

Set up devices and inputs

• Connect the device
Connect your audio interface and make sure that, if they are needed, any drivers are correctly installed and up to date. Open Audio MIDI Setup to check that the device is working.

• Configure GarageBand
Go into GarageBand's Preferences and locate the Audio/MIDI section. Make sure the device you have connected is chosen for audio input and output.

• Arm the track
Select the audio track and make sure the input channel that's selected is the same one your mic or instrument is plugged into. Play or speak and you should see the level meters jumping.

Specific projects | Making a podcast

When making a podcast you would probably include some backing music as a music bed, perhaps automated to be quiet when you're speaking. You can also embed artwork that is also used as chapter markers, and even embed URLs that become clickable at certain points in the podcast.

interface conflicts. Add to this the fact that it is designed to be seamlessly inter-operable with the other iLife applications and you've got a one-stop music production solution sitting right there on your Mac.

To its original feature set, GarageBand 2 added the ability to use musical notation – essential for anyone working with classically trained musicians who might need to read music off a stave rather than a screen. It also featured the ability to record up to eight tracks

at once, making it useful for recording, say, a whole drum kit with multiple mics, or several musicians playing together. Or course, for this you'd need an audio interface with up to eight inputs – but they are relatively common and inexpensive. Version 2 also included the ability to automate various parameters such as volume and pan, to transpose audio and MIDI and to import MIDI files. Last but not least in this impressive upgrade of features were tools for the timing and pitch of recordings.

GarageBand 3 brought podcasting to the masses, with new podcasting features that made it simple to embed artwork, chapter markers and even URLs into your productions. It also had a new set of music beds, sound effects and the 'ducking' effect, which automatically reduces the volume of a backing track when you start to speak, just like you hear on commercial radio. Version 3 also came with over 200 one-shot sound effects and jingles, plus the ability to integrate with iChat to record remote interviews, which is a really handy feature.

In the fourth version, released as part of iLife '08, GarageBand was able to automate instruments and tempo, to create and export iPhone ringtones and the new Magic GarageBand feature. This is designed for people who want to get up and running straight away, and presents you with a choice of preset musical styles like blues, latin and rock. If you choose one you will see a 'stage' full of instruments, each of which you can customise and all of them play preset musical parts for you to jam over. If you like you can even switch to regular view and work with the project as a conventional GarageBand project.

GarageBand 5 is part of iLife '09 and saw some interface and workflow refinements, as well as project templates for much quicker and easier setup. It also features Artist Lessons, a selection of free and fairly inexpensive downloadable videos where leading musicians take you through music lessons at different levels. When you're viewing these you have many options, such as the ability to loop and repeat parts

Specific Projects | Scoring a movie

By importing a movie file into GarageBand you can view it while composing music over the top, using loops, software instruments and real recordings like vocals or guitars to underscore the on-screen action. When you're finished, export the whole project to disk or to iDVD for burning.

What you'll need for...
• Podcasting

GarageBand ships with some great sound effects, which you can find by opening the Loop browser and clicking the FX tab to filter the list.

	Name	Tempo	Key	Beats	Fav
	Ambient Synth 01	124	–	4	
	Beach Sound Effect 01	–	–	00:40	
	Crowd Applause 01	–	–	00:28	
	Crowd Applause 02	–	–	00:33	
	Crowd Sound Effect 01	–	–	00:38	
	Crowd Sound Effect 02	–	–	00:37	
	Office Sound Effect 01	139	–	4	
	Phone Sound Effect 01	–	–	00:01	
	Phone Sound Effect 02	–	–	00:24	
	Phone Sound Effect 03	–	–	00:25	
	Sci Fi Texture 01	–	–	00:06	
	Sci Fi Texture 02	–	–	00:07	
	Sci Fi Texture 03	–	–	00:17	

To import your own sounds you could drag them from the Media browser or desktop then add audio plug-ins to mangle the sound. Or you could time stretch and pitch stretch the audio to make it sound weird.

of the video, a tuner for your guitar, and the ability to set the volume levels of each part of the presentation. It's designed to be as easy as possible, and there are some free lessons on offer to get you started learning either the piano or guitar.

GarageBand has two basic kinds of tracks – 'real instrument' tracks, which record audio from either your built-in mic, an external mic or from a source like a guitar through an audio interface, and 'software instrument' tracks that are triggered by MIDI from an external keyboard or by using the built-in MIDI loops. The advantage to using software instruments is that they are guaranteed to be in tune and sound great, since they exist virtually within your Mac. Any track can be edited and you can use the excellent built-in effects like reverbs, delays, equalizers and distortions to create special effects. There's even a special guitarist section where you can use a virtual stomp box of guitar pedals to get a really good electric guitar sound. Of course, you're not limited to just recording

"Mixing tracks is quite simple, and you can use the Volume sliders on each track to change the relative gain, and solo or mute tracks"

guitars through these – you could experiment and try recording your voice through them for some weird and wonderful results.

Typically you might mix and match these two types of tracks in a music project, perhaps using looped beats to underscore a production, and then add keyboard parts from a MIDI keyboard through a software instrument and finally guitars and vocals onto a 'real' instrument track over the top. Mixing tracks is quite simple, and you can use the Volume sliders on each track to change the relative gain of each track, or solo or mute tracks as you wish. Finally there's a master track where you control the output of the whole production, and you can add global effects (which will process every track at the same time) as well as performing creative automation, say

to fade a track in or out. When you're done you can export a track directly to iTunes or out to disk, or burn it straight to a CD. Movies you've added new soundtracks to can be exported to iWeb for upload to the web or to iDVD for burning to disc using any of its excellent themes.

Composing music for film projects is something that, until recently, was the preserve of professionals and those with access to top-end equipment and studios. You may be surprised to learn that GarageBand actually has some great tools in this area and provides pretty much everything you need to start creating music for your own movies. At its simplest, this involves importing a movie file into a movie track, of which you can have one per project. Then, you record and compose

▶

What you'll need for...
• Podcast jingles

GarageBand installs by default with some jingles. These are entertaining bits of music that you can drag from the Loops section into an audio track when making a podcast to begin and end it, or to bridge between different sections of the show.

Jingles are just regular audio files, so you can actually use any music as a jingle. If no jingles appear on your Mac then you may have to re-run the installer, selecting only the jingles option.

What you'll need for...
• Songwriting

The important thing when it comes to songwriting is a sense of structure. Zoom out to get an overview of your song and see how it fits together.

Consider an intro, verses, choruses, a middle eight and an outro. Is it too long or too short? Could it be made more interesting by adding harmonies? Is it too cluttered with competing parts? Is it catchy enough? These are all things to think about when writing songs.

What you'll need for...
• Recording real instruments

To record real instruments and vocals you will need some way to get sound into the Mac. This could be the Mac's line-in or, preferably, a proper audio interface. These start at as little as £50. Many don't even require drivers and draw power over USB. Plug in a mic or a jack lead and you're all set to record pro-quality sound.

your music along with the movie, viewing the video in a special window as you work to help you see what's going on. You don't have to be a musical genius to do this of course, and that's where loops come in. By dragging loops from the browser into a project, you can quickly 'paint' a drum part, for example, over several minutes and be sure that it will loop seamlessly and stay perfectly in time. As well as the loops that come with GarageBand there are many sample collections available, some of which come in Apple Loops format, ready sliced, processed and tagged to drop straight into GarageBand projects. They are fairly inexpensive, cover many musical styles and will provide you with hours of new inspiration. When you start a new project, one of your options is to use a project template called Movie. This will automatically open with all the

> ## "By dragging loops from the browser into a project, you can quickly 'paint' a drum part and be sure that it will loop seamlessly"

right screen elements visible like your Movies folder and, importantly, any movies you have made in iMovie '08 or '09 and shared to the Media browser. You can drag a movie into GarageBand's Movie Track and its soundtrack will be automatically split off and displayed as a separate audio track. It's then easy to drag loops into the timeline to build up a musical soundtrack. Or, to plug in a MIDI keyboard or a real instrument like a guitar or a microphone and record some original material over the movie. This can really help you to achieve a unique end product that won't sound like anyone else. The video playback window can

be made to float by double-clicking on its track icon and, once it's floating, you can manually resize it. This is great if you have a second monitor and you want to watch the film at full size while you compose. By using the Video Markers feature, revealed by double-clicking in the Movie Track's control section, you can add markers that help you navigate longer projects. After all, different parts of a film require different pieces of music or different atmospheres, so you will probably want to zoom around quite a lot. Remember that you can easily copy and paste whole sections of music around by selecting them on the

MAKE MUSIC ON YOUR MAC
GARAGEBAND
NO EXPERIENCE NEEDED

Magic GarageBand

Magic GarageBand is designed for those who just want to jam away from the word go without worrying about setting anything up. Choose a style and the software will load the relevant instruments and parts for you to accompany on guitar, keys or vocals. You can even swap instruments by clicking on them.

Recording vocals

GarageBand can record audio in through your Mac's built-in microphone, but for better quality you will need to connect either a USB microphone or a USB audio interface and connect a regular microphone to it. Then it's simply a case of creating a new audio track, making sure it's set to read from the correct input and hitting Record. Most interfaces also handle MIDI, or you may want to use a USB MIDI keyboard that can carry the note data from the keys you play to be recorded on MIDI tracks. It can then play back software instruments like pianos or synths.

Add loops to GarageBand

• Select your loops

Gather together the loops you want to add to the library. If they are on a CD or DVD, copy them to the desktop or a secondary drive.

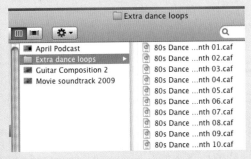

• Drag the loops

Drag the loops or the folder containing the loops from the Finder into the Loop browser in GarageBand. You'll then be told that the loops will be moved into the Apple Loops folder.

• Drag single loops

Individual audio files can be dragged into the Loop browser to be converted to loops. You are prompted to rename the file as well as adding tags and choosing whether it is to be a loop or a one-shot sound.

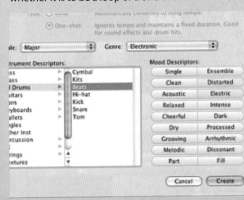

Musical notation

Scoring is traditionally quite difficult, but GarageBand puts all the tools you need at your fingertips. With a MIDI part played in or dragged and dropped, double-clicking it will normally open it in Piano Roll view. But if you click Score View alongside it, you can view the MIDI notes on a musical stave. If you play back the project you will see the playhead pass over the notes. You can pick up one or more notes on the stave and right-click to alter the note type, as well as dragging left or right and up or down to change the position and pitch of the note. You'll even hear the results played as you drag them.

timeline and dragging them to a new location while holding down the Option key to save time. It could be that you want to write some music for someone else to play, like a cellist or a piano player. Many musicians are unfamiliar with musical notation, but with GarageBand it's easy. If you have a MIDI part that you have perhaps played in by hand or got from a pre-recorded loop, you can double-click it to open it in the MIDI editor, then press the Score tab to view it on a stave. If you then select Edit>Print, you can print the musical score or export it as a PDF, all properly formatted for other musicians to read. By clicking on the notes and other musical figures while the score is still in its editable form, you can change the notes, rests, ties and many other elements by using the symbol palette that pops up. By selecting notes you can drag their durations left or right to

make them longer or shorter. An absolute must for those of a classical music background and essential for anyone serious about selling their music for film or television production.

When your soundtrack is complete, you have several options. If you choose Share>Export Movie To Disk, you get to choose from various different size and quality options to output the movie complete with its new soundtrack. There are settings for iPod, Apple TV and more, plus the option to manually choose compression settings if you're comfortable with that. Alternatively you could send the movie with its new soundtrack directly to iDVD for burning, or to iWeb to upload to your MobileMe account or other FTP site. You can also export the movie to iTunes, ready to be played on your Mac, iPod, iPhone or Apple TV with a simple sync required to add them to your chosen device.

▶

Specific projects | Recording electric guitar

GarageBand '09 has a preset available to start a new electric guitar project, which will create an audio track complete with a classic set of stomp box effects and an amp. Create some beats and maybe a bassline and riff away over the top through the effects.

What you'll need for...
• **Soundtracks**

GarageBand's built-in software instruments are great for scoring, and of course you'll need a film to work with as well. The software is quite happy running everything together so you can compose music to picture without leaving GarageBand.

An audio interface will be necessary to record some good quality guitar or vocals, and a MIDI keyboard to play the built-in software instruments.

Hidden behind GarageBand's friendly interface are some more advanced features and techniques that might surprise you. Musical notation is something that many modern musicians, even those with some classical training, aren't too familiar with. However, transcribing MIDI parts to a musical stave can be very useful sometimes – especially when you need to write music for others to play. In the film scoring world, musical scores are still very much an important part of the working process. At the other end of the scale, you might just want to print a score out for someone who is learning to play. Either way, it's possible in GarageBand. There are also a few other tricks on offer; one is to use templates to get up and running quickly. Let's say you always like to write to a beat and use a piano and a guitar. Create a project with a drum loop already loaded, a software instrument track with a piano connected, and a guitar track with your favourite pedals already attached as insert effects. Instead of having to set it up by hand you can be off

recording in seconds, spending more time being creative and less time pressing buttons. It's also a good idea, if you have set up a track just the way you like it, to save the instrument or track as a preset using the Save button at the base of the Track Inspector section. If you are a guitarist you might want to use GarageBand's built-in tuner, which you can access by selecting it in the LCD-style display at the base of the window. Notes you play – or even sing – into the software will now be displayed so you can get perfect tuning every time.

iCandy
iPhone 3G

iPhone 3G

We're quite prepared to acknowledge the iPhone 3G as
Apple's finest 2008 release and, possibly, its best product yet.

Tutorial: Use Artist Lessons in GarageBand '09

With the iLife '09 suite, GarageBand not only gets a fresh new look, but also a brand new purpose – as an educational tool…

Task: Buy, download and use Artist Lessons
Difficulty: Beginner
Time needed: 20 minutes

Just when you thought that there was nothing else that Apple could add to GarageBand, it comes up with an idea that puts a whole new spin on the basic purpose of the software. Not content with merely adding bespoke lessons in basic piano and guitar, presented by Apple's own teacher, the new version of the software takes the education concept even further by having actual recording artists teaching you their songs step-by-step, one-to-one.

These Artist Lessons do not come bundled with the software – they are available to download from Apple's online store at a cost of £3.95. If you want a taste of a lesson, however, you can try the free basic lessons that come with GarageBand '09. At the time of writing there are still only eight to choose from, but if you want to expand your repertoire with one of the featured songs, or you just want to fantasise about being alone in a room with Sara Bareilles and a piano, here's how to go about it!

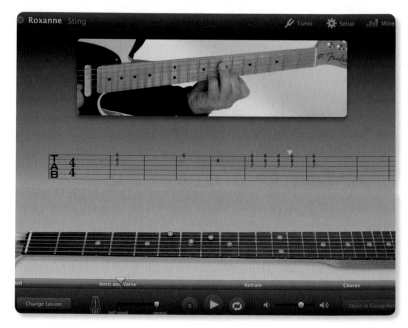

Step-by-step | GarageBand Artist Lessons

1: Access the Lesson Store

From GarageBand's new opening screen, select Lesson Store from the sidebar and click the Artist Lessons button at the top of the window. Clicking Preview will give you an idea of whether you want to go ahead or not.

2: The hard bit

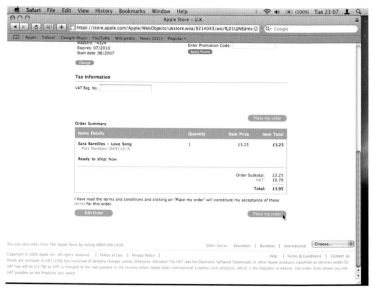

Press the desired lesson's Add To Cart button and click Checkout. This opens Safari and routes you to the Apple Store, where you'll be asked to log in and enter your payment details. Click Place My Order to complete the transaction.

Music lessons in GB

Modes definitely
In Learn mode, the various chords and sections of the song are outlined, while Play mode features a full backing band for you to play along with

Mix it up
Use the Mixer panel to solo, mute or alter the volume of the band, the teacher, or yourself

Regain control
The lessons effectively monopolise your Mac. To get back to normal running click the X button and you will return to the intro screen

Knowledge base

Use cycle mode
To loop a section of on-screen notation, enable the cycle mode, then click underneath the first measure of the section you want to loop. Hold the Shift key and click the remaining measures until the whole region is highlighted. The lesson will then cycle round that segment, allowing you to practise it indefinitely.

Notation, notation, notation
The lessons are totally interactive, each note or chord played can be set to be displayed on-screen underneath the tutorial video window in the notation type of your choice

Transport of delight
Skip to the required section of the lesson by dragging the playhead along the timeline bar. You can select on-screen measures and enable the cycle mode to loop a required section

Slow it down
When playing along, use the Tempo slider to slow the track down if necessary, then you can slowly build back up to normal speed as your playing improves

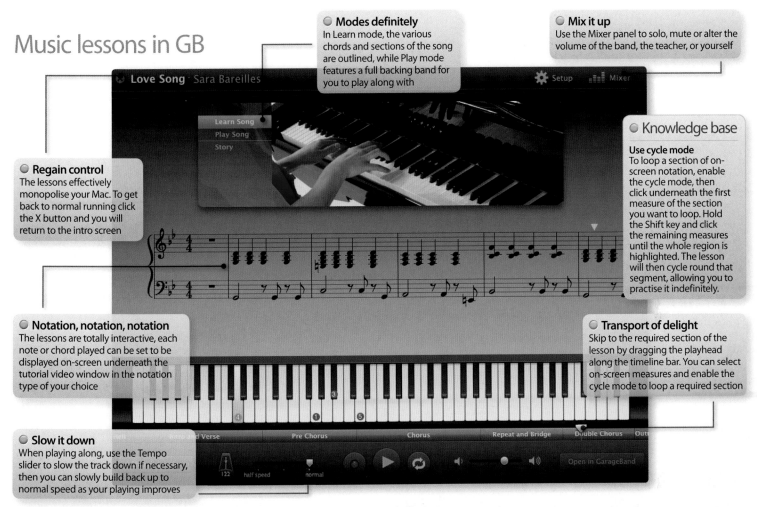

3: Download

Click the Download button in the Thank You window that appears. This will download and install the lesson to your computer. Once the download is complete, simply double-click to run the lesson.

4: Setup

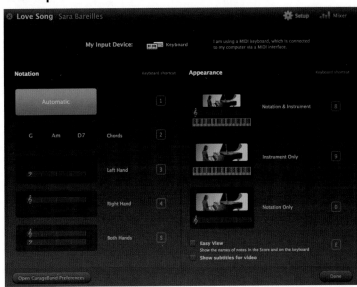

Click Setup to access the various view options, determining whether you view the instrument and notation along with the video. There are also options for left-handed versions and subtitles.

Tutorial: Set up guitar stompboxes in GarageBand

The new features in GarageBand allow you to add vintage effects when recording guitar parts so you can lay down classic sounding licks any time you want

Task: Set up an effects rig for recording guitar parts
Difficulty: Beginner
Time needed: 20 minutes

 GarageBand '09 has had more than just a cosmetic makeover; Apple has decided to take the already awesome engine of this music workstation and add some really impressive new features. One of these is the ability to create a custom guitar rig from synthetic stompboxes modelled on vintage equipment. Previously, to do this you would have needed to buy third-party software and run it as a plug-in, but now it's all right there and available as soon as you load GarageBand. The effects are easy to load, control and manage, so you can really add a bit of extra sparkle to guitar tracks with minimum effort. On top of that you also get to choose from a set of vintage modelled amps so you can further perfect the sound you want. We'll take you through the set-up procedure so you're off to a head start, but the rest is up to you. To get the exact sound you want from your axe it's well worth taking a while to go through all the effects to see what they offer. Rock on.

Step-by-step | GarageBand Stompboxes

1: Grab your axe

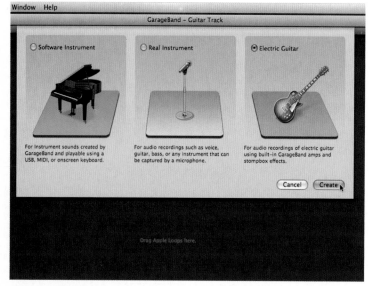

● Set up your guitar so that you're ready to record. Normally this requires a special USB guitar lead or an audio interface. Load your existing or new GarageBand project and hit the plus button to add a new track. Click Electric Guitar and then Create.

2: All about the panel

● Your new track will be created and on the right you'll see a new panel where you can select amps and effects. If it's not visible click on the 'i' to bring it up. Click on an effect to bring it into the bottom window and change the settings. Double-click to see all effects.

Create a stompbox in GB

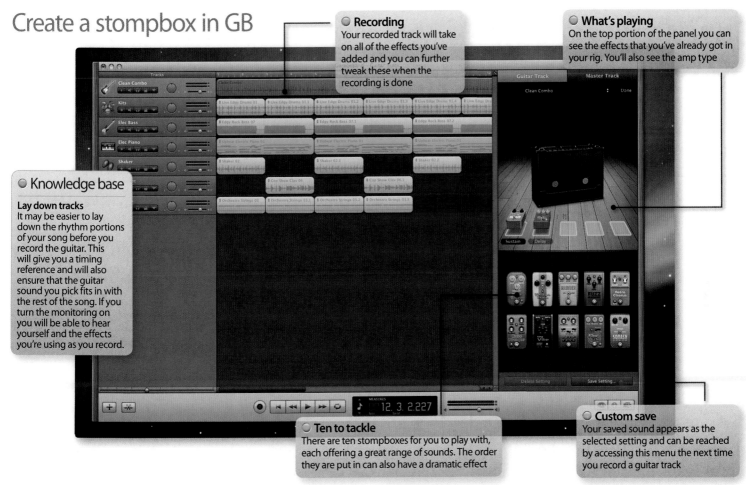

Recording
Your recorded track will take on all of the effects you've added and you can further tweak these when the recording is done

What's playing
On the top portion of the panel you can see the effects that you've already got in your rig. You'll also see the amp type

Knowledge base

Lay down tracks
It may be easier to lay down the rhythm portions of your song before you record the guitar. This will give you a timing reference and will also ensure that the guitar sound you pick fits in with the rest of the song. If you turn the monitoring on you will be able to hear yourself and the effects you're using as you record.

Ten to tackle
There are ten stompboxes for you to play with, each offering a great range of sounds. The order they are put in can also have a dramatic effect

Custom save
Your saved sound appears as the selected setting and can be reached by accessing this menu the next time you record a guitar track

3: Drag and drop

● With all of the effects showing you can pick which one you would like to add to your rig next. Then just drag and drop it into the window above. You can also drag effects into a different order from here, as that will affect the sound too.

4: Save that sound

● Once you've got the perfect sound you can save it as a preset by clicking the Save Setting button, naming your sound and then clicking Save. Try and pick names that are easy to remember and similar to the sound the guitar makes, like Light Fuzz and Chorus. Now you can recall the sound any time you like.

Tutorial: Create ringtones from a template

A feature in GarageBand '09 makes it even easier to create a ringtone for your iPhone without any of the previous hassle. Here's how to make ringtones from a template

My First Ringtone.m4r

Task: Create an iPhone ringtone in GarageBand

Difficulty: Beginner

Time needed: 10 minutes

There's been a long-running saga over user-created iPhone ringtones, starting with third-party apps that made it possible, then Apple's somewhat flawed method of buying ringtones from the iTunes Store. Then the possibility to use GarageBand for ringtone creation came into play and things got that bit easier.

Now, the GarageBand method just got even simpler with a preset template option that puts everything you need in one place, so you can quickly throw together a musical snippet ready to be added to iTunes and synced to your phone. For this tutorial, we'll be using a preset jingle from the GarageBand Loops library, but it's just as easy to record an instrument using your Mac's built-in microphone. Regardless of the ringtone style you choose, this tip will help you save time and make the most of your iPhone and GarageBand.

Step-by-step | GarageBand Make iPhone ringtones from a template

1: Prepare the project
Launch GarageBand and select iPhone Ringtone from the side panel. Now select Example Ringtone to load a default ringtone. Hit the Choose button to begin and choose a name and location for your project.

2: Basic setup
GarageBand will load with an example ringtone. There is a single loop on the timeline and a yellow Cycle Region set that determines the length of the ringtone. Delete this existing loop.

Produce a ringtone in GarageBand
Use templates in GarageBand to make iPhone ringtones

Real audio & instruments
If you fancy getting a bit more creative, why not add an instrument track or vocal recording to your ringtone? You're free to add as many tracks as you like

Cycle Region
This yellow region can be turned on and off by clicking the Cycle button at the bottom of the interface. It will loop any audio within it, which is perfect for previewing a ringtone and required for exporting

Knowledge base
Advanced options
You can add as many tracks as you like to your ringtone and even include your own voice and instruments if you wish. You can also add non-copy protected music to a ringtone too by dragging it to the timeline and cutting it down to fit. This rules out most songs downloaded from iTunes, but anything you've ripped from CD should work fine.

Tempo and time
Click on the note icon on this window and select Time so you can see your project ordered in seconds. This will help you stay within the 40-second limit

Lots of loops
There are hundreds of effects and loops available within the GarageBand Loop browser (accessed by clicking the Eye button in the bottom-right) that are perfect for mixing a great ringtone or alert sound

3: Choose your sound
You can now add a new loop or set of loops from the Loop browser by dragging them to the timeline, or record your own. Make sure whatever you choose is within the yellow Cycle Region.

4: Send to iTunes
Check your loop by playing it back and make sure it loops properly (extend the yellow Cycle Region if needed, but no longer than 40 seconds). Now head to Share>Send Ringtone To iTunes.

Create your own iLife sounds

With much more than music-making on the menu, it's time to dig deeper and get more from GarageBand

"Did you know that GarageBand has far more to offer than simple musical composition?"

So you've made pretty good use of the iLife apps, but you've never really dabbled with GarageBand. Perhaps you don't have a musical bone in your body or are quite content dropping iTunes tracks into movies and slideshows in order to provide adequate backing.

This is all well and good, but did you know that GarageBand has far more to offer than simple musical composition? While it is the ultimate practise tool for the amateur musician, more and more professionals are finding its intuitive interface and no-nonsense performance a very easy way to turn everything from ideas to complete compositions into pro-sounding products.

As you will see from our 'Artist tip' boxouts over the next few pages, GarageBand provides a veritable arsenal of tools for all kinds of production purposes, all wrapped up in the kind of slick application we've come to expect from Apple.

But what if you've never played an instrument, are tone deaf and can't get your head around music? Fear not. If you like, you can even forget about music in GarageBand entirely. Not only is there the opportunity to record podcasts in iLife's Audio app, but you can go so far as to shun all composition work in favour of creating brilliant sounds for your movie and DVD projects, without having to know the difference between staccato and legatto.

Did you know the sounds of lasers in George Lucas's *Star Wars* came from recording a hammer hitting wires on a radio tower? Or that many movies have used the sound of raw meat hit with a broom handle to simulate the impact sound of a punch? Regardless of your musical skills, you can easily record the sound of a particular tool crashing into an object and, hey presto, you have your own custom sounds for movies. Even if you don't fancy getting your hands dirty with any audio recording, you can still use GarageBand's extensive suite of tools

and generators to produce some amazing sounds right out of the box, with no specialist equipment required at all.

From a musical point of view GarageBand comes up trumps for original music, even without any formal training or understanding of the way notes and chords work. The addition of Magic GarageBand in iLife '08 means that anyone can now put together a pro-sounding musical part without touching an instrument or singing a note. If you've ever listened to music in your life, you have the requisite skills to produce songs for your iLife projects in GarageBand.

Thinking of your Mac as a blank canvas, you'll be surprised to hear that with iLife and GarageBand you have all the equipment to create pro-quality effects, jingles and songs with no additional peripherals or laborious training needed. Read on to discover the hidden talents of the app that you may have previously overlooked, but soon won't be able to live without.

So what can you use with GarageBand?

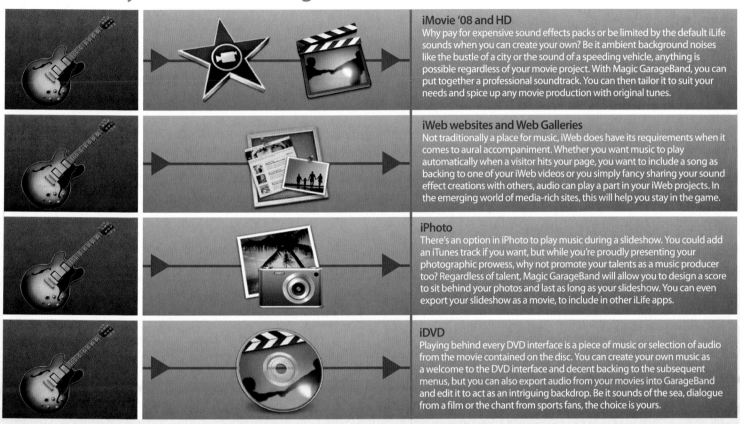

iMovie '08 and HD
Why pay for expensive sound effects packs or be limited by the default iLife sounds when you can create your own? Be it ambient background noises like the bustle of a city or the sound of a speeding vehicle, anything is possible regardless of your movie project. With Magic GarageBand, you can put together a professional soundtrack. You can then tailor it to suit your needs and spice up any movie production with original tunes.

iWeb websites and Web Galleries
Not traditionally a place for music, iWeb does have its requirements when it comes to aural accompaniment. Whether you want music to play automatically when a visitor hits your page, you want to include a song as backing to one of your iWeb videos or you simply fancy sharing your sound effect creations with others, audio can play a part in your iWeb projects. In the emerging world of media-rich sites, this will help you stay in the game.

iPhoto
There's an option in iPhoto to play music during a slideshow. You could add an iTunes track if you want, but while you're proudly presenting your photographic prowess, why not promote your talents as a music producer too? Regardless of talent, Magic GarageBand will allow you to design a score to sit behind your photos and last as long as your slideshow. You can even export your slideshow as a movie, to include in other iLife apps.

iDVD
Playing behind every DVD interface is a piece of music or selection of audio from the movie contained on the disc. You can create your own music as a welcome to the DVD interface and decent backing to the subsequent menus, but you can also export audio from your movies into GarageBand and edit it to act as an intriguing backdrop. Be it sounds of the sea, dialogue from a film or the chant from sports fans, the choice is yours.

Let's start with the basics. While GarageBand can record, import and edit audio, produce podcasts and more, at its heart it's a tool for making music. Should you be inclined you can connect a microphone, keyboard or even a drum kit to your Mac and build up a coherent piece of music to your heart's content.

If you can, you surely have by now, so we're not going to focus on the die-hard musos here. Instead we want to explore just how the non-musician can make something that doesn't sound like a drug-enduced prog rock experiment from the Eighties. You can do this by using Magic GarageBand, and the good news is that it's also easy.

Opening up GarageBand presents you with a number of options and, in this case, we're after a new Magic GarageBand project. Unlike the daunting appearance of a regular GarageBand project, Magic GarageBand offers a simple, attractive fascia to the grunt behind it. Start by picking a genre of music from blues to funk, rock to reggae, and you're away. You can opt to create a snippet, perfect for podcast and video jingles, or a complete song for adding

to a slideshow, DVD interface or credits sequence. Once you click the Audition button you're into the fun part, selecting what you want in your song from a variety of instrument parts. Everything fits coherently and you can pick your instrument on the fly while the track is playing. Don't like the lead guitar? Replace it with a brass section, and so on.

At no point are you asked about bars, pitch or tempo. Of course, being an iLife app, the option to delve further is completely possible. Simply click Create Project and, as if by magic, all the parts from your track are loaded into

a traditional GarageBand project that would likely have taken you hours via conventional methods. Neatly arranged into verse and chorus parts, you can either export the track via the Share menu immediately or play around and perfect things as you wish. If you're a complete GarageBand beginner, you can check out our guide to the interface over the page and also the GarageBand Creative Companion guide free on the disc, to grasp the basics.

From the main GarageBand screen you can work with the timeline as you would in iMovie HD, selecting individual clips ▶

Artist tip: John Mayer
"It's a practise tool. I just wish I had this when I was 13 or 14 – I would have locked myself in my room forever and just gone around and around playing on it. That's the cool part." Apple Keynote favourite John Mayer was brought on stage at Macworld to help Steve Jobs introduce GarageBand, and played guitar over a number of loops in a number of different styles. The Grammy award-winner appreciates GarageBand as a tool for practise and fleshing out ideas on the Mac. Learn more at **www.johnmayer.com**.

"Magic GarageBand offers a simple fascia to the grunt behind it"

The GarageBand interface explained

Instrument info
Information for the selected instrument/track is shown on the right when the 'i' button is highlighted. This allows for different effects and styles to be added to a track

Tracks
Each instrument in GarageBand has its own track shown as a single line on the main window, like this guitar part

Loops
Any sound that plays in your GarageBand project is displayed as a green or blue segment. Green is for software/Midi instruments and blue is for real or recorded instruments

Editing and loops
Depending on the selected option, this space is reserved for selecting loops or taking a closer look at the selected track. Here users can edit a recording or notes

"Once satisfied, you're free to export to any of the iLife apps"

and dragging them into position as you wish. An invaluable tool, especially if you want to trim your music to a specific length, is the Split tool (Apple+T). This allows you to select a specific point in one or a number of musical parts and split them in order to remove selections or delete unwanted parts. You can also drag loops in GarageBand to extend them if you need your music to last a little longer.

Once satisfied with your music, you're free to export to any of the iLife applications or simply save as an MP3 to add manually to a number of applications. Of course, you can save your project and come back to it later if you want to make any changes and then re-export to your chosen application. It's certainly worth playing with your song once it's saved, as it will provide a valuable insight into the

workings of the project and software as well as, hopefully, allowing you to further enhance the sounds you have created to perfect them before adding them to your chosen creative project. You're free to do anything you wish to any of the

Top tip

iLife preview
When you save a song in GarageBand, you are given the option to save with an iLife preview. This will allow you to use the song in other iLife projects via the Media browser without having to export the project as an audio file. This can come in particularly handy when you're testing out different music and effects with an iMovie or iDVD project.

tracks – add effects from the Track Details window to enhance sounds, or even add completely new tracks and instruments to round off your music.

If you're only planning to create a snippet of a song to use as a jingle or intro tune, you may wish to record a vocal over the top of your Magic GarageBand project. This can easily be performed by adding a new real instrument track from the Track menu and assigning your built-in microphone or audio interface to it. If you want your voice to be heard over multiple instruments, it's often a good idea to duplicate your vocal track (Apple+D) and then hold Alt while clicking and dragging the recorded loop onto the new track . This will double up your vocal, but watch out for extremely high volume levels that may occur when using this technique.

Built-in microphone
Most modern Macs have a built-in microphone, which you can use to record vocals and sound effects in GarageBand

MIDI keyboard
For greater control over your input, a MIDI keyboard makes it easy to play software instruments and record them in GarageBand

Keyboard
Using musical typing in GarageBand you can turn your keyboard into a piano, playing keys like notes

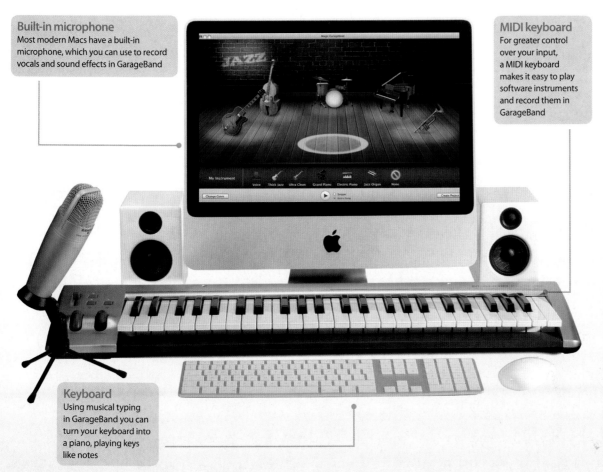

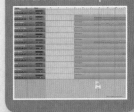

Step-by-step
MIDI files
Hunt down your favourite songs online and use them in your GarageBand projects as MIDI files

1 A quick Google search for your chosen song and MIDI file should bring up a host of options. Select a site and click the link for it in your chosen browser.

2 Your browser will now load the file using QuickTime, or a QuickTime browser plug-in. If it's the song you're after, you can now continue by downloading it to your HD.

3 Load a new GarageBand project and locate your MIDI file in the Finder. Now simply drag the file onto the GarageBand timeline and it will load all the instruments required, as well as the music loops.

With most new Macs, you have at your disposal a complete audio-editing suite with the basic tools to get the sounds you want into the software. There's the built-in mic found in iMacs and the MacBook line up, right through to the audio-in port that allows for all sorts of devices to send their sound to GarageBand for recording. Even the humble USB or wireless keyboard can be used as a handy input device using the Musical Typing feature (Shift+Apple+K).

Bereft of any physical instruments, you have an entire orchestra of possibilities within GarageBand that can be controlled in a number of ways. Musical Typing is one, allowing the user to press corresponding keystrokes to play notes. There's also a simple software keyboard (Apple+K), which you can use by clicking on keys with the cursor to play notes.

If you're not interested in inputting your own notes, you can always take a tip from the professionals. All over the web are files known as MIDI. MIDI stands for Musical Instrument Digital Interface and is a prevailing standard in music

that allows instruments and computers to communicate by reading musical notes as MIDI notes. We're not looking at anything this complex, however – we're simply going to harness the input of others to create our own tunes.

A quick Google search for MIDI files should produce a wealth of links to download from, with previews available online and (in most cases) via QuickTime when the MIDI file is clicked. You will often have to Ctrl+click on a link and choose Download Linked File to get hold

of a MIDI file to avoid it automatically playing in Safari. Once you have a MIDI file downloaded, the real magic can begin.

Simply open a blank GarageBand music project and drag your MIDI file into the interface. Before your eyes you will see the complete track appear in front of you with all the parts split into instruments. From here you can either export the whole thing as an MP3 or get in and cut tracks, change instruments and more. You can even edit the tracks to put your own stamp on the song, which can be a good idea if you're using copyrighted material as you will be heading into a legal minefield should you wish to promote the music online or commercially. This is another ▶

Top tip

Vocal effects
It's easy to add effects to your own voice by selecting one of the preset vocal instruments in GarageBand, or using the Generators from the Track Details window. The Vocal Transformer generators can do anything to your vocal recordings from adding a deep bassy sound through to turning you into a chipmunk. Perfect for voiceovers and podcast sounds.

"You have an entire orchestra of possibilities within GarageBand that can be controlled in a number of ways"

Jargon Box

Make sense of the gibberish found within modern-day musical production

Track
Each instrument in a GarageBand project has its own track on the timeline and will be labelled as Vocals, Guitar, etc.

Software/Real Instrument
A software instrument's sound is produced by GarageBand and can be triggered with a keyboard. A real instrument is recorded via a microphone or line-in and covers vocals and guitar parts.

MIDI
Musical Instrument Digital Interface. A standard for transferring musical notes into a digital format, usually via a keyboard or other MIDI instrument.

Generator
A generator contains a number of preset effects to alter the sound of a track and can provide anything from echo through to vocal adjustments.

Reverb
An abbreviation of reverberation, reverb simulates an acoustic space and adds a more 'live' feel to sounds.

Loop
A loop is software or real instrument audio on the GarageBand timeline containing sounds or music. Loops can be cut, resized and deleted at will.

Tempo
The speed in beats per minute that a track plays at. Modern dance music is typically 120BPM, while soul and rock vary from around 60 to 100BPM.

Equaliser (EQ)
An EQ allows for the adjustment of different frequencies for a specific instrument or recording and can help enhance the overall sound of a track. EQ can be used to improve bass or treble sounds and even remove unwanted frequencies entirely, such as hiss and rumble found in recordings.

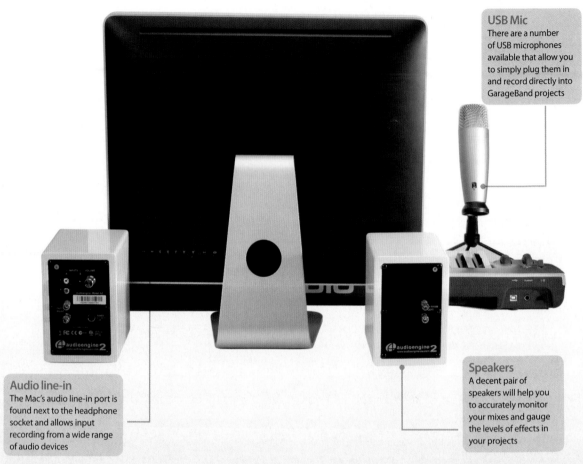

USB Mic
There are a number of USB microphones available that allow you to simply plug them in and record directly into GarageBand projects

Audio line-in
The Mac's audio line-in port is found next to the headphone socket and allows input recording from a wide range of audio devices

Speakers
A decent pair of speakers will help you to accurately monitor your mixes and gauge the levels of effects in your projects

unique way to produce a pro product without having a degree in music or an advanced knowledge of editing software.

Regardless of your setup, impressive effects aren't far away in GarageBand. It's an idea to check out those on offer to begin with, if anything to make sure you're not wasting time creating a sound you already have in your possession.

That check aside, let's take a look at just what can be achieved in a few simple clicks of the mouse. First there's recording, which can be as simple as recording your

own voice into the Mac's built-in mic, or as involved as recording the sound of birds calling outside your window. The Mac's built-in mic will do a pretty good job with simple sounds and can even stretch to outdoor work if you're on a laptop, but it does have its limitations.

Should you wish to push things a little further, invest in a USB mic, portable audio recorder or simply a microphone adaptor for your iPod. Once recorded, you can drop these sounds into GarageBand for touching up.

In most cases where you're not recording directly into GarageBand, the process will be as easy as dragging and dropping an audio file onto the timeline. If you do plan to record directly into the app, a trip to System Preferences is required in order to choose your input from the Sound menu. Then, in GarageBand's preferences, select the System Setting option for both input and output. Once you're set up, you need to add a new track from the Track menu and select Real Instrument. Select your input from the Track Details drop-down menu and click the Record button. The process is the same if you have recorded to an external device, however, you will need to connect the recorder to your Mac's line-in socket with a mini-jack cable and set Audio Line-in as the input for your track.

Most recorders will let you play back your recording, which can then, in turn, be recorded by GarageBand. However, the only drawback with this is that some digital devices use a hard drive or memory card, which you will need to attach to your Mac in order to move the audio files.

Artist tip: Jason Mraz

With a MacBook Pro and GarageBand, Jason Mraz has been inspired by iTunes to release more digital EPs. "I can make them at home, I can make them anywhere I want at low cost. It's so easy to do that now," he says. Making the most of GarageBand's recording features, most of his new album was developed and demoed in the iLife app. "I can record something in a hotel room that might actually be quite brilliant that I can just dump into the studio." **www.jasonmraz.com**

Step-by-step
Amazing backing
Create incredible background sounds with one simple click of the mouse in GarageBand

1 Create a new software instrument track with a GarageBand project open and click the 'i' button to open the Track Info screen on the right of the interface.

2 Select one of the Synth Pads from the instrument menu and then hit Apple+K for the software keyboard or Shift+Apple+K for the musical typing keyboard.

3 Hold down a note on the software keyboard or through musical typing and listen to it evolve as it is held. Select a synth that works for you before hitting Record and playing your chosen note.

An alternative to such a device is to use your digital camera or camcorder to record external sounds and then import them in the traditional way. If there's no audio recording function, record a video and remove the movie track from GarageBand when you import.

There are many options available when it comes to recording. When using a microphone for your iPod, the recordings are generally stored on the iPod and then transferred into iTunes when docked. You can then add these files to a GarageBand project using the Media browser (button next to the 'i' on the right of the interface) and selecting your iTunes library from under the Audio tab. From here, you can

simply drag and drop the sounds you have recorded into the precise position you wish them to appear within your project. With sounds recorded or imported into GarageBand you don't have to simply leave them as they were when recorded, you can add any number of additional sounds or begin playing with the make-up of your sound in general. From the same Track Details menu you chose your input from, you can pick a variety of effects Generators, which can do anything from adding echo to a sound through to increasing or decreasing the pitch. If you fancy giving yourself a deep and bassy movie trailer vocal, record your normal voice and then add the Vocal Transformer

generator with its Deep Soulful preset. This is just one of many possible options and it doesn't stop at vocals. By using any of the generators available, you can make simple or drastic changes to any sound in your project to provide the effects you're looking for.

There are a number of preset instruments available in GarageBand that will save you from touching the generators at all. These presets can add polish to the spoken word at a practical level and bounce sounds back and forth from left to right for more diverse tweaks.

Aside from recording, you can create incredible sounds purely using the instruments present in GarageBand. Tap out piano notes on the software keyboard for a basic introduction sound for a podcast, or hit weird and wonderful chords using musical typing and a string ▶

Artist tip: Eryka Badu

GarageBand provided the inspiration for Erykah Badu's latest album. On a MacBook she pieced together vocal recordings and sent them to producers, who performed their work and sent them back. Speaking to **Apple.com**, Badu said: "I learned how to use GarageBand by trial and error, I hate reading instructions, so I just figured it out. It's like somebody stuck a plug in the back of my neck and uploaded a program to learn how to use GarageBand. It was automatic. Everything on that Mac was automatic."

"A vocal recording with a suitable amount of reverb can act as a decent internal monologue for characters in your movie"

Step-by-step
Scoring a movie
Make movie soundtracks a breeze with GarageBand's built-in movie scoring facility and movie track

1 Open a new GarageBand project and pick a movie from the GarageBand Media browser, under the Movies tab. Drag the movie onto the timeline.

2 The GarageBand Movie Track will now appear with your movie's frames in it. A track below will include any audio that may be present within your movie file.

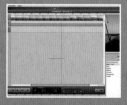

3 You can now add loops, sound effects and jingles to the GarageBand project and move them to the precise point required in your movie. You can preview the movie at any time by pressing Play.

GarageBand instrument effects explained

Learn how to make subtle or drastic changes to your tracks with our guide to the effects found in GarageBand, to help make a difference to your instruments and recordings for any purpose

Amp Simulation
A variety of amplifier sounds perfect for replicating classic guitar sounds, but also great for adding effects to vocals.

Auto Wah
Another useful guitar effect that can be applied to a number of rhythm instruments in a number of styles.

Automatic Filter
Commonly used in dance music, the Automatic Filter gradually adjusts the frequency of an instrument over time to produce a unique effect.

Bass Amp
Perfect for adding a richness to any track, but ideal for bass guitar parts.

Bass Reduction
As the name implies, this effect will remove certain bass frequencies from a track.

Bitcrusher
Destroy your audio for a retro sound that can replicate that of an Atari or AM Radio.

Chorus
By repeating and detuning the original sound, the chorus effect creates a wider sound as if many instruments are playing at once.

Distortion
Provides a crunchy sound similar to that of a megaphone for vocals and other sounds.

Flanger
Like the Chorus effect, but with even more detuning of the original instrument sound.

Overdrive
Another guitar enhancer that boosts sound, this also works well with software instruments.

Phaser
By reproducing original sounds and offsetting them, this effect creates a wooshing sound.

Speech Enhancer
Adjust the way vocals sound by adding one of the many Speech Enhancer effects.

Track Echo
As you would expect, this effect adds a variety of echos to a track.

Track Reverb
Short for reverberation, this effect adds space to sounds and provides a live feel.

Treble Reduction
For sounds that are too tinny, use this effect to reduce the treble frequencies.

Tremolo
Add a wavering effect to your instruments.

Vocal Transformer
From a chipmunk to a deep soulful voice, you can change your vocal recordings as well as other sounds using this fun effect.

---

instrument to add a *Psycho*-style sting to your movie project. A little play is all that's required to come up with some truly unique effects and remember, you're free to change your sound as you wish even after it's been recorded.

Switch the instrument, turn off specific effects, even cut out certain notes using the editor if you wish – the options are all available to you. Beginner users are likely to get the most mileage from simple-held notes played by the synth instruments found among GarageBand's software instruments. With lead and pad instruments available, these undulating sounds can be as musical or cinematic as you require and will suit many a purpose when adding sounds to iMovie. Many of the Pad synths actually evolve sonically as you continue to hold the note, so you could easily put together a sound bed for a movie scene with one press

of a button. Synths also make handy accompaniments to vocal recordings. For a sinister voice-over you could easily effect your own speech and then record a swirling synth sound on a separate track to add to the intensity. This is another facet of GarageBand that comes in handy: multiple track recording. Rather than having to worry about all the sounds in one go, you can record one part at a time and layer them together for a polished final output.

A movie score can make or break a movie, and there's no reason this shouldn't be true for your movie project. Of course, you can easily drop an MP3 onto the iMovie timeline and trim it to fit your project, but GarageBand provides many more options for both music and effects in your movie. Instead of worrying about additional audio in iMovie other than the sound in your video clips, export your movie and drag it into a new GarageBand project from the Media browser. From here, a Movie track will appear in GarageBand with the frames of your movie and its audio displayed along the top of the timeline. This makes it easy to add music and sound effects to the precise points you wish them to play. You can also very easily record a commentary for your movie, which you may wish to add as an extra on your DVD project. Simply record

your voice over the video as it plays back in the Preview window.

Recording vocals directly into movies offers creative opportunities, too. A vocal recording with a suitable amount of reverb can act as a decent internal monologue for characters in your movie, as well as narration to accompany the things happening on screen. Once you've added all the audio required, you have the same export options for your movie in GarageBand as you would expect in iMovie, allowing you to send the video, complete with new soundtrack, to iTunes, iWeb, iDVD or to a location on your Mac's HD ready to be shared with others or shown off in all its glory using Front Row.

Top tip

Podcast jingles
Using Magic GarageBand, recording your own instruments or working from an imported MIDI file you can quickly put together a jingle for use in your podcasts. You can even record your voice over the top of a jingle in order to introduce an episode. Once you've created a jingle, you're free to cut it down to fit into your project and add alternative vocal parts and effects.

> "There are a number of preset instruments available in GarageBand, which will save you from touching the generators at all"

Why not try?

Take the next step with your music and effects creation and invest in some tools to help you make the most of your audio productions

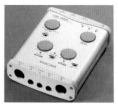

MIDI keyboard
A USB-powered device that allows you to input musical notes and sounds using piano-style keys.
We recommend: M-Audio Oxygen 8 v2 www.m-audio.com

Audio interface
A USB or FireWire device that allows for input from microphones, guitars and other instruments.
We recommend: Tascam US-122 www.tascam. com

USB microphone
For perfect recording it's best to get hold of a decent external mic, especially for recording vocals.
We recommend: Blue Snowball www.bluemic.com

Speakers
Great for monitoring your mixes, a decent set of speakers will make a world of difference.
We recommend: harmon/kardon Soundsticks II www.harmonkardon. com

USB/Guitar lead
A soundcard in a cable, this lead will connect a guitar and other instruments without need for an interface.
We recommend: Lightsnake USB Cable www.soundtech.com

Loop disc
Learn from the best with a professionally produced loop disc to add to your library and inspire you.
We recommend: Loop Masters Artist Series www.loopmasters.com

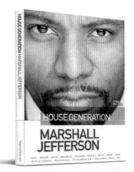

As we mentioned before, there's no need to buy any more equipment in order to create impressive music and effects with GarageBand. If, however, you're looking to take your craft to the next level, there are a number of inexpensive additions you can make to your setup that will also benefit you in other applications.

If you want to record instruments or regular microphones into GarageBand there are a number of methods. The first is to invest buy a USB microphone like Blue's Snowball. This is an excellent mic for podcasting and will also allow you to record live instruments like acoustic guitars and vocals. Powered by USB you won't need to attach the mic to the mains and, after installing required drivers, the microphone will be available for recording into GarageBand.

If you want to use more than one microphone or those with standard microphone connections, you would be well advised to buy an audio interface. These devices can handle input from many sources including mics, guitars and electric keyboards. Once again, a USB/FireWire audio interface will likely be powered by the connection to your Mac, so no mains supply is required.

Artist tip: Fall Out Boy

Patrick Stump of Fall Out Boy is an avid GarageBand user, often bouncing tracks from the app and using them live on stage via an iPod. He says: "The beauty of GarageBand is that it's only limited by what you want to do with it. Ultimately, you can do anything. It's a sequencer and you can record and edit audio. And it runs on my laptop. I've composed and recorded on the plane and on the Bullet Train in Japan. It's made me so much more prolific because I don't have to think about where and when I can record or write music. I can do it anywhere."

Guitarists don't need to head down the interface route if they have access to a LightSnake cable, however. This unique lead connects an electric guitar directly to your Mac's USB port and turns your Mac into a digital guitar amp. A USB keyboard will offer a similar service and provides basic control over notes but also pitch bend and modulation, which add differing effects to a software instrument. If you really want to get creative you can even use the keyboard as a drum kit with a drum instrument loaded in GarageBand.

Of course, you will need to hear the audio you're creating, but sometimes headphones and the Mac's built-in speakers just don't cut it. A decent set of

speakers will allow you to hear how your music and effects will sound to others to help you perfect your mix. Finally, if you need inspiration or want to continue to add to your own creations, you can't go wrong with a professionally created disc of Apple Loops or effects. Apple provides its own Jam Packs for a number of musical styles, but there are plenty of alternatives for you to add to your loop library.

GarageBand is indeed one of the more complex of the iLife applications, but that doesn't mean it shouldn't be used. Take these tips on board and bear them in mind the next time you're about to export a project – you may discover a whole new stage in your creative productions.

"Sometimes the Mac's built-in speakers just don't cut it"

Podcast preview
Double-click the podcast track to open the Track Info pane, which contains the Podcast Preview window. You can use this to check how your podcast will play back

Knowledge base

Editing markers
To shift a marker's position, click the Start Time in the Edit window and enter a new start time. You can resize marker regions in the podcast track by dragging their left or right edges, or you can move whole regions by dragging them. Delete markers by selecting the marker or marker region in the Edit window and pressing the Delete key.

Knowledge base

Video podcasts
A podcast episode containing a video or movie file is known as a video podcast. These are created by importing a movie file from the Media Browser into GarageBand, creating the soundtrack and adding markers and URLs in the same way you would with a conventional enhanced podcast.

Episode information
The Episode Info pane is just below the Podcast Preview window. Information entered here is viewable in iTunes when the podcast is downloaded

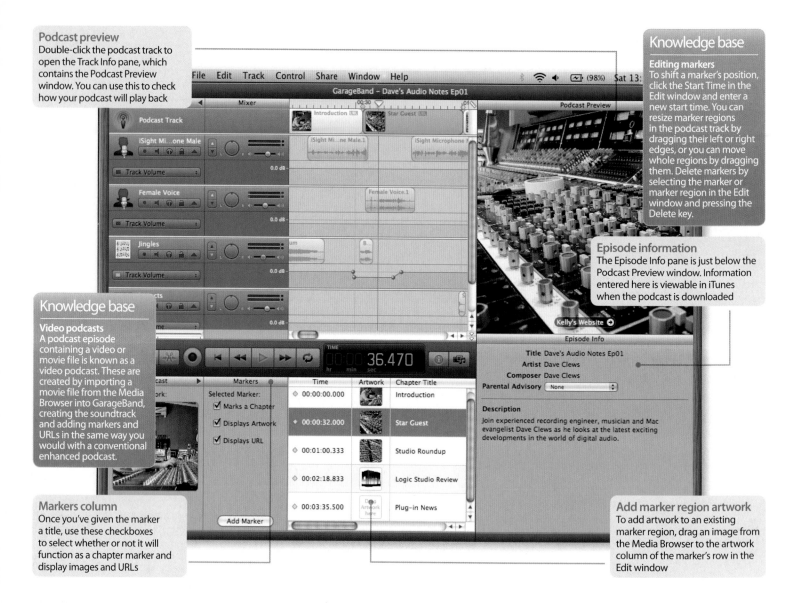

Markers column
Once you've given the marker a title, use these checkboxes to select whether or not it will function as a chapter marker and display images and URLs

Add marker region artwork
To add artwork to an existing marker region, drag an image from the Media Browser to the artwork column of the marker's row in the Edit window

Tutorial: Enhance a podcast in GarageBand

GarageBand's podcasting potential is remarkable, especially when you discover how easy it is to add images, chapter markers, links to external websites and even videos…

Task: Enhance your podcast with links and images
Difficulty: Intermediate
Time needed: 60 minutes

🎸 Podcasts are the best thing since sliced bread if you're a closet radio show host. But why limit yourself to just audio when you're broadcasting yourself to the world at large? This is clearly the question Apple had in mind when it provided GarageBand users with the ability to turn a basic audio podcast into an interactive visual extravaganza. Whether you're doing a roundup of your favourite recipes or putting together your own review show, adding images that play back along with your audio content is simplicity itself. Now a podcast can be a slideshow, a travelogue or even a mini TV show. As with the advent of the iPod video and iPod touch, video podcasts are just as feasible as those created using static images.

When you create a new podcast episode in GarageBand, an empty podcast track is displayed at the top of the Arrange window, and this is where you view, manage and edit your marker regions. These break the podcast up into chunks in a similar way to how a DVD is split up into chapters, which makes it easier for your listeners to navigate through the content of your episode. Each region can be given a title and designated as a chapter marker, and you can even set a different image to be displayed for each region.

If you want your audience to know more about a particular topic, adding an external website's internet address (URL) is a great way of allowing them to access sites which are pertinent to your theme. The URL appears when the podcast is viewed, and when the viewer clicks on it their web browser will automatically open on the intended webpage.

With all this added visual impact, enhanced podcasts make for a totally different audience experience, so let's check out how to make one!

Step-by-step | **GarageBand** Learn how to insert GarageBand's Sound FX into your podcasts

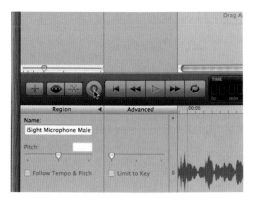

1: Create a new podcast
Launch GarageBand and select New Podcast Episode from the splash screen. Record-enable a voice track and record in some audio content.

2: Add jingles and SFX
Click the eye button to open the loop browser, and audition jingles and sound effects by clicking on them. Drag ones you like onto the jingles track.

3: Prepare podcast track
Select the podcast track and click the button to open the Media Browser. Click the scissors button to open the Edit window.

4: Add cover image
Add a cover shot for your podcast by dragging the required photo from the Media Browser onto the Episode Artwork field.

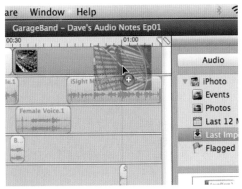

5: Picture this
Drag more images from the Browser into the podcast track to mark specific points. Align each one so it appears where you want it.

6: Chapter markers
To add a marker manually, position the playhead at the point where you want to add one, then click the Add Marker button.

7: Magic marker
The marker region appears in the podcast track at the playhead position, and the start time appears in the marker's row in the Editor.

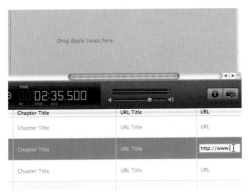

8: Add a URL
To add a URL to the marker region, click the placeholder text in the URL column of the Edit window and type in the URL.

9: Add URL title
Do the same in the URL Title field to give the URL its own title. This is displayed instead of the actual URL when viewing the podcast.

Tutorial: Create a film score in GarageBand

If you've created an original movie, why not create your own original movie score? Get musical and give your home movies a soundtrack lift in GarageBand

Task: Import a movie into GarageBand and create a film soundtrack to accompany it
Difficulty: Beginner
Time needed: 15 minutes

The reason Macs are amazing is because the guys at Apple think of pretty much everything. They know that we're all creative at heart and need to utilise things that improve, and not hinder, the process. So, if you're a budding filmmaker and want to add your own original score to an iMovie project using GarageBand, the process should be totally seamless and incredibly simple. And it is very simple.

Once you've completed a movie in iMovie you can export the file to your Movie folder, and access it from within GarageBand. Some drag-and-drop action will have it cued up and ready for some musical magic in no time at all. Now it's just down to you and your imagination to get the ball rolling, and have that movie sounding like Quincy Jones himself has just spent the last few hours sat at your Mac. Easy.

As usual, we'll give you the steps you need to get going…

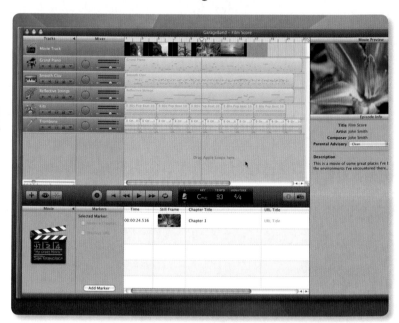

Step-by-step | GarageBand Create a film score

1: Start at the beginning

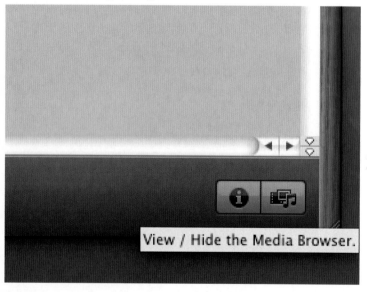

View / Hide the Media Browser.

● Create a brand new GarageBand project. Open the Media browser by clicking the Media Browser button in the bottom corner of GarageBand. This will slide open a new window on the side of GarageBand.

2: Pick Movies

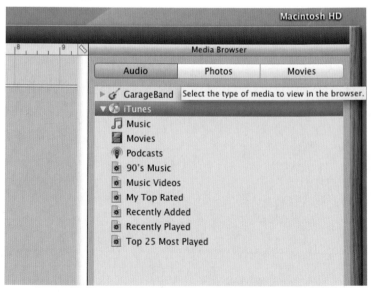

● There are three tabs at the top of the newly appeared window. Click on Movies on the right and you will be able to navigate until you get to the movie that you want to make the score for.

Create a soundtrack for your movie

Use the playhead
Use the playhead to track your progress through the movie. The window on the right will give you a larger image of where you are in the film

Volume
It sounds obvious, but you don't want the soundtrack to overpower images or drown out audio from the movie. Finding the perfect balance can be hard, but it's worth it

Loops
Drag-and-drop loops to get a quick-themed sound into your movies. You can shorten them if need be, or double them up

Knowledge base

Sections
Breaking your movie into sections can be extremely helpful. It means that you can concentrate on a particular section rather than recording for the whole movie in one go. Use the Loop button to repeat sections over and over until you get a feel for it, then begin recording or adding other sounds.

Tempo
Tempo can really affect the mood of the piece. Luckily this can be automated, so that you get a range of tempos in one score

3: Drag and drop

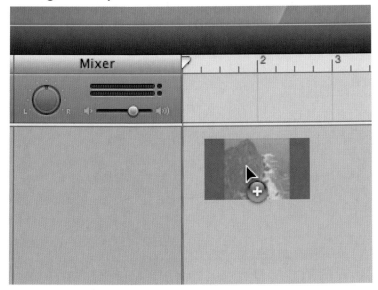

● Now just drag and drop the movie file into the main Arrange page of GarageBand. An overview will then be generated, so you can see the film progress as you add sounds to it.

4: Get creative

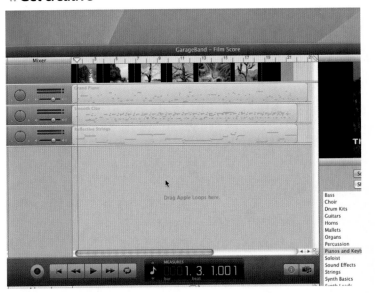

● Now that the film is in, you can add all the music and effects that you need. There are of course the Apple loops if you're not much of a musician, or you can record software and real instruments.

 GarageBand

Tutorial: Label your favourite loops in GarageBand

GarageBand ships with over a thousand Apple Loops, but how on Earth do you keep track of your favourites?

Task: Learn to label and search for your favourite Apple Loops

Difficulty: Beginner

Time needed: 10 minutes

In among the 1000+ Apple Loops in GarageBand's Factory library, there are sure to be ones that you really like, or that you'd like to earmark for future projects. But the problem is that there's so much choice, and it can be difficult to find a particular loop again once you've clicked away from it. Realising this, Apple has incorporated a favourites system within the Loop Browser to help you keep tabs on the loops you like most. If you always want to be able to access a particular loop in future projects, you can leave it in the Favorites list for as long as you like. However, if you only need to earmark a loop for a short while, removing it from the Favorites list is just as easy as putting it there in the first place – so there's no excuse not to make your best tracks ever now!

Follow these easy steps, and before long this may well become your favourite GarageBand feature.

Step-by-step | GarageBand Favourites

1: Open Loop Browser

○ Launch GarageBand and click the eye button to reveal the Loop Browser (the special Search window for finding and auditioning Apple Loops). There are three different views to choose from: Column, Button and Effects.

2: Audition loops

○ In Button view, hit a category button to bring up a list of loops that fit that category. The list appears in the right-hand search results window. Click on a loop to listen to it, and click again to stop it.

Sort your favourite Apple Loops

Move closer
To avoid having to scroll right, you can move the Fav column further to the left, nearer the loop names, by dragging the column header over to where you want it to be

Favourites in view
Choose Favorites from the first column, and select the desired subcategories. The advantage of Column view is that listed favourites are restricted by keyword. This is handy if you have a lot of favourites

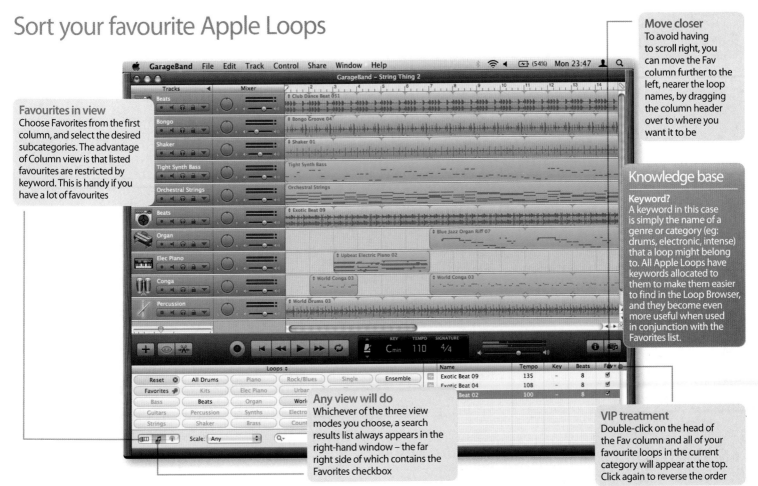

Knowledge base

Keyword?
A keyword in this case is simply the name of a genre or category (eg: drums, electronic, intense) that a loop might belong to. All Apple Loops have keywords allocated to them to make them easier to find in the Loop Browser, and they become even more useful when used in conjunction with the Favorites list.

Any view will do
Whichever of the three view modes you choose, a search results list always appears in the right-hand window – the far right side of which contains the Favorites checkbox

VIP treatment
Double-click on the head of the Fav column and all of your favourite loops in the current category will appear at the top. Click again to reverse the order

3: Check the box

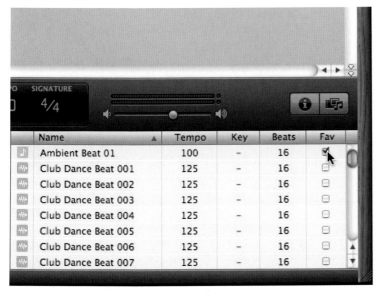

When you find a loop that you want to add to your Favorites list, scroll to the far right-hand side of the search results window. Check the desired loop's 'Fav' checkbox to add it to the list.

4: View favourites

When you hit the Favorites button now, all the loops of the boxes you checked will be listed in the Search Results window. To remove a loop, simply uncheck the box again and it will disappear from the list.

GarageBand

Knowledge base

Monitor effects
When you record a vocal into GarageBand, the vocals are recorded to disk dry – without any effect. The effects are only applied on playback from the disk. This type of effect is known as a 'monitor effect', and the approach pays dividends because it leaves you free to change the effect without changing your original basic recording.

Automated madness
As with most plug-in parameters in GarageBand, the Pitch and Sound sliders in the Vocal Transformer can both be automated by plotting automation curves. Trust us – this is fun!

Pitch slider
This control alters the pitch of the source vocal. Measured in semitones, it has a total range of four octaves, allowing the potential for some fairly extreme pitch-shifting effects

Feedback protection
Feedback is where sound from the speakers is picked up by the mic, and re-transmitted through the speakers in an endless squealing loop. Use this setting to minimise the risk

Sound slider
This slider can best be described as a 'windpipe width' control, with higher values sounding thin and squeaky, while lower settings result in a booming character

Knowledge base

The Vocal Transformer applications and settings Used subtly, the Vocal Transformer effect can be used to benefit backing vocals you have recorded yourself. Slight adjustments can simply make you sound like someone else singing, allowing for a more blended sound. More extreme settings bring us into the realm of gender-bending androids, chipmunks or Darth Vader – great for wacky effects for use in podcasts!

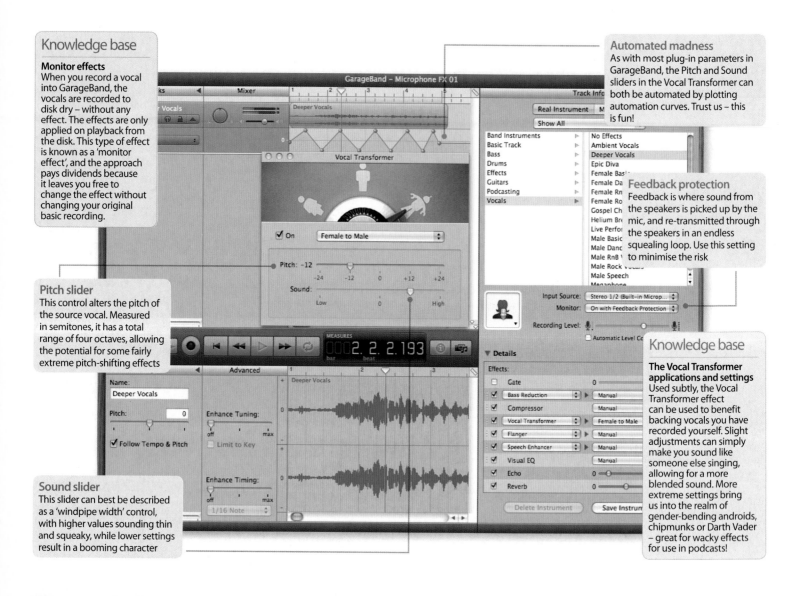

Tutorial: Use microphone effects in GarageBand
We take a whistle-stop tour of some of the special effects GarageBand places at your disposal for use when recording with a microphone

Task: Explore GarageBand's microphone effect plug-ins
Difficulty: Beginner
Time needed: 30 minutes

GarageBand comes with a range of plug-in settings crafted to bring out the best in certain types of microphone input signal. Whether you're male or female, an operatic diva or a rock star, GarageBand has a setting in there somewhere for you. This makes podcasting a breeze, as it's possible to create a professional-sounding voiceover very quickly. Not only that, but there are enough highly amusing voice-changing effects on board to keep your inner child happy for days on end.

The microphone effects presets are found in two categories in the Preset list for new Real Instrument tracks. The Podcasting section contains a selection of presets geared towards the type of microphone used, mainly based around the Speech Enhancer plug-in. Conversely, the Vocals section contains a variety of presets tailored towards sung vocals, and a few of these include the wacky Vocal Transformer plug-in. So let's track down some of the more interesting settings on offer…

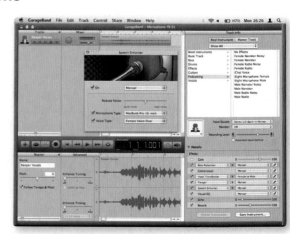

Step-by-step | GarageBand Explore microphone effects

1: Open project
First you need to open, or create, a new GarageBand project. Now select Real Instrument Track and click Create.

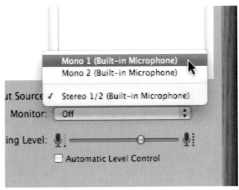

2: Set source
Now set the Input Source to the Built-in Microphone. Or you can select an external microphone if you have one connected.

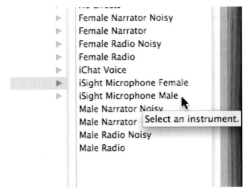

3: Voiceover setting
For a voiceover recording, select the Podcasting category and pick the preset that most applies to your recording environment.

4: Make changes
Click the Details disclosure triangle to reveal the Effects, and click the pencil button next to the Speech Enhancer plug-in.

5: Feel the noise
Use the Reduce Noise slider to estimate the likely amount of background noise the system will have, to compensate for when you're recording.

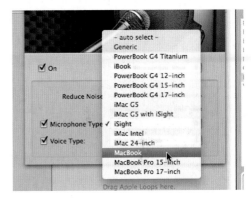

6: Select mic type
The microphone list includes optimised settings for certain models of built-in Mac microphones. If yours is not on the list, select Generic.

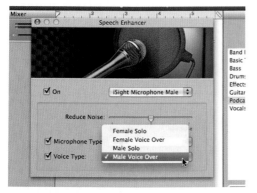

7: Select voice type
Here you can specify whether the voice is male or female, solo singer or voiceover style, to further refine the settings.

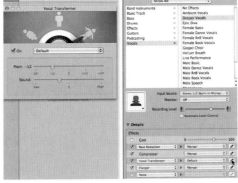

8: Vocal setting
Alternatively, select a preset from the Vocals category. We've chosen Deeper Vocals. Call up the Vocal Transformer window with the pencil button.

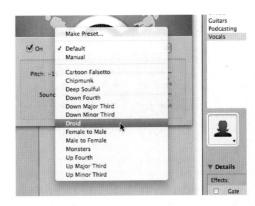

9: Experiment!
Again, there is a list of preset settings to choose from. These make good starting points for your own experiments!

GarageBand

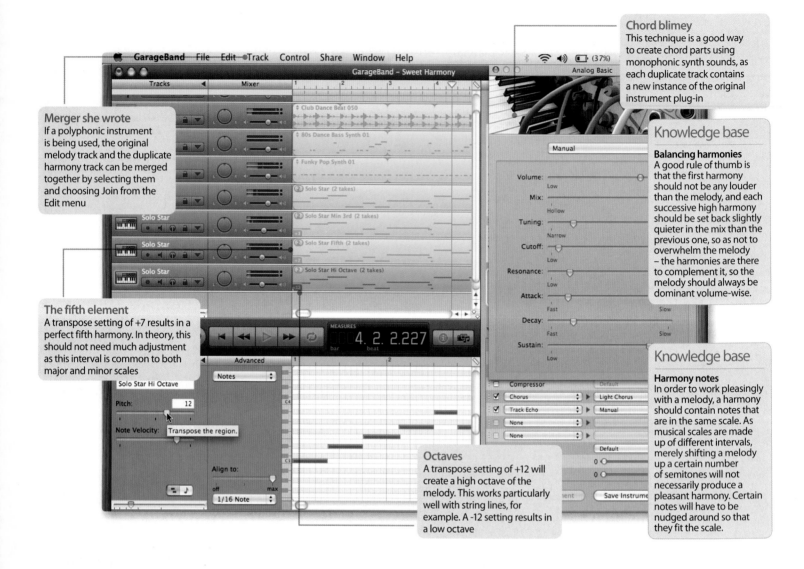

Chord blimey
This technique is a good way to create chord parts using monophonic synth sounds, as each duplicate track contains a new instance of the original instrument plug-in

Merger she wrote
If a polyphonic instrument is being used, the original melody track and the duplicate harmony track can be merged together by selecting them and choosing Join from the Edit menu

Knowledge base

Balancing harmonies
A good rule of thumb is that the first harmony should not be any louder than the melody, and each successive high harmony should be set back slightly quieter in the mix than the previous one, so as not to overwhelm the melody – the harmonies are there to complement it, so the melody should always be dominant volume-wise.

The fifth element
A transpose setting of +7 results in a perfect fifth harmony. In theory, this should not need much adjustment as this interval is common to both major and minor scales

Knowledge base

Harmony notes
In order to work pleasingly with a melody, a harmony should contain notes that are in the same scale. As musical scales are made up of different intervals, merely shifting a melody up a certain number of semitones will not necessarily produce a pleasant harmony. Certain notes will have to be nudged around so that they fit the scale.

Octaves
A transpose setting of +12 will create a high octave of the melody. This works particularly well with string lines, for example. A -12 setting results in a low octave

Tutorial: Create MIDI harmonies in GarageBand

Suffering from lacklustre leadlines and mediocre melodies? We reveal how to use a simple MIDI track duplication technique to make sweet harmony in your GarageBand projects

Task: Create harmonies by duplicating MIDI tracks
Difficulty: Beginner
Time needed: 30 minutes

So you've got your groove on, the bass is pumping and you've added a keyboard melody line – but something's missing. If your lead part sounds a bit on the thin and lonely side, one way to beef things up a bit is to add some harmonies. But how do you go about it?

A good technique is to make a copy of the original part on another track, then transpose the copy by a few semitones to create a harmony. This may sound simple, but how well it works will depend on the scale of the melody and the key of the song. Invariably, some of the notes in your newly generated harmony will have to be shifted about in pitch to fit the scale, but satisfactory results can be achieved with just a small amount of jiggling about. Here we show you an easy way to generate basic harmonies with MIDI track duplication to get your tracks, well, back on track!

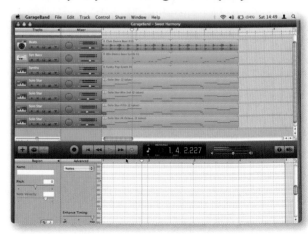

Step-by-step | GarageBand Create harmonies with MIDI track duplication

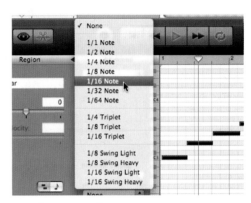

1: Open GarageBand session
Open your project and set up a new software track to record your melody part onto. Here we've chosen a monophonic synth software instrument.

2: Create original part
Record in your melody, either from a MIDI keyboard or using the Musical Typing feature (Shift+Apple+K) to play notes in from your Mac keyboard.

3: Edit original part
Double-click the original to open it in the Edit window. Getting the part exactly how you want it at this stage will save time later.

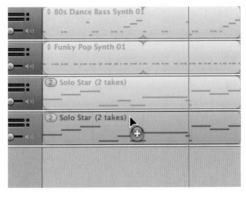

4: Duplicate track
With the original track selected, choose Duplicate Track from the Track menu. The track will contain a new instance of the same software instrument.

5: Duplicate part
Hold down the Option key and drag the original part onto this new track to make a duplicate. Rename it in the editor if desired.

6: Open duplicate in Edit window
Double-click on the duplicate part to open it in the Edit window, then click once in the Edit window to make it active.

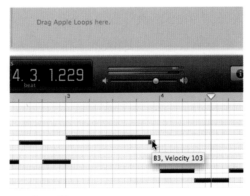

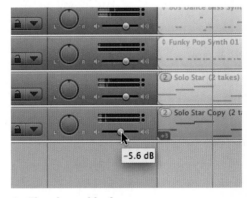

7: Transpose
With the track playing in cycle, move the Pitch slider around until you hear a harmony. A three-semitone interval represents a minor third.

8: Identify wrong notes
Listen out for notes that don't fit, click to select one, then drag it up or down one semitone at a time until it sounds right.

9: Check and balance
Continue shifting notes until the harmony part sounds correct. Then use the track Volume slider to sink the level back slightly behind the melody.

Tutorial: Fix audio problems with GarageBand's EQ

If you have recorded your own audio for a music track or podcast, you can fix minor problems easily by using an EQ

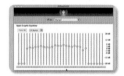

Task: Load and use the AUGraphic Equalizer to fix minor sonic imperfections

Difficulty: Intermediate

Time needed: 30 minutes

The great thing about GarageBand is that you're your own boss. It's your composition, and GarageBand has the facility to affect audio in so many different ways that you can do pretty much anything you want. This flexibility also lends itself to fixing problems you may encounter with audio files. Your main weapon against basic sonic anomalies is EQ. GarageBand has a useful visual EQ that deals in curves, but also has a much simpler (and often more effective choice) in the form of AUGraphic EQ. If you're an avid podcaster you may have recorded an interview using a dictaphone then imported it, but often this can sound too hissy. This is where you can use the EQ to drop out the high frequencies, eliminating the hiss. If you recorded music from a live show and find that the bass is all you can hear, you can drop the lower frequencies out to get rid of the overwhelming bass and top up the higher and middle frequencies. Experimentation is the key here, and the results can be astounding.

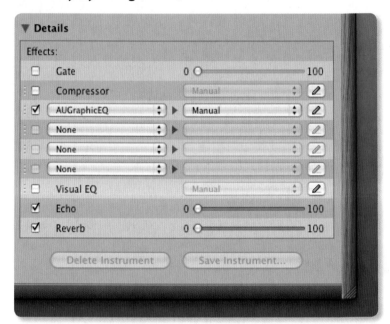

Step-by-step | GarageBand Fix with EQ

1: Record

● Select the track that contains the audio you want to fix. You may need to drag and drop or import audio from another place first.

2: Triangulate effects

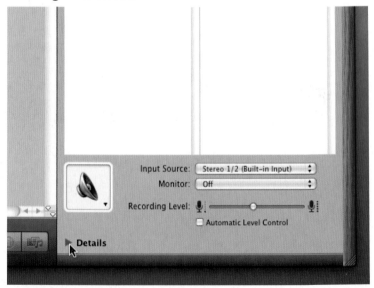

● On the right-hand pane of GarageBand, click the Details triangle to see all the effects you can add to the track you have selected.

Save spoiled sound with EQ

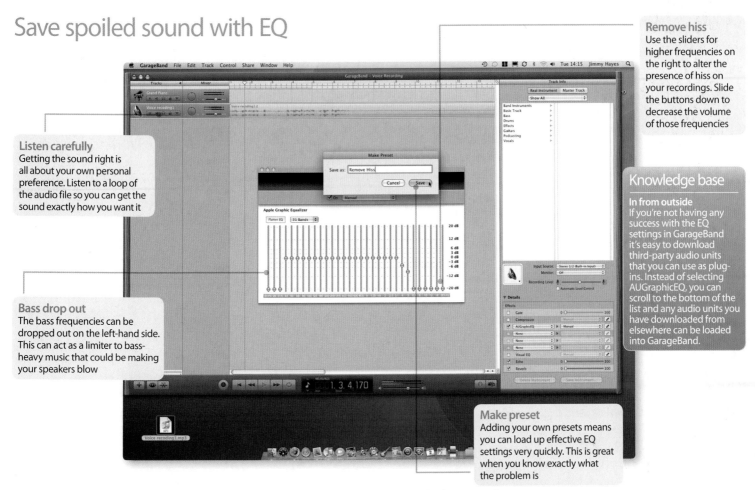

Remove hiss
Use the sliders for higher frequencies on the right to alter the presence of hiss on your recordings. Slide the buttons down to decrease the volume of those frequencies

Listen carefully
Getting the sound right is all about your own personal preference. Listen to a loop of the audio file so you can get the sound exactly how you want it

Bass drop out
The bass frequencies can be dropped out on the left-hand side. This can act as a limiter to bass-heavy music that could be making your speakers blow

Knowledge base

In from outside
If you're not having any success with the EQ settings in GarageBand it's easy to download third-party audio units that you can use as plug-ins. Instead of selecting AUGraphicEQ, you can scroll to the bottom of the list and any audio units you have downloaded from elsewhere can be loaded into GarageBand.

Make preset
Adding your own presets means you can load up effective EQ settings very quickly. This is great when you know exactly what the problem is

3: Drop down

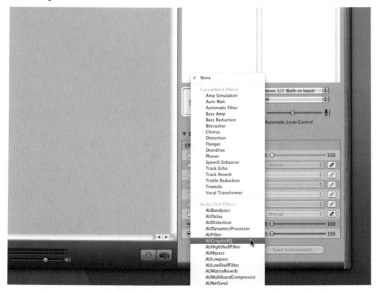

● Use the drop-down menu and scroll down until you see AUGraphicEQ. Click on this and you will see it as a ticked (meaning activated) effect.

4: Click the pencil

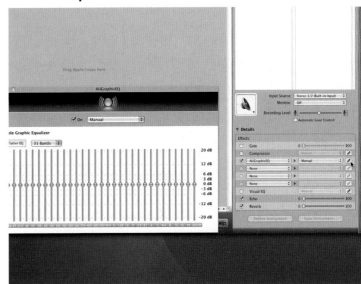

● Click on the Pencil icon to the right of AUGraphicEQ and you'll see the EQ window. You can now use sliders to alter the sound of the track you selected.

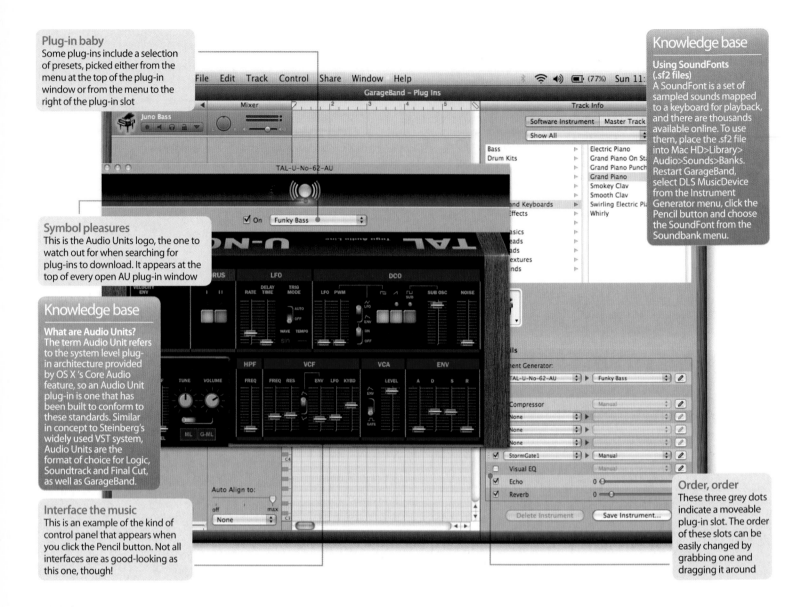

Plug-in baby
Some plug-ins include a selection of presets, picked either from the menu at the top of the plug-in window or from the menu to the right of the plug-in slot

Knowledge base

Using SoundFonts (.sf2 files)
A SoundFont is a set of sampled sounds mapped to a keyboard for playback, and there are thousands available online. To use them, place the .sf2 file into Mac HD>Library> Audio>Sounds>Banks. Restart GarageBand, select DLS MusicDevice from the Instrument Generator menu, click the Pencil button and choose the SoundFont from the Soundbank menu.

Symbol pleasures
This is the Audio Units logo, the one to watch out for when searching for plug-ins to download. It appears at the top of every open AU plug-in window

Knowledge base

What are Audio Units?
The term Audio Unit refers to the system level plug-in architecture provided by OS X 's Core Audio feature, so an Audio Unit plug-in is one that has been built to conform to these standards. Similar in concept to Steinberg's widely used VST system, Audio Units are the format of choice for Logic, Soundtrack and Final Cut, as well as GarageBand.

Interface the music
This is an example of the kind of control panel that appears when you click the Pencil button. Not all interfaces are as good-looking as this one, though!

Order, order
These three grey dots indicate a moveable plug-in slot. The order of these slots can be easily changed by grabbing one and dragging it around

Tutorial: Using Audio Unit plug-ins in GarageBand

GarageBand already ships with several built-in instruments and effects, but you can easily expand its palette of sounds by adding processors from other manufacturers…

Task: Enhance GarageBand by adding some third-party Audio Unit plug-ins
Difficulty: Beginner
Time needed: 30 minutes

In terms of bundled content, GarageBand can happily take pride of place in the line-up of iLife applications. The impressive stack of music-making and signal-processing devices it ships with is more than enough to keep most new users busy for a while. So it may come as a surprise to learn that as well as being a fully featured audio and MIDI sequencer and podcast studio, GarageBand is also a fully fledged Audio Units host. This means that it is capable of running Audio Units plug-ins from third-party manufacturers, in addition to the pile of processors it already comes with as standard. This greatly expands the program's creative potential – so if you're beginning to run out of inspiration using the supplied instruments and effects, it may well be time to broaden your horizons. There is a wealth of AU plug-ins available on the internet, including not only effects processors such as reverbs, choruses, phasers, filters

and delay effects, but also a large number of software instruments (although there are one or two limitations with these).

While GarageBand can use any software synth that conforms to the Audio Units standard, some Audio Unit instruments that would normally be capable of responding on multiple MIDI channels can only be triggered on channel 1. This means that multitimbral instruments, such as MOTU's Mach Five and Native Instruments' Kontakt, are not ideally suited for use in GarageBand. And one last word of warning – once you discover how much stuff there is out there and how easy it is to expand GarageBand's sonic armoury, you may well spend all your time collecting new plug-ins and not making any music! A simple Google search or a browse across some of the digital music making sites online should provide you with a decent shopping list right away. So with that distraction in mind, let's take a look at how to use Audio Units.

Step-by-step | GarageBand Enhance GarageBand by adding third-party Audio Unit plug-ins

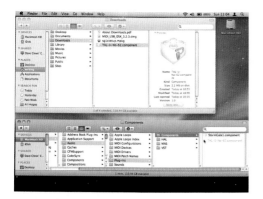

1: Browse for plug-ins
Google for free AU plug-ins, or go to www. kvraudio.com for a continually updated list of freeware, shareware and commercial releases.

2: Hit download link
Once you've found a suitable plug-in, check that it's compatible with your system. Some older AU plug-ins may not run on Intel machines.

3: Run installer
Run the Installer if one is included in the download. If not, click the magnifying glass in your browser's Downloads window to locate the downloaded files.

4: Install manually
If there is no Installer, drag the plug-in component file from your Downloads folder into Mac HD>Library>Audio>Plug-ins>Components.

5: Launch GarageBand
The software will scan the plug-ins folder while initialising. Any new additions it finds will be added to the plug-in list for use in the program.

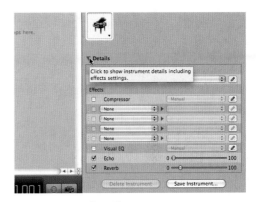

6: Open Track Info
In your GarageBand project, click the 'i' button to open the Track Info pane. Click the Details disclosure triangle to reveal the plug-in slots.

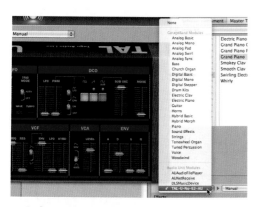

7: Select instrument
If you added a new software instrument, it should now appear in the Instrument Generator pop-up menu. Click the Pencil button to view the interface.

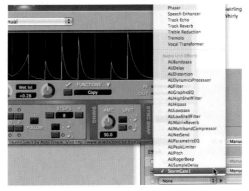

8: Select effect
Click the pop-up menu in any one of the four effects slots and choose your new plug-in from the Audio Unit Effects portion of the menu.

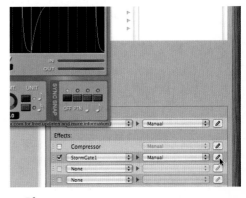

9: Play away
Click the Pencil button to view the plug-in's controls. This will enable you to make changes to the sound – just like any of GarageBand's standard plug-ins.

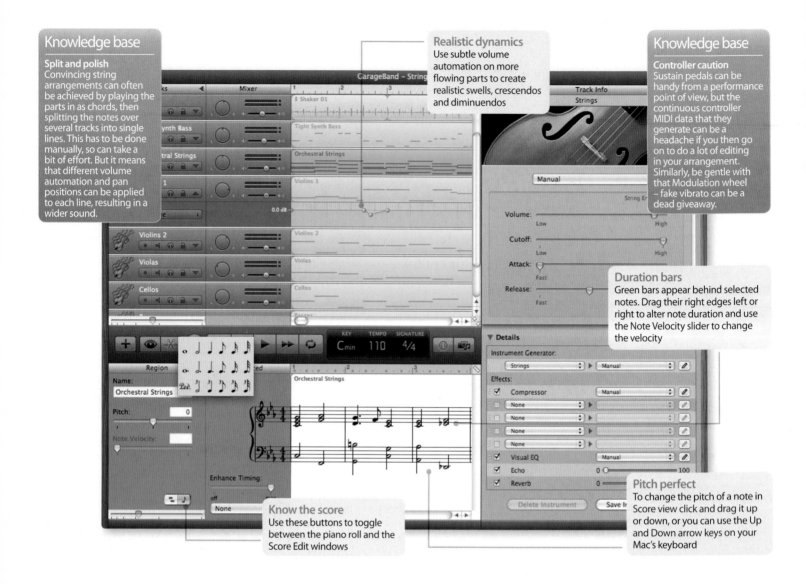

Knowledge base

Split and polish
Convincing string arrangements can often be achieved by playing the parts in as chords, then splitting the notes over several tracks into single lines. This has to be done manually, so can take a bit of effort. But it means that different volume automation and pan positions can be applied to each line, resulting in a wider sound.

Realistic dynamics
Use subtle volume automation on more flowing parts to create realistic swells, crescendos and diminuendos

Knowledge base

Controller caution
Sustain pedals can be handy from a performance point of view, but the continuous controller MIDI data that they generate can be a headache if you then go on to do a lot of editing in your arrangement. Similarly, be gentle with that Modulation wheel – fake vibrato can be a dead giveaway.

Duration bars
Green bars appear behind selected notes. Drag their right edges left or right to alter note duration and use the Note Velocity slider to change the velocity

Know the score
Use these buttons to toggle between the piano roll and the Score Edit windows

Pitch perfect
To change the pitch of a note in Score view click and drag it up or down, or you can use the Up and Down arrow keys on your Mac's keyboard

Tutorial: Program great string parts in GarageBand

Creating realistic-sounding string parts in GarageBand can sometimes be a bit of a challenge. Read on, and soon all your projects will have strings attached…

Task: Get the most out of GarageBand's string sound
Difficulty: Beginner
Time needed: 45 minutes

Whether you do dance tracks or movie scores, strings are always a classy addition to any music project. Yet even with all the advances in music technology that have been made over the years, they remain one of the trickiest instruments for a computer to imitate.

Sadly, the version of GarageBand that ships with your Mac is not particularly blessed in the orchestral sound department, sporting only four variations on the same basic ensemble string sound, and no solo instruments at all. That said, there are one or two tricks you can utilise to make your string parts more convincing. Follow this tutorial and hopefully you'll soon be coming to an agreeable arrangement. For best results you'll need a keyboard with a decent velocity response – this means that the volume level and intensity of the sound changes depending on how hard you hit the keys.

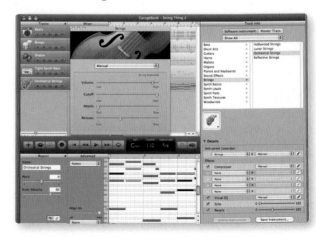

Step-by-step | GarageBand Create convincing strings with GarageBand

1: Launch GarageBand
Open your music project and create a new Software Instrument track. Change the Grand Piano to Orchestral Strings.

2: Play your part
Record in your part and use your keyboard's Velocity sensitivity to control the dynamics as much as you can.

3: Open Editor
Select the part you wish to edit in the Arrange window, and click the Scissors button to open the Matrix Editor.

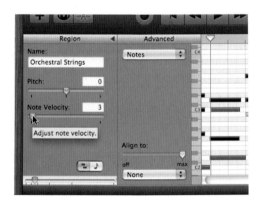

4: Trim Velocity
By selecting notes that are too quiet or too loud, you can simply use the Velocity slider to bring them back into line.

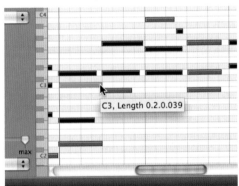

5: Adjust note length
Create a more flowing, legato effect by clicking and dragging the ends of notes to the start of the following ones.

6: Tweak Reverb
Click the 'i' button to open the Track Info pane. Click the Details Disclosure triangle and adjust the Reverb slider. Be careful not to overdo it though!

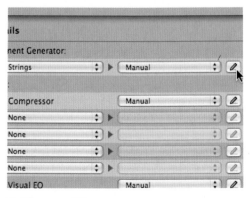

7: Show settings
Click on the Pencil button in the Instrument Generator slot, which will reveal the string instrument settings.

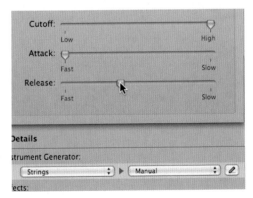

8: Adjust Release
Play with the Release parameter a bit to suit the speed of your performance (slower for legato, faster for a more staccato sound).

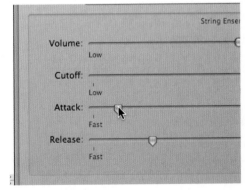

9: Adjust Attack
For most up-tempo parts, a fast Attack will be required. Move the slider to the right for a slower, more expressive start to the sound.

Pan-demonium
When two duplicated regions playing exactly the same sound are panned left and right, one side should differ slightly in tone, pitch or timing for the effect to work properly

Knowledge base

The Join command
By definition, Join is used to join multiple regions into one single region. Purple Real Instrument regions can be joined as long as they are adjacent to each other on the same track, in which case a new AIFF file is created. Green Software Instrument regions can be joined while on the same or different tracks, while blue Apple Loop regions can't be joined.

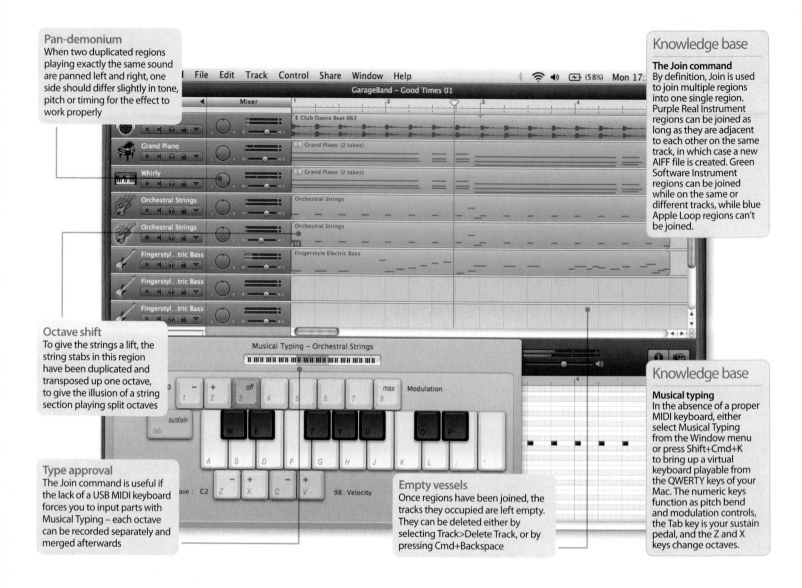

Octave shift
To give the strings a lift, the string stabs in this region have been duplicated and transposed up one octave, to give the illusion of a string section playing split octaves

Knowledge base

Musical typing
In the absence of a proper MIDI keyboard, either select Musical Typing from the Window menu or press Shift+Cmd+K to bring up a virtual keyboard playable from the QWERTY keys of your Mac. The numeric keys function as pitch bend and modulation controls, the Tab key is your sustain pedal, and the Z and X keys change octaves.

Type approval
The Join command is useful if the lack of a USB MIDI keyboard forces you to input parts with Musical Typing – each octave can be recorded separately and merged afterwards

Empty vessels
Once regions have been joined, the tracks they occupied are left empty. They can be deleted either by selecting Track>Delete Track, or by pressing Cmd+Backspace

Tutorial: Merge tracks in GarageBand

GarageBand's Join and Duplicate commands are two of the basic building blocks of MIDI editing – discover how to use them to copy, merge and manipulate track data

Task: Discover the basics of track duplication
Difficulty: Beginner
Time needed: 30 minutes

When using computer sequencing programs such as GarageBand, it's vital to have flexibility when editing – you need to be able to manipulate the data on the tracks as freely as possible if you're going to get the best out of the software. This flexibility is exactly what GarageBand has in spades. One of the more useful functions, namely the ability to duplicate tracks and merge regions, has been around since the first revision of the software in 2004. In everyday use, these two features have a wide number of potential applications – for instance, the Merge facility is useful when piecing together string arrangements, or recording hard-to-play parts in sections and sticking them together into a complete performance afterwards. The Duplicate command, on the other hand, is good for creating handmade stereo and delay effects, as well as harmonies. Here we reveal some basic steps that highlight these techniques.

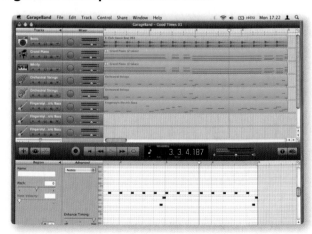

Step-by-step | GarageBand Join and duplicate tracks and regions

1: Open project
First, load up or create a GarageBand project. We'll start with a project already containing a drum loop and a couple of keyboard parts.

2: Duplicate track
We'll duplicate this piano part to create a stereo effect. Click the track's header and select Duplicate Track from the Track menu.

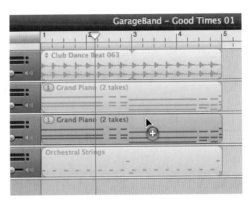

3: Copy regions
This duplicates the track and its settings, but not the regions it contains. To copy the regions, hold down Alt and drag them to the duplicate track.

4: Split pan
Use each track's pan pot to split the tracks left and right in the stereo image. Change the sound on one side to avoid phasing.

5: Get funky
Now to record a funky bassline. On a new Software Instrument track, select a bass sound and record in the first few notes.

6: Duplicate again
Duplicate the track as before, but not the regions this time. Instead, record some more notes to fill the gap in your bassline.

7: Fill in
Continue adding new tracks and filling in notes until the bassline is complete, but split it across several tracks.

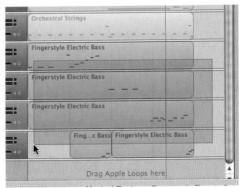

8: Select regions
To merge all the bass parts into one, select them by either Shift-clicking or by drawing a bounding box around them.

9: Join multiple parts
With all required parts now selected, simply select Edit>Join to merge them into one region. It's that easy to use the Join and Duplicate commands!

iDVD

Features

Tutorials

iDVD is an unsung hero in the iLife suite. It may not be the application you choose to create amazing projects, but quite often it's the one you turn to for finishing them. It's easy to use, has great features and does its job extremely well.

Tutorial: Burn your movie to disc with Magic iDVD

Share your movies on a keepsake DVD complete with slideshows in a matter of minutes with iDVD's brilliant Magic iDVD feature. It takes the hassle out of disc burning…

Magic iDVD

Task: Burn a disc in iDVD with Magic iDVD
Difficulty: Beginner
Time needed: 20 minutes

There are many ways to share the movies you make in iMovie, such as emailing, adding them to an iWeb page or uploading them to YouTube. However, the original and best method is to burn them to a DVD using iDVD. If you're willing to get your hands dirty, you can add all sorts of incredible extras to your disc but, if you simply want a stylish disc containing the media you choose, the Magic iDVD option is your best bet.

In this tutorial we'll show you how to add your finished iMovie projects to iDVD, add slideshows and how to burn your disc. You can select from a number of themes in iDVD to enclose your movies and photos, and you can even pick the music to play behind your slideshows. When you're done it's simply a case of dropping in a blank DVD and letting your Mac do the rest of the work. Before you know it you'll have an amazing DVD to share with friends and family. It could even make a unique gift for someone!

Step-by-step | iDVD Burn with Magic iDVD

1: Add your media

● Launch iDVD and select the Magic iDVD option to show the Magic iDVD screen. Start by naming your disc and then selecting a theme. Now use the Photos and Movies tabs to find the movies and iPhoto Events you want to drop into the vacant squares.

2: Background music

● With your movies and photos added you can now pick some music to play behind the slideshows you have selected. Choose a song under the Audio tab and drag it on top of the relevant slideshow. Now click the Create Project button in the bottom-right of the screen.

Use Magic iDVD in iDVD

Theme chooser
Pick from the numerous iDVD themes by using this slider and select theme collections by using the drop-down menu

Media drop zones
You can add movies, photos and music to these drop zones to include them in your final DVD

Knowledge base

Export movies
To include movies in your Magic iDVD project you need to have access to them from the Media pane. You can select videos from iMovie from the Event Library or export clips from iMovie using the Share menu and add them from any location on your HD. If you have exported movies on your Mac add them to your Movies folder. Now add them in Magic iDVD.

Preview
Before committing to your chosen theme you can take a look at what your disc will look like by clicking this button

Create Project
Click this button when you are done adding media to set iDVD creating your DVD interface automatically

3: Finished product

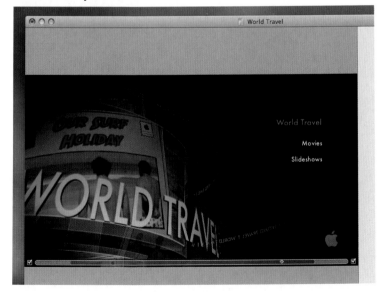

● Your disc will now be automatically built in iDVD with menus created for movies and slideshows. Check through the disc and preview it if you wish by clicking the Play button at the bottom of the screen. You can adjust any elements of the interface, including titles, by clicking on them.

4: Burn to disc

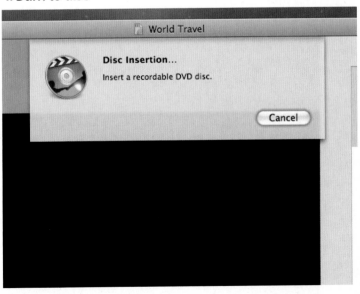

● When you are happy with the way your project looks, click the circular button next to the Play button to launch the burning process. Now you will be prompted to insert a blank disc which, when done, will initiate the burning of your project.

 iDVD '09

● Comment markers

iMovie's new comment markers are merely for adding comments to frames for guidance – attached comments will not appear in the finished DVD

● Skip to marker

You can skip to a previously inserted chapter or comment marker at any time by clicking this triangle and selecting the required name from the pop-up menu

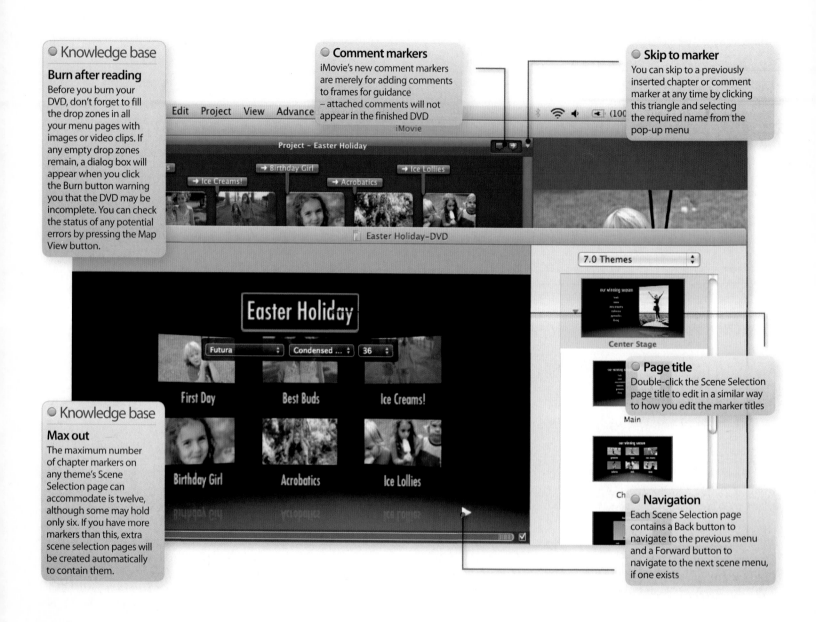

● Knowledge base

Max out

The maximum number of chapter markers on any theme's Scene Selection page can accommodate is twelve, although some may hold only six. If you have more markers than this, extra scene selection pages will be created automatically to contain them.

● Page title

Double-click the Scene Selection page title to edit in a similar way to how you edit the marker titles

● Navigation

Each Scene Selection page contains a Back button to navigate to the previous menu and a Forward button to navigate to the next scene menu, if one exists

Tutorial: Use iMovie chapter titles in iDVD

With the latest version of iMovie, you can now send projects directly to iDVD complete
with inserted chapter markers…

Task: Insert chapter markers in iMovie '09 for use in iDVD

Difficulty: Beginner

Time needed: 60 minutes

There are a large number of improvements to iMovie '09 that will certainly bring a smile to the faces of those who were disappointed with iMovie '08's comparatively limited feature set. There's no doubt that iMovie '09 has done a lot to redress the balance, and one of the most useful things to have been added back in is the ability to place chapter markers at specific places within a project, which can then be carried over when exporting the project directly to iDVD. This enables viewers of your disc to be able to skip back and forth between different sections of your movie, just as they would with a commercial DVD. The only ways to do this in an iMovie '08 project was to either

use iMovie '06 to place the chapter markers and then export the project to iMovie '08, or to export an iMovie '08 project into GarageBand as a video podcast, place markers there and then export to iDVD – either of which was a fairly arduous process. Fortunately, iMovie '09 consigns all of this to history, so here we illustrate the new, easy way to create chapter markers in iMovie and export them within the project to iDVD, where they will be picked up and included in the design of your finished disc. When you next want to burn a DVD, remember this handy tip to make the transfer from iMovie to iDVD as seamless as possible and more enjoyable for your viewers too.

Step-by-step | iDVD | Insert chapter markers into your project

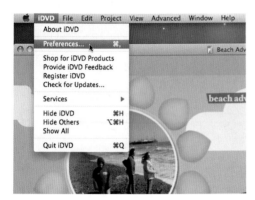

1: Set up iDVD
The first task is to check that iDVD is configured to recognise chapter markers, so launch iDVD and select Preferences from the iDVD menu.

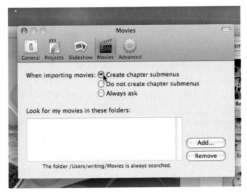

2: At the movies
In the Movies tab, make sure that 'Create chapter submenus' is selected from the 'When importing movies' options.

3: Launch iMovie
Now you can quit the iDVD program and open up the iMovie project that you wish to burn to disc to make your DVD.

4: Express preferences
Open iMovie Preferences by selecting Preferences from the iMovie menu. Alternatively, use the Cmd+, shortcut, which selects Preferences in any app.

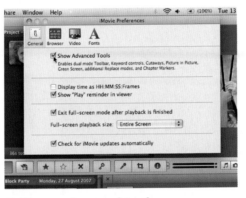

5: Show advanced tools
Tick the Show Advanced Tools checkbox in the General pane. Among other things, this will allow you to insert chapter markers into your project.

6: Close window
Close the Preferences window. You should now see two buttons in the top-right corner of the Project browser. The orange one is to add chapter markers.

7: Drag and drop
Click on the orange button and drag a marker to the desired frame. An orange chapter marker appears above the filmstrip, titled numerically.

8: Name chapter
Type a chapter name for the marker. You can re-title a marker at any point by double-clicking it and typing a new title.

9: Add more markers
Continue to add as many chapter markers as you like, up to a maximum of 99. Move them around by dragging them to their new position.

iDVD '09

10: Export to iDVD
When satisfied with the number and placement of your markers, send your movie to iDVD by choosing iDVD from the Share menu.

11: Twiddle thumbs
This stage can take a while, depending on the complexity of your project, so make sure you put the kettle on at this point!

12: Open sesame
After the conversion process has completed, iDVD will automatically open with your movie in a brand new project.

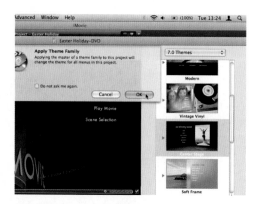

13: Change the theme
Change themes if desired by selecting a new theme from the sidebar on the right. Click OK in the box that appears.

14: View chapters
Double-click on Scene Selection to view your marked chapters, or select the Chapters page from the themes sidebar.

15: Edit marker title
The marker names correspond to those you set up in iMovie. To edit a marker's title, first click to highlight the marker in question.

16: Type new name
Pause, then click again to enter a new title for that chapter. Without the pause, iDVD will interpret a double-click and begin a preview of that chapter.

17: Edit font
To change the look of the marker titles you can use the drop-down menus to choose a new font type, style and size.

18: Burn DVD
When you're happy with the way your DVD is laid out, insert a blank DVD-R and click the Burn button to create your DVD.

iCandy

iCandy
Faster. Greener. Still mini

Faster. Greener. Still mini.

Not only has it seen a speed bump and additional ports but the mini also becomes the world's most energy efficient computer

MUSIC & MOVIES - PAGE 244

Menu

Chapters

Extras

iDVD:Movies

Whether its classy content or cool covers you're after, you may be surprised at what iDVD can bring to your iLife

I f you were a salesman, and the components of iLife were your wares, you'd probably use iMovie and iPhoto to wow the punters. Or perhaps GarageBand if they had unkempt hair and a rebellious look. But you'd probably keep iDVD back until you were closer to a sale, offering to 'throw it in' to make the package look sweeter and more attractive, rather than leading with it. That would do the program's possibilities a great disservice.

As an established part of the iLife bundle, with a previous seven versions behind it, iDVD not only has the looks and style to appeal to the casual onlooker, but an in-depth range of features that should draw in the more ambitious users too. Without extension, iDVD can be used to create so much more than was ever possible before. There are just so many possibilities.

Before you even leave the confines of the DVD-Video specification you can add beautiful picture galleries to your discs, or interactive games and quizzes, which viewers can enjoy with their remote controls. There's no need to stop there either. iDVD lets you add data to the disc, creating the perfect multimedia distribution platform for your audio-visual masterpieces. By using these features it's possible to create a disc viewable across Mac, PC and the standalone DVD player, making the best of each platform. What's better than tucking into a 21st Century portfolio?

In short, iDVD can stand proudly with its compatriots, a strong selling point in its own right, and the means through which programs like iMovie reach their ultimate audience. Whether that's your grandmother's TV, a paying customer, a prospective employer, or any of a million alternatives, is up to you. ▶

Photos & Extras - Page 246

& beyond

DVD Inlays & Covers - Page 248

15. 06. 03

Do more with: Movies & Music

Menu
Chapters
Extras

Theme choice: Vintage vinyl
Perfect for: Audio compilations, iPod-ready movies, DVD extras

Our Picnic

"DVD maintains a lead of 90,000 titles, making it the natural choice for your content too"

DVD has established rapidly, so much so that while the technology can certainly be described as mature, it still has the fresh good looks of youth. That's not to say there aren't challengers, but even after Blu-ray emerged the bloodied victor over HD-DVD, it is still only just breaking its way into the mainstream.

Nibbling at DVD's other flank is the possibility of internet distribution, but that simply doesn't offer the quality, reliability, portability or flexibility of the 12cm disc at the best of times, and certainly not for small runs. iTunes now allows for rentals but it remains to be seen how this will affect DVD sales going forward.

So, as the others struggle to get off the starting blocks, DVD maintains a lead of 90,000

titles, making it the natural choice for your content too. Even with such a healthy lead, distributors aren't resting on their laurels. Jim Gianopulos, CEO of 20th Century Fox, took to the stage with Steve Jobs at his last MacWorld keynote to announce that his studio will be releasing DVDs that include iPod-tuned versions of their films too.

For the uninitiated, that means that if you prefer to watch on an iPod all you need to do is copy the iPod optimised file to iTunes and sync, side-stepping the process of "ripping" the video, which is both excruciatingly slow and dubiously legal. This is an example you can easily follow in your projects too. Better still, your MP4s won't be laden with the irritating digital rights

management (DRM) that fetters commercial projects. All you need to do is pop the disc into your computer, open the disc through Finder and drag the file into your copy of iTunes.

You can take advantage of this ability with any project, whether it's to add high-res images, MP3 files, or even documents. Just remember that not everyone has a Mac. Yet…

Have you tried?

Making a music DVD
If you're putting together a music DVD then there's many more features you can add, on top of the obligatory Rapid zoom. Why not use iMovie to add lyrics to a version of your latest masterwork, and include it on the disc as a karaoke version? Another option is to add your latest MP3s into the data portion.

Adding iPod-ready video
Peter Griffin and family present their take on George Lucas's space-based film in this DVD. But it is remarkable for more than just the edgy fourth-wall breaking humour. What really marks this disc out for Apple fans is its status as the first ever DVD to include an iPod-ready MP4 file, something worth adding to your own discs.

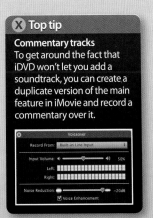

Fun in the sun

Step-by-step | iPod-ready content

With video-capable models spreading like wildfire, isn't it time you made it easier for them?

1 Once you've created your masterpiece in iMovie, choose Share>Export Using QuickTime. Select iPod from the Export To menu.

2 With iMovie still running click Share>Media browser, and make sure you choose to publish your film as a Large file, not a Medium file.

3 Create an iDVD project using the Large video file, and click Advanced>Edit DVD-ROM Contents. Now import the MP4 file.

"What really marks this disc out for Apple fans is its status as the first ever DVD to include an iPod-ready MP4 file"

Do more with: Photos & Extras

On Vacation

Menu
Chapters
Extras

Weekend Away

The Pier

Skati...

Theme choice: Sunflower
Perfect for: DVD quiz, family tree, interactive games

"Static menu pages are a great way to add extra information or bring it to life"

For many people their first experience of a VCR involved a top-loading machine that required your physical presence to stop and start the cassette, as remote controls were only just creeping their way into the public consciousness.

This period lasted only a few short years, however, before the device that revolutionised all our viewing habits – the remote control – entered our lives. It will no doubt remain until the end of time, or until voice control is perfected – it's hard to say which will be first. Anyway, the point of this digression is to highlight one of the things that makes DVD special – it was designed in an age when the remote control was commonplace, and so, interactivity is possible through very basic means, essentially arrow keys.

PlayStation owners who are used to 3D graphics may sneer at the word 'interactive' in the context of DVD menus, but one of the most successful games on that console is *Buzz*, a straightforward quiz game that picked up a BAFTA, as well as proving there is a vast audience for games that make quiz shows leap out of your television and into your living room.

While the power of the PlayStation gives *Buzz* a bit of an advantage in terms of game design, as do the special controllers, each title in the series has to be specially programmed by skilled engineers. iDVD makes it possible to design and write your own quiz game, effortlessly working around the restrictions of DVD specification to create a project that works on any DVD player.

And there's more to DVD interactivity than fun and games. Static menu pages are a great way to add extra information or bring it to life, as with the family tree project shown on the right. The up-down-left-right navigation is simple enough for anyone to use with a basic DVD remote or computer keyboard, but flexible enough for any number of methodical projects to be carried out. You just need to start building.

Have you tried?

Top Trumps DVD games
Back at school we always knew who had the longest throw-in or which car had the best acceleration, yet we didn't always have much experience at professional football or behind the wheel of supercars. *Top Trumps* had all the answers we ever needed, and its legend lives on in the form of this DVD game chocked with quizzes and clips. Why not take a trip down memory lane?

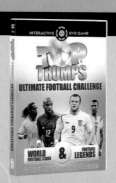

Using the iDVD map
Building a quiz in iDVD involves creating a very long tree-like disc structure, which can be a little confusing to navigate. Luckily you can switch to iDVD's Map view at any time to make sure things are working okay. It's not a bad idea to add Title Menu buttons to every page too, so users don't get buried in trivia.

Top tip

Old themes
You might find some of iDVD's old themes greyed out from versions 1-4. To bring them back to life, click on one and choose to download and install it from the internet.

The Wedding Day

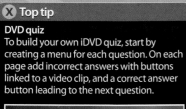

Top tip

DVD quiz
To build your own iDVD quiz, start by creating a menu for each question. On each page add incorrect answers with buttons linked to a video clip, and a correct answer button leading to the next question.

Step-by-step | Create a family tree

iDVD automatically creates hierarchically arranged menus, so why not use them?

1 Begin a new project in iDVD and choose a plain template, without too much clutter, from the old themes section to get you started.

2 Choose Import. Add one of the backgrounds supplied, depending on how many branches this part of the family tree will need.

3 Create submenus for each relative you are adding to the tree, and drag the photos of your relatives onto the waiting icons.

"iDVD makes it possible to design and write your own quiz game, effortlessly working around the restrictions of DVD specification"

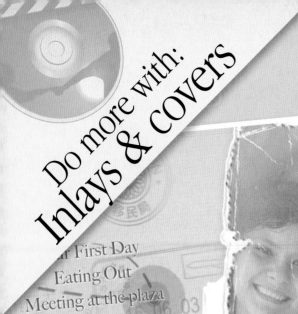
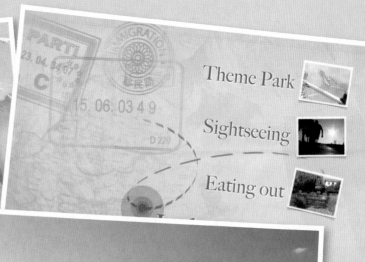

Do more with: Inlays & covers

Theme choice: Travel
Perfect for: Extracting art for inlays

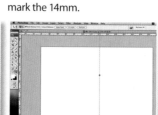

Italy 2008 - Extras

Lucca & Sylvia   Out on the hills   Going h

iLife projects are characterised by their professional sheen, and Apple's exquisitely crafted templates go a long way to making your discs stand head and shoulders above the competition. For all of their beauty, however, you don't see them until the discs are already in the player.

The problem is, once your superdrive spits out your still-warm disc, it's all too easy to scribble a title on the surface and stuff it in a plastic wallet. It's certainly quick, but what about the head and shoulders dilemma? Don't forget: you never get a second chance to make a first impression.

Step forward the good people of MacKiev, who redress the balance with its fabulously friendly application – The Print Shop. For little more than the price of a couple of commercial discs, this program helps turn your Mac into a DVD production line. The masterstroke that makes this possible is the inclusion of a full set of DVD label and box templates to match those in iDVD, so in a few brief clicks you can have a DVD with a perfectly printed surface and case design. Just type the title and the text, drop in your pictures, and off you go!

While that's certainly an elegant solution, on a system so popular among designers it's certainly not the only one. If you'd rather work with InDesign or Photoshop, for example, then it's easy to create your own DVD Inlay template. There aren't any printer compatibility problems either; open DVD cases are smaller than a sheet of A4 paper, so you can create full-bleed designs, even without a borderless printer.

Then, after choosing the program you're going to use to design your packaging, you simply cut the sheet to fit, open the DVD case so the clear film pops away from the box, and slide it in. Simple!

⊗ Top tip
Casing the problem
There are many ways to buy blank DVD media, but the most cost-effective is on spindles. For a more professional product you can buy cases from record stores, or in bulk from specialists like **www.discworlduk.co.uk**.

Step-by-step | Create your own box

If you have any graphics software to hand, design a DVD sleeve and give your disc the pro look

1 A standard plastic DVD case is 273mm by 183mm, so set the size accordingly. In Photoshop you would do this in Document Setup.

2 Before you start playing, you need to add guides to show you where the 14mm spine is. Drag from the ruler to mark the 14mm.

3 Remember, anything goes. But it's traditional to have the title written on the spine, and the front of the box.

Have you tried?

Surface printing
Many printers are capable of printing directly onto a DVD surface, and disc manufacturers like Verbatim have kept pace-selling discs with good-quality, white, printable surfaces for reasonable prices. Check your printer's manual to see whether you can print discs, or if you're in the market for a new printer, be sure it can.

iMac updated The new iMac looks just the same but boasts more processing power and up to 8GB RAM

iCandy
iMac updated

 iDVD

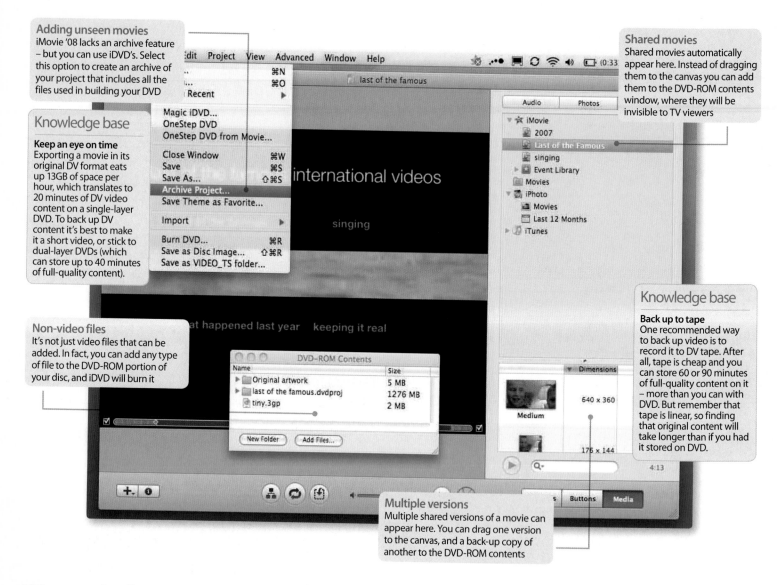

Adding unseen movies
iMovie '08 lacks an archive feature – but you can use iDVD's. Select this option to create an archive of your project that includes all the files used in building your DVD

Knowledge base

Keep an eye on time
Exporting a movie in its original DV format eats up 13GB of space per hour, which translates to 20 minutes of DV video content on a single-layer DVD. To back up DV content it's best to make it a short video, or stick to dual-layer DVDs (which can store up to 40 minutes of full-quality content).

Non-video files
It's not just video files that can be added. In fact, you can add any type of file to the DVD-ROM portion of your disc, and iDVD will burn it

Shared movies
Shared movies automatically appear here. Instead of dragging them to the canvas you can add them to the DVD-ROM contents window, where they will be invisible to TV viewers

Knowledge base

Back up to tape
One recommended way to back up video is to record it to DV tape. After all, tape is cheap and you can store 60 or 90 minutes of full-quality content on it – more than you can with DVD. But remember that tape is linear, so finding that original content will take longer than if you had it stored on DVD.

Multiple versions
Multiple shared versions of a movie can appear here. You can drag one version to the canvas, and a back-up copy of another to the DVD-ROM contents

Tutorial: Back up your videos in iDVD

iDVD isn't just for presenting movies, you can also use it to archive original footage and viewers will never know the difference. Here we show you how…

Task: Archive your videos to iDVD

Difficulty: Beginner

Time needed: 20 minutes

iDVD is a great tool to present movies. But what happens to the original material that was imported from your digital video camera? Or the multiple versions of the movie you created in iMovie? Usually when you transfer your movie to iDVD that content is discarded.

But it's possible to archive your digital content alongside your video. You can add content to your DVD that will remain invisible to anyone viewing the DVD on a TV, but it can be retrieved from a PC or a Mac – an ideal way to back up associated files. Whether you opt to do this to provide added benefits to your DVD viewers or decide to simply back up your projects in a more creative and efficient manner, this is a handy tip to save space on your Mac.

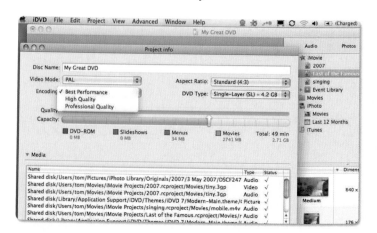

Step-by-step | iDVD Archive videos to iDVD

1: Prepare your video
To export a movie from iMovie to view on DVD, select Share>Media Browser. Now choose the Medium or Large settings.

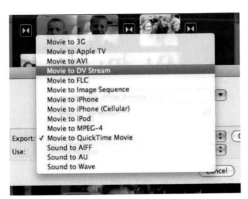

2: Store a DV stream
To copy higher quality DV footage, select Share>Export using QuickTime. Now select Movie to DV Stream from the options.

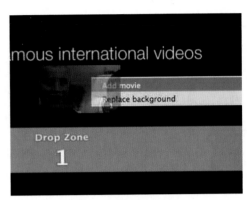

3: Add the movie to iDVD
Create a new project in iDVD. Click the Media button and select the Movies tab. Drag the shared video over the DVD canvas in the iMovie section.

4: Add more movies to the canvas
Continue adding movies to the DVD menu by dragging them from the Media browser over the canvas in the iMovie section.

5: Add extra content
Choose Advanced>Edit DVD contents. Click the New Folder button in the window. Double-click its name to rename it as 'Original artwork'.

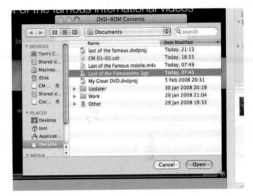

6: Navigate to the extra files
Click the Add Files button. Navigate to the original DV file to add it. You can also drag files from the Finder over the window.

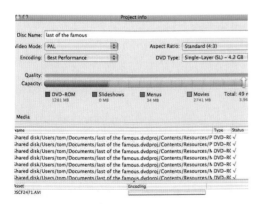

7: Check available space
Select Project>Project Info. In this window you can see how much space is taken up by the video and DVD-ROM portions of the disc.

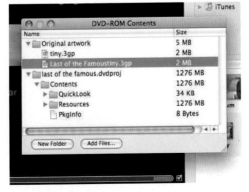

8: Reduce space
If your files exceed your DVD's capacity you can drop items from the DVD-ROM Contents window. Select an item and press the Delete key.

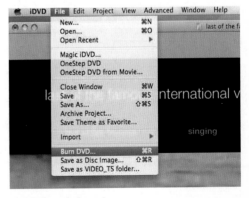

9: Upload the site
To burn your disc select File>Burn DVD. The video contents will appear on the DVD menu, but only Mac or PC owners get to see the underlying files.

Tutorial: Align objects with guides in iDVD

Aligning objects in your iDVD menu smartens its appearance and makes it easier to navigate – here's how to straighten things out

Keeping objects aligned in an iDVD project doesn't just make menus look neater, it also has a practical benefit: it makes them much simpler to navigate. Until the arrival of iDVD '08, one of the program's weaknesses was the fact you couldn't align items easily – users were reduced to tricks such as dragging the iDVD window slightly off-screen to check against the edge of the screen that objects on the iDVD canvas were aligned with each other.

iDVD '08 solves all this through its dynamic alignment guides. These don't appear all the time, but instead they pop up automatically as one canvas object nears another to help you align the left-hand, right-hand or centre of one with another object.

iDVD '08 doesn't just make sure objects are neatly aligned horizontally; it also vertically aligns, and can even ensure objects are spaced apart evenly. This simple tutorial will teach you how to play it straight.

Step-by-step | iDVD Align objects neatly in iDVD

1: Add buttons

● Open an iDVD project. Add buttons to the menu by dragging them from the media zone over the main canvas. You can configure your buttons by dragging a Buttons style from the Buttons tab over the buttons.

2: Vertical alignment

● So far, so untidy. Drag a button below another and a vertical yellow guide appears through the centre, top or bottom of both buttons as those parts of the object align. Release the object when this line appears.

Straighten up in iDVD

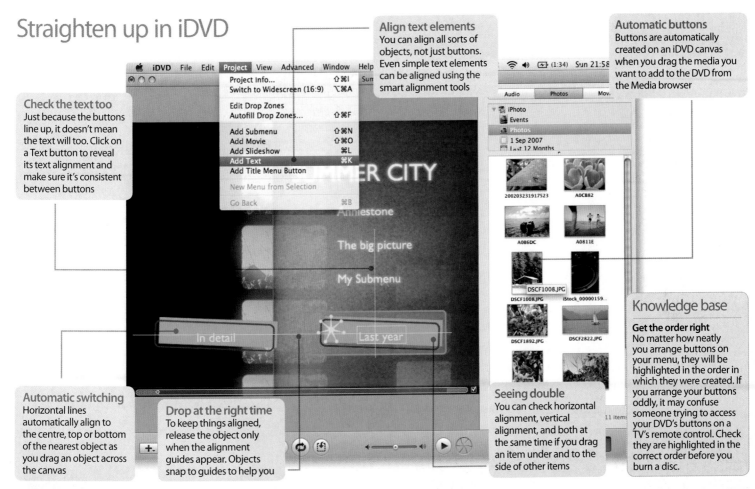

Check the text too
Just because the buttons line up, it doesn't mean the text will too. Click on a Text button to reveal its text alignment and make sure it's consistent between buttons

Align text elements
You can align all sorts of objects, not just buttons. Even simple text elements can be aligned using the smart alignment tools

Automatic buttons
Buttons are automatically created on an iDVD canvas when you drag the media you want to add to the DVD from the Media browser

Automatic switching
Horizontal lines automatically align to the centre, top or bottom of the nearest object as you drag an object across the canvas

Drop at the right time
To keep things aligned, release the object only when the alignment guides appear. Objects snap to guides to help you

Seeing double
You can check horizontal alignment, vertical alignment, and both at the same time if you drag an item under and to the side of other items

Knowledge base

Get the order right
No matter how neatly you arrange buttons on your menu, they will be highlighted in the order in which they were created. If you arrange your buttons oddly, it may confuse someone trying to access your DVD's buttons on a TV's remote control. Check they are highlighted in the correct order before you burn a disc.

3: Horizontal alignment

● Drag an object to the left or right of the object you want to line it up with. As you do, a horizontal line will appear through the centres, tops or bottoms of both objects to show that they line up.

4: Equal spacing

● Alignment guides also help to equally space multiple objects: as you move an object in the canvas towards two other aligned objects, arrows appear on the alignment guides when they are spaced apart equally.

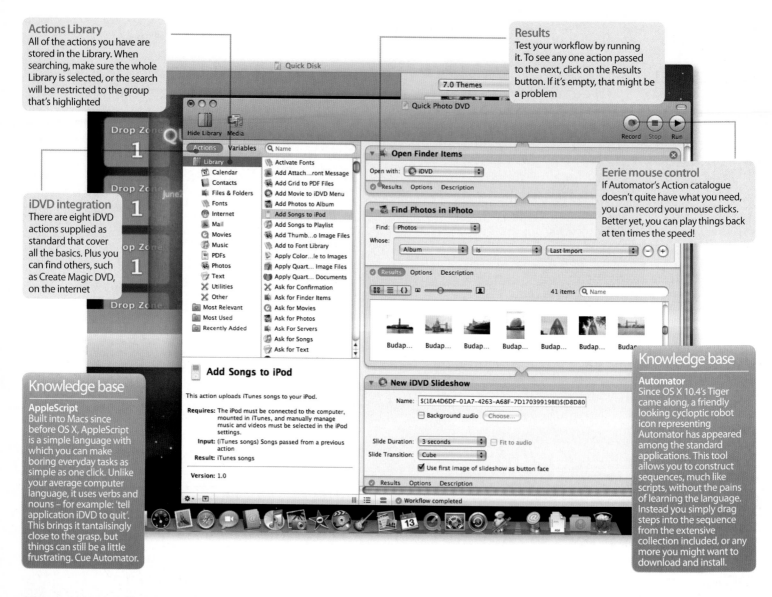

Actions Library
All of the actions you have are stored in the Library. When searching, make sure the whole Library is selected, or the search will be restricted to the group that's highlighted

Results
Test your workflow by running it. To see any one action passed to the next, click on the Results button. If it's empty, that might be a problem

iDVD integration
There are eight iDVD actions supplied as standard that cover all the basics. Plus you can find others, such as Create Magic DVD, on the internet

Eerie mouse control
If Automator's Action catalogue doesn't quite have what you need, you can record your mouse clicks. Better yet, you can play things back at ten times the speed!

Knowledge base

AppleScript
Built into Macs since before OS X, AppleScript is a simple language with which you can make boring everyday tasks as simple as one click. Unlike your average computer language, it uses verbs and nouns – for example: 'tell application iDVD to quit'. This brings it tantalisingly close to the grasp, but things can still be a little frustrating. Cue Automator.

Knowledge base

Automator
Since OS X 10.4's Tiger came along, a friendly looking cycloptic robot icon representing Automator has appeared among the standard applications. This tool allows you to construct sequences, much like scripts, without the pains of learning the language. Instead you simply drag steps into the sequence from the extensive collection included, or any more you might want to download and install.

Tutorial: Create an iDVD photo disc automatically

Everyone wants to see your pictures when you've just taken them, but there isn't always time to burn a photo DVD. Now your Mac can do it for you...

Task: Create an Automator workflow to back up your latest photos
Difficulty: Beginner
Time needed: 30 minutes

No really, it can! Like all good students, it just needs you to show it what to do once and after that it can be trusted to get on with things alone. Better still, it's a lot less likely to rush off to the pub as soon as the loan cheque arrives. But enough of the cheap stereotyping; how can iDVD possibly be any more helpful than it already is? There's only one way, and that's through bespoke scripts. None of us work in exactly the same way, but we all have certain repetitive tasks we tire of. The example here is making a disc of your most recent photos, but as you'll see, there are plenty of chances to tailor the automated workflow to your requirements.

The first step is making that series of instructions, and as ever Apple has provided an elegant solution that eradicates the need for tedious coding. All we need to achieve can be accomplished using the drag-and-drop Automator tool included with OS X.

In this tutorial we'll build a workflow by dragging a series of actions into place in a certain order. You will be using the Action Library to choose which action you wish your Mac to carry out. Some of these actions perform simple tasks, like locating files in the Finder and telling the next action where it is. Others are able to search though iPhoto catalogues and add songs to a playlist or, and this is the crux of it, even invoke some iDVD commands.

Because each step passes what it finds or does onto the next one, you don't need to be there while your computer gets on with the things you have 'trained' it to do. That's not to say that it isn't fascinating, and a little spooky, to watch your Mac working away without your guiding hand there. The point is that you can spend the time elsewhere if you wish, and your trusted Mac can take one of your many chores away from you by producing an iDVD photo disc all by itself!

Step-by-step | iDVD Create photo discs in iDVD

1: Get started
Begin by launching iDVD as you normally would. Choose the Create A New Project option since the file we'll be creating will coexist with the action.

2: A sensible spot
Give your template a simple generic name, like 'Quick Disc', and save it somewhere where you won't accidentally delete it before moving on.

3: A touch of style
Select your favourite theme (simple ones work best) and give your disc a title that would be suitable whenever you use the disc. Now save it.

4: A bit of action
Quit iDVD and launch Automator. You're automatically offered a choice of how to start your new workflow. Select Custom and click Choose.

5: First move
Click the Utilities subsection of the Action Library. At the top of the next column you'll see Ask For Confirmation. Drag this to the main area.

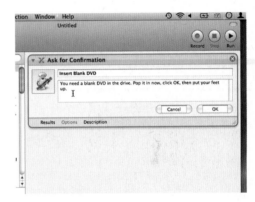

6: Preparing the user
Type a message to the user of your action in the box. In your own words, remind them to put a blank DVD in the drive.

7: My first program
Click the Run button at the top to test the workflow. Now your dialog box appears. You get feedback in the bottom ... ch action's box.

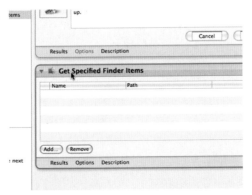

8: The next step
Now bring files into play. Click on the word Library, then type 'Get Finder' in the search field. Pick Get Specified Finder Items.

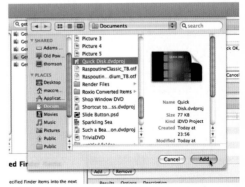

9: Locating your template
Click the Add button in the corner of your new action, and use the pop-out menu to locate the iDVD file you created earlier.

10: Open the template

Having located the file, add the Open Finder Items action to the workflow to take the file and open it. Choose iDVD in the application drop-down menu.

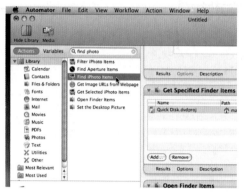

11: Get the photos

So far, our action only opens an empty document. Now drag the Find Photos in iPhoto action into the workflow to locate the images you want.

12: Pick your pictures

To give the option of a slideshow, where you can add more images, simply drag the iPhoto album from the Media pane onto the page.

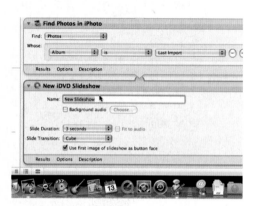

13: Scripting iDVD

Follow this action with the New iDVD Slideshow, choosing your favourite settings, but delete and remove all the text in the Name field.

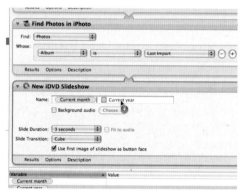

14: Variation on a theme

Select the Variables list (next to the search field), and from the Date & Time section drag the Month and Year to the Name field.

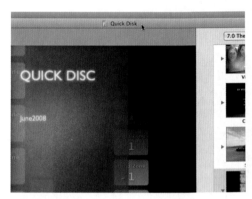

15: Trial and success

Run the workflow again. It's vital that after you do, you don't click on anything in iDVD. Make sure you switch straight back to Automator.

16: Big brother

Click Record in Automator. Now click on the iDVD icon on the dock, then on the Project menu. And finally, select Autofill Drop Zones.

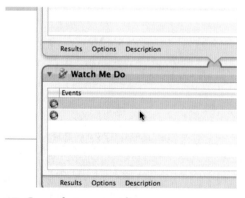

17: Complete recording

Afterwards, click on the floating Stop icon. Repeat the process to create a following action to initiate the Burn process, remembering to stop afterwards.

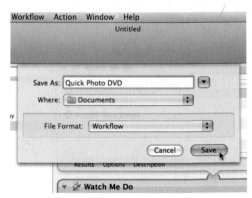

18: Save and reuse

Save the action in Automator, run it if you want to make a disc and when you come back from your cuppa, close iDVD without saving it.

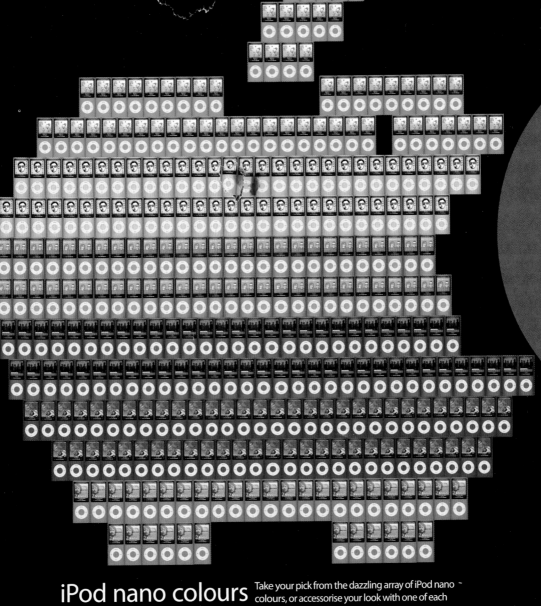

iPod nano colours Take your pick from the dazzling array of iPod nano colours, or accessorise your look with one of each

On your free CD

The best creative resources, how... ...or your iLife apps

It's not just a great book of iLife guides you're getting, there's more to be found on your free CD. Once you load up the CD attached to the opposite page, you'll discover a world of creativity from bonus PDF guides to exclusive creative resources you can add to your iLife media libraries and use for whatever purpose you wish. A selection of royalty-free sounds, images and iLife templates are included on the disc as well as a series of tutorial files to help you better follow the guides in the book. The disc interface will guide you through the necessary steps to install the content you like the look of and, of course, you can come back to the disc any time you need an extra hit of inspiration.

Free GarageBand Handbook

We've taken a selection of the best GarageBand guides and compiled them into a useful PDF handbook that you're free to take anywhere. Store it on your Mac for reference when you feel like making music, or print out its pages and keep them near to your computer as an essential guide. Whether you want to put together a podcast, record a score for your latest iMovie project or simply write some music, this handbook offers everything you need.

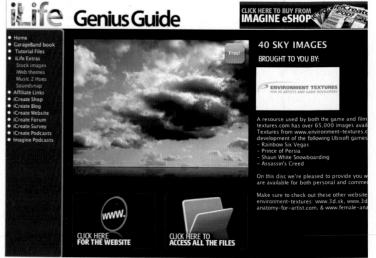

iWeb themes to customise your site

While the default Apple templates are brilliant when it comes to making a wide variety of websites in iWeb, you can always do with a little extra. On your free CD you'll find free iWeb themes which you can add to the default collection that comes with the app and customise as you wish. Don't stick with the norm, make your site stand out from the crowd today!

Free creative resources for iLife '08 and '09

Images and sounds make up the basics of any iLife project. As a creative Mac user, you're likely to have a bank of such media to hand but, when you need that extra kick, we've included a great range of free, professionally produced audio files and images for you to add to your projects. If you need an image to use as a backdrop for an iWeb site, a simple piece of music for a podcast jingle or a wild sound effect for your iMovie creations, you'll find it and more among our creative resource collection on your free disc.